THE FRAMERS' INTENTIONS

THE
FRAMERS'
INTENTIONS

*The Myth of the
Nonpartisan Constitution*

ROBERT E. ROSS

*University of Notre Dame Press
Notre Dame, Indiana*

University of Notre Dame Press
Notre Dame, Indiana 46556
undpress.nd.edu

Copyright © 2019 by the University of Notre Dame

Published in the United States of America

Library of Congress Cataloging-in-Publication Data
Names: Ross, Robert E., 1981–, author.
Title: The Framers' intentions : the myth of the
nonpartisan Constitution / Robert E. Ross.
Description: Notre Dame, Indiana : University of Notre Dame Press,
[2019] | Includes bibliographical references and index. |
Identifiers: LCCN 2019002908 (print) | LCCN 2019015519 (ebook) |
ISBN 9780268105525 (pdf) | ISBN 9780268105518 (epub) |
ISBN 9780268105495 (hardback : alk. paper) |
ISBN 0268105499 (hardback : alk. paper)
Subjects: LCSH: Political parties—United States—History—18th century. |
Political parties—United States—History—19th century. | Constitutional
history—United States. | United States. Constitution. 1st Amendment. | United
States. Constitution. 12th Amerndment. | Founding Fathers of the United States.
Classification: LCC JK2260 (ebook) |
LCC JK2260 .R67 2019 (print) | DDC 342.73/07—dc23
LC record available at https://lccn.loc.gov/2019002908

∞ *This paper meets the requirements of ANSI/NISO Z39.48-1992
(Permanence of Paper).*

CONTENTS

ACKNOWLEDGMENTS

This project is the product of countless individuals to whom I owe a debt of gratitude for their efforts on my behalf.

I wish to thank my colleagues and teachers at the University of Houston, where this project began from a question posed in a seminar on political parties, and at Utah State University, where it was finally completed. First and foremost, I am deeply indebted to Jeremy Bailey, who exemplarily embraced the role of adviser and mentor. Jeremy taught me how to be a scholar, and I constantly recognize his influence on my work. I express my gratitude to Michael Zuckert, Jeffrey Church, and Richard Murray, who read various versions of the manuscript and provided invaluable feedback. I am grateful for Andrea Eckelman, Sarah Mallums, Bruce Hunt, Roger Abshire, Marcia Beyer, Luke Williams, and Markie McBrayer, who offered encouragement and support through the initial stages of the project. At Utah State University, I owe Peter McNamara, Tony Peacock, Damon Cann, Michael Lyons, and Josh Ryan my gratitude for pushing me to complete the project.

The University of Notre Dame Press has made this project a reality. I owe thanks to my editor, Eli Bortz, the staff, and the reviewers: all of you made valuable comments that vastly improved the manuscript. *Publius: The Journal of Federalism* has given permission to reprint a portion of chapter 6, which is a revision of "Federalism and the Electoral College: The Development of the General Ticket Method for Selecting Presidential Electors," *Publius* 46, no. 2 (2016): 147–69. Likewise, *Polity* has given permission to reprint a portion of chapter 7, which is a revision of

"Recreating the House: The 1842 Apportionment Act and the Whig Party's Reconstruction of Representation," *Polity* 49, no. 3 (2017): 408–33.

Finally, I would not have completed this project without the support of my family. My parents, Charles and Sandra Ross, offered support and encouragement no matter how obscure my project seemed to them. Likewise, Harold and Teresa Kunz provided as much support as in-laws could possibly give. To my children, Nathaniel and Scarlett, thank you for patiently waiting for me to finish working before requesting my return to the good life. Finally, my wife Erin was my constant amid persistent uncertainty. Thank you for loving me through it all.

Antipartyism and the Constitution

Reassessing the Constitution-against-Parties Thesis

It is well known by party scholars that many members of the founding generation held deep antiparty sentiments and aimed to design a constitutional system that would exclude political parties. The Constitution is silent on parties, and most scholars have interpreted this as a hostile silence. The new constitutional system was intended to include a level of popular sovereignty but not through mass participation by way of political parties. Rather, institutions were designed to limit popular influence and mute party competition.[1] Competition among various interests and institutional features like the division and separation of powers would constrain and contain party conflict and dialogue.[2] With the Constitution's ratification, democracy in the United States was intended to proceed without the intervention of political parties. However, political parties developed quickly, and the intention of designing a constitutional government without political parties was short-lived. Even more to the point, many of the founders who expressed antiparty sentiments, such as James Madison and Thomas Jefferson, were also central in creating the first political parties. Political parties have an unsettled place in American constitutionalism

1

because they are deemed useful, if not necessary, to politics, even for those who seemingly despise them.

Contemporary society faces the same party paradox as the founding generation. For all the claims against partyism and partisan obstinacy, parties are embraced because they provide salutary benefits for the political process at every level of government. While political parties and an institutionalized party system were never intended to be a prominent feature in the American constitutional order, American politics are fundamentally structured and organized by political parties and a system of partisan competition for elected offices.[3] Unlike any other institution in American politics, political parties have the capacity to divide while also providing a mechanism for unity across the vast nation. At the national and local levels, parties play a pivotal role in electing candidates and recruiting political leadership, educating citizens by transmitting political information and values, and governing by organizing individuals and groups into majorities. Yet parties threaten the overall needs of the nation because they represent only partial or special interests. As James Madison warned, "The public good is disregarded in the conflicts of rival parties, and . . . measures are too often decided, not according to the rules of justice and the rights of the minor party, but by the superior force of an interested and overbearing majority."[4] Political parties are institutionalized features of American constitutionalism, and attempts to promote or strengthen parties and the party system because of their utility must be reconciled with the clear attempts to eliminate or circumscribe their influence in politics and vice versa.

Given the promise and peril of partyism for politics, the purpose of this book is to understand how political parties became deeply entrenched in a constitutional order that was intended to work against them. The notion that the Constitution was intended to work against political parties, or what the historian Richard Hofstadter calls the Constitution-against-parties thesis,[5] has long been a pillar of American political and constitutional development. The primary aim of this book is to address how the framers interpreted the Constitution in relation to the emergence of the first political parties in the United States. To a large extent, the turn to political parties came in response to the Constitution's promise of popular sovereignty and majority rule. Political actors interpreted the Constitution and constructed constitutional meaning to ensure political and electoral outcomes were achieved through majoritarian, albeit partisan, means. In this way, early political parties were not necessarily antithetical to the Constitution, and the turn to partyism can be understood as a legitimate part of the constitutional order rather than an aberration of it. However, to successfully situate the development of partyism within the early constitutional system, we must reassess the prominent Constitution-against-parties thesis.

THE CONSTITUTION-AGAINST-PARTIES THESIS

There is no shortage of examples detailing the way in which antipartyism influenced the framers in creating our constitutional system. Thomas Jefferson remarked that the "addiction [to a political party] is the last degradation of a free and moral agent."[6] In his Farewell Address, George Washington discussed the "baneful effects of the spirit of party," fearing that parties would dangerously divide the country just as they had divided his cabinet.[7] The 1787 constitutional system was the result of both political thought and political experience regarding parties. Localized parties under the Articles of Confederation were riddled with mischief, as the loose confederation of states failed to produce harmonious policy and, in many instances, united on a shared interest or passion with nothing to prevent them from unjustly violating the rights and interests of other individuals or a minority group.[8] Shortly after adoption of the Articles of Confederation, it became clear that they were insufficient to successfully govern the separate states. Many individuals, including Madison, observed that the governments under the Articles of Confederation and of the separate states were not sufficiently neutral in regard to the various interests and factions, as parties invaded the rights of others and pursued interests that were adverse to society as a whole.[9] A major impetus for the constitutional convention was this insufficiency of the Articles and the failures of the state constitutions to control the negative effects of party on law and policy. It was these concerns that produced the Constitution against parties. Hofstadter writes:

> While most of the Fathers did assume that partisan opposition would form from time to time, they did not expect that valuable permanent

structures would arise from them which would have a part to play in the protection and exercise of liberties or in reconciling the stability and effectiveness of government with the exercise of popular freedoms. The solution, then, lay in a nicely balanced constitutional system, a well-designed state which would hold in check a variety of evils, among which the divisive effects of parties ranked high. The [founders] hoped to create not a system of party government under a constitution but rather a constitutional government that would check and control parties.[10]

According to this thesis, the 1787 constitutional design was intended to mute partisanship and party competition. One of the essential advantages of the Constitution over the Articles of Confederation was the newly designed union's ability to break and control partisan conflict and factional politics by multiplying the number of parties and distinct interests. Madison's Federalist No. 10 is perhaps the clearest articulation of this constitutional principle. For Madison, parties were susceptible to becoming factions, and factions were likely to be the vehicle by which narrow special interests could impose their will at the expense of both minority rights and the public good.[11] The new Constitution was designed to promote the election of particular individuals, those of solid reputation and character who were not subject to capricious, partisan convictions. In Madison's words:

> The great desideratum in Government is such a modification of the Sovereignty as will render it sufficiently neutral between the different interests and factions, to control one part of the Society from invading the rights of another, and at the same time sufficiently controuled itself, from setting up an interest adverse to that of the whole Society.... An auxiliary desideratum for the melioration of the Republican form is such a process of elections as will most certainly extract from the mass of the Society the purest and noblest characters which it contains.[12]

As a further guard against parties in the newly conceived "extended republic," the number of representatives in Congress would ensure that even if an individual with "unjust or dishonorable" purposes were elected, he would be incapable of subverting the public good for private interest. The system was intended to be suprapartisan with no one party or interest being capable of controlling government.

An institutionalized party system developed relatively quickly in the United States despite the long-standing opposition to the idea of political parties. Shortly after the Constitution was ratified, the Federalist and Republican Parties emerged as a result of competing interests and understandings of constitutional principles. The turn to parties, even by those who openly despised them, was understood as necessary to overcome the disequilibrium in Congress due to competing sectional interests and beliefs in the extent of the new national government's power.[13] While parties emerged as a necessary device, it was understood that their use would be temporary. That is, they would no longer be necessary once constitutional and political disputes were settled. President Jefferson famously called for partisan conciliation in his first inaugural address, asserting that "we are all Republicans, we are all Federalists," with a shared commitment to constitutional principles like union and representative government.

According to the Constitution-against-party thesis, politics reverted back to the original, antiparty constitutional design following the rise of the Democratic-Republicans and the demise of the Federalists. The election of 1800 brought the Democratic-Republicans to national power in dramatic fashion. The Federalists could not challenge the Democratic-Republicans' majority status in the House of Representatives and the Senate, and they failed to run a presidential candidate against President James Monroe's reelection bid in 1820. This period, often referred to as the Era of Good Feelings, featured one-party politics and a return to constitutional normalcy. However, one-party politics lasted only as long as the Democratic-Republicans could maintain unity. By 1824, their unity dissolved and political parties and partisan competition once again became necessary.

According to the Constitution-against-parties thesis, after the election of 1824, these second-generation politicians viewed partyism and partisan competition as both necessary and a political good. Antipartyism in American constitutionalism was fully replaced with an understanding of partyism as a political good, and a new form of constitutionalism was adopted that included political parties and an institutionalized party system. Based on this early transition to partyism, many scholars have recognized the essential roles parties assume in American democracy.[14] Specifically, political parties and a party system are looked to as the means by which representative government is workable in a large, complex society.[15] The Constitution-against-parties thesis concludes that the acceptance of an institutionalized party system completely deviated from the original constitutional design because, according to Hofstadter, the founders "did not expect that valuable permanent structures would arise from [political parties] which would have a part to play in the protection and exercise of liberties or in reconciling the stability and effectiveness of government with the exercise of popular freedoms."[16] In so doing, partyism in the United States rejected a long history of antiparty constitutionalism.

POLITICAL PARTIES AND AMERICAN POLITICAL DEVELOPMENT

Political parties became a resilient feature in American politics. Beyond their benefits to the electoral process, political parties and an institutionalized party system are an integral part of how we understand the development of American politics. Our party system provides a distinct way of understanding the "American" in American political development. The history of American politics is essentially a genealogy of political parties. We can speak of different eras throughout American history in terms of the party competition transpiring at that time. The founding era can be understood in terms of the Democratic-Republican and Federalist Parties; the Civil War era, in terms of the Republican and Democratic Parties. Scholars have looked to political parties to help describe developments in politics because parties serve as a means of analyzing shifts in governing authority and changes in institutional forms.[17] This is the case because political parties are pragmatically adaptable to changes in politics, altering their organizations, identities, and strategies in response to the structure and needs of the electorate.[18] Consequently, parties both shape and are shaped by politics at the state and national levels, and they have become central in understanding American political and constitutional development.

The emphasis on parties as a way to understand developments in American political history has two distinct approaches. The first approach is to determine "party eras," or the nuances of individual party politics when parties adapt (or fail to adapt) to prevailing political circumstances. The second approach is to determine changes in the party system. Regarding the first approach, parties will respond, both successfully and unsuccessfully, to changes in institutional arrangements, established commitments, and new policies and politics. This process results in parties reconstructing or reconstituting themselves and is often highlighted by shifts in the coalitions forming the party's base support. For example, leading up to the Civil War era, the Whig Party gave way to the Republican Party because the emerging Republican Party created a new coalition with support from the Whig, Know-Nothing, and American Parties, as well as some Democrats in the Northeast and Northwest.[19] Following this first approach, party history is disaggregated based on dominant coalitions, and party eras are constructed according to, as A. James Reichley aptly titled his book, the life of the parties.[20] Often these party eras are understood in tandem with shifts in electoral behavior as parties shape and are shaped by the electorate.[21] Karen Orren and Stephen Skowronek describe this approach:

> The orthodox version of this theory highlights five major breakthroughs coming at intervals of roughly thirty years and centering around the elections of 1800, 1828, 1860, 1896, and 1932. These framed five extended periods of political order or regimes—the Jeffersonian, the Jacksonian, the Republican, the Progressive, and the New Deal. Each of these regimes affirmed in its own way the same basic cultural commitments to democracy and capitalism, but each also framed a distinctive universe of political and institutional action.[22]

Parties are an organizing concept by which to understand the transitions between competing electoral coalitions and the politics and policy created during these eras of particular parties' ascendancy. History is brimming with both salutary examples and dangerous errors committed by parties attempting to achieve political ideals and improve political practices.

The first approach also helps us understand politics between party eras. Parties in one era can be further understood by reconciling their existence with parties of the past and identifying instances of continuity or change in values, beliefs, attitudes, and interests. Sydney M. Milkis has argued that the rise of modern presidential politics, starting with

President Franklin D. Roosevelt, was correlated with the demise of traditional party politics during the Progressive Era. That is, the rise of presidential politics consolidated and expanded the role of the national government at the expense of political parties and their traditional role in previous eras.[23] Certain presidents during the contemporary era, such as Richard Nixon and Ronald Reagan, attempted to limit the excesses of the national government. However, they found it difficult to do so because of the diminished influence of political parties and because partisan conflict narrowly confined to the executive and legislature replaced party practices that once enabled citizens to redefine constitutional principles and reorganize governmental institutions.[24]

The second approach to understanding party development focuses on general developments in the party system rather than the nuances of particular parties. The two-party system in the United States has been relatively constant despite the fact that individual parties are always in flux. Due to ideological traditions, electoral rules, and institutional design, two major parties have regularly competed for national power, and two major parties have won the majority of elected offices. Defining the U.S. party system is a function of there being two durable parties, regardless of what they are called. Or, as John H. Aldrich explained, a party system can be defined by its "strategic interaction. The system of political parties consists of all and only those parties whose actions help determine the outcome, and whose actions are contingent upon the (anticipated) actions of all other parties, and vice versa."[25] The United States is considered a two-party system because third parties or their candidates, like Ralph Nader in 2000, do not have durable impacts on the system over time.[26]

Using this second approach, Aldrich conceptualized party development by looking at institutional changes in the party system that altered the strategic interaction between the parties. According to Aldrich, the party system started with temporary congressional alliances (the founding era). However, the two-party system did not fully emerge until the Whig Party became a viable national competitor of the Democratic Party in the late 1830s, thereby institutionalizing a system based on competition between mass political parties. This system gave way in the 1960s when the institutional form of the two-party system changed from competitive mass parties to competitive candidate-centered parties.

This change was highlighted by a decline in the "party-in-the-electorate" and an increase in "party organization."[27] And even though reforms during the 1970s attempted to put control of party nominations in the hands of the people, party organization, particularly interest groups, ideological activists, intense policy demanders, and state party leaders, still maintained primary control over the nomination process.[28]

POLITICAL PARTIES AND THE CONSTITUTION

Despite the literature on developments in both political parties and the party system, the majority of party development accounts rest on the fundamental assumption that the Constitution was designed to work against parties. Parties are understood to be exogenous to the constitutional order, and early political parties were not considered legitimate features of the constitutional structure.[29] During the 1820s, the tone of party discourse changed and political actors began to understand the place of parties within the constitutional order. Proponents of partyism looked to parties as an additional check on government and holding elected officials accountable. Parties began to have an accepted place within the constitutional system. Their use and existence worked for rather than against the Constitution. During this time, the Constitution-against-parties thesis was replaced by, as Hofstadter labeled it, "the idea of a party system." Party constitutionalism did not become legitimate until the idea *and* practice of party government combined under a new constitutional order.

These explanations of the movement from antipartyism to party constitutionalism add much to our understanding of American political development. However, these accounts miss important features of this movement from the Constitution's hostile silence on parties to incorporating partyism into the constitutional order. The acceptance of partyism during the Jacksonian era did not break the constitutional silence on political parties because the Constitution still made no explicit mention of them even after their acceptance. The relationship between political parties and the Constitution is more than what is, or is not, written in the document. An account of how political actors understood the Constitution in relation to the adoption of parties is needed to fully understand the development of partyism within the constitutional system. The

Constitution-against-parties thesis assumes that political actors understood the Constitution differently once partyism was accepted and that they viewed it as a break from the founders' Constitution. A complete understanding of party development must center on the Constitution and how those participating in the movement toward partyism understood the role of political parties in the constitutional order.

The pages that follow examine how political actors understood the Constitution in relation to the emergence of political parties and the acceptance of partyism. They detail how political actors used the Constitution to strengthen party practices rather than work against them. Put differently, when parties became accepted, party government advocates, like Martin Van Buren, attempted to work parties into the constitutional order rather than replace it. According to Gerald F. Leonard, Van Buren considered himself "a thoroughly conservative defender of Jeffersonian constitutional orthodoxy. He was faithful to Jefferson's view that there were two eternal, constitutional parties, one a party of the people and of states'-rights, strict-constructionist majoritarianism, the other a party of the aristocracy and of consolidationist, anticonstitutional elitism."[30] Early party developments were understood in relation to the central features of the constitutional order: majoritarianism, the principle of popular sovereignty, and federalism. Consequently, as partyism became accepted, it was viewed as a continuation and fulfillment of the founders' Constitution rather than a deviation from it. What this book provides is an early constitutional history that accounts for partyism and the constitutional developments preceding the acceptance of party government that allowed the party system to flourish and fulfill the constitutional commitment to popular sovereignty and majority rule. Thus the central contention of this book is that during the time when the Constitution was supposed to work against party government, political actors conscientiously turned to parties and partyism because of their concern with constructing a political majority and ensuring majority rule. Parties were intentionally worked into American constitutionalism to ensure that a majority party could make a legitimate claim to represent the country's opinions, interests, and constitutional interpretations.

The following pages also provide a different way of understanding the process by which the Constitution is given meaning. An account of how nonjudicial actors create constitutional meaning is needed to explain the place of political parties in our constitutional tradition. Constitutional history is more than how the Supreme Court has interpreted the Constitution. The judiciary arrived relatively late to the party scene; party politics were well established before the Supreme Court began applying the Constitution to party practices. The individual states primarily challenge party practices because Congress, with the exception of campaign finance, has left party regulation to them. During the nineteenth century, state regulation increased, raising the question of how far states could go in regulating parties without infringing on the constitutional rights of parties, candidates, and voters.[31] Prior to state regulation, parties were considered private organizations and free to control their membership, election campaigns, nominations, and party platforms. In 1866, California and New York passed the first laws regulating party practices. Other states quickly followed, responding to accusations of party corruption. At this time, parties were understood as public entities subject to the Constitution rather than private organizations protected by it. Parties turned to the judicial system when they deemed state regulations violated their constitutional rights, and the judiciary began to apply the Constitution to party practices. However, the institutionalization of the party system predates political party case law. Party jurisprudence cannot explain the early constitutional development of political parties.

The jurisprudential model for understanding partysim needs to be supplemented with a model that explains the way other political actors understand the Constitution and elucidate its text. The political process can also provide meaning to the Constitution. This political model is referred to as a "constitutional construction."[32] Rather than rely on legal norms, a constitutional construction addresses indeterminacies or ambiguities in the text. According to this interpretive approach, political actors attempt to "elucidate the text in the interstices of discoverable, interpretive meaning, where the text is so broad or so underdetermined as to be incapable of faithful but exhaustive reduction to legal rules."[33] For example, in the early republic prior to judicial interpretation, political actors dealt with constitutional indeterminacies in the freedom of speech, freedom of the press, and freedom of association clauses. These clauses were used to elucidate important constitutional meanings to determine the nature and scope of the political tools available to the emerging opposition Republican Party. A constitutional construction can account for the political process of incorporating an extraconstitutional party doctrine into our constitutionalism. Most accounts of party development fail to address the problem of parties in constitutional terms because of the acceptance of the Constitution-against-parties thesis. In addition, this thesis misses these early constitutional developments demonstrating how political actors understood majority rule to work through a party system as part of a larger turn to democratic principles and public opinion. Our party system's constitutional foundation needs to be understood as a result of political actors creatively making a constitutional meaning more explicit while remaining faithful to the existing text, thereby constructing a Constitution that supports the two-party system.

Organization of This Book

Chapter 1 provides a brief historical account of the antipartyism tradition. Partyism has been a perennial political problem, as political theorists have mostly taken two approaches to the problem of parties: eliminating them or controlling their effects. The latter approach has been the foundation of the Constitution-against-parties tradition, as scholars turned to Madison, who was influenced by David Hume, and Federalist No. 10 for an articulation of this position. Partyism in the United States did not take hold until political actors turned to parties and the party system as a political good rather than a danger needing to be eliminated or circumscribed. Political parties and a party system are not necessarily inevitable in politics. Rather, they are the result of choice, and the party system that emerged during the Van Buren era was the result of decades of deliberate constitutional constructions and creations that grounded partyism within the constitutional system in the United States.

Chapter 2 provides a brief history of political parties before the Constitution. Forms of partyism existed during the colonial era and as states developed their own constitutions after independence. Colonial partyism emerged based on institutional antagonism between executive power and the assembly. This form of partyism reflected the Whig and Tory division that emerged in British politics. As states developed their own constitutions, many significantly reduced executive power to avoid institutional conflict between the governor and assembly. Partyism, then, developed in various degrees within state legislatures. Based on demographics, geography, and voting patterns in the legislatures, there was a spectrum of two-party development from highly organized to more loosely organized partyism. Leading up to the constitutional convention, those involved in the creation of the Constitution had varying exposure to partisan conflict and party competition, including Madison, who viewed local partisanship as a major impediment to governance under the Articles of Confederation. It was from this environment that partysim emerged following ratification of the Constitution and the beginnings of competition arising from the nature and scope of national politics and governance.

Chapter 3 examines the constitutional construction of the First Amendment's protection of speech and the press. Its focus is not on how the Supreme Court has interpreted the constitutional meaning of these particular guarantees but on how political actors used the First Amendment to ground early party practices. Specifically, the Alien and Sedition Acts of 1798 provided a first test of the First Amendment's meaning by criminalizing organized opposition. The Sedition Act was a direct challenge to the constitutionality of an opposition party. The Federalists aimed to suppress party and oppositional forces rather than simply prosecute seditious libel. The debates surrounding this controversial act revealed indeterminacies in the meaning of the First Amendment. These indeterminacies were overcome by a constructed constitutional meaning of the freedom of speech and press, grounded in an argument for the need of organized opposition and party competition.

Chapter 4 explores the creation of the Twelfth Amendment in response to the 1800 presidential election and the electoral college tie between Thomas Jefferson and Aaron Burr. With the First Amendment being understood as supporting an opposition party forming a majority, the Twelfth Amendment can be understood as allowing for this new majority to elect a president who reflects their collective voice. Following the Constitution, the House of Representatives resolved the election of 1800 in a contingency election, which revealed the possibility of the House selecting a president not supported by popular will. While current scholarship on the Twelfth Amendment understands it in terms of political parties, these accounts primarily assume any relationship between the amendment and the parties was either inadvertent or temporary. Congressional debates over the Twelfth Amendment reveal a different understanding of political parties. While the Democratic-Republicans held majorities to unilaterally pass the amendment in Congress, they designed it around a recognized role for political opposition in the electoral process because they understood they would not always be in the majority. The Democratic-Republicans understood the fluidity of party politics and agreed on a system that helped ensure majoritarian election outcomes without disadvantaging a competitive opposition party in the process.

Chapter 5 considers the party building efforts of both the Democratic-Republican and Federalist Parties. By most accounts, the rise of the Democratic-Republicans and the fall of the Federalists was a restoration of the Constitution designed to work against political parties. The Democratic-Republican Party was intended to be the party to end all parties, and the postrevolution Era of Good Feelings and one-party electoral competition was a return to a nonpartisan constitutional order. However, the same constitutional understandings and electoral strategies the Democratic-Republicans used to achieve majority status were available to the Federalist Party as they assumed their new role as an opposition, minority party. After the Federalists' electoral defeat in 1800, Alexander Hamilton went to great lengths, albeit unsuccessfully, to establish more effective electioneering party practices that would have moved the Federalist Party closer to the form of contemporary political parties. Not all Federalists agreed with Hamilton's party building plan, and after his death, the Federalists largely abandoned efforts to increase their electoral support. The Federalist Party's demise was not due to general antiparty sentiments and party illegitimacy. Rather, the party failed to adhere to the evolving political norms and accepted methods of political opposition, thereby hastening its exit from the political landscape.

Chapter 6 examines the development of Article II, Section 1, and the rules pertaining to the electoral college, specifically, the decision to allocate electoral college votes by the general-ticket method. The purpose of the Twelfth Amendment was incomplete without connecting it to the electoral college and the method of selecting electors. The Twelfth Amendment was meant to ensure that the results of the House contingency election reflected popular will. However, it could not ensure that the actual election results reflected popular will without accounting for how the states elected presidential electors and allocated their votes. Following the contested election of 1824, an amendment was proposed that required states to elect presidential electors by district. Debates over the amendment centered on Article II, Section 1, and the most appropriate method, either the district or general ticket method, for constructing a majority in the electoral college. The amendment was ultimately rejected because the district method was understood to break and undermine the majorities within the separate states. As a result, political actors understood Article II, Section 1, to allow states and political parties to maximize their influence within a federal system of presidential selection.

Chapter 7 addresses the constitutional construction of Article I, Section 4's times, places, and manner clause. While state legislatures have plenary power over selecting presidential electors, Congress "may at any time by law make or alter" the selection of representatives, and with the exception of the place of electing senators, the scope of this power remained unsettled. Initially states experimented with various methods for electing representatives to the House, including at-large elections and multimember districts to provide urban areas with more representatives. However, in 1842, Congress, for the first time, added a requirement to the Apportionment Act that required representatives to be elected by single-member districts. Debates on the single-member district mandate raised questions regarding Congress's constitutional power under the times, places, and manner clause. These debates connected the issue of representation with political parties, and the single-member district mandate was understood to provide better representation to minority parties and contribute to a fairly functioning party system. These debates anticipated later social science with Duverger's law in that the requirement for single-member districts created conditions conducive to the institutionalization of a two-party system.

The conclusion connects these early constitutional developments with the Twenty-Fourth Amendment. The Twenty-Fourth Amendment is the only portion of the Constitution containing language that even approximates a reference to political parties by explicitly addressing primary elections, which are fundamentally controlled by political parties. This amendment solidifies the existence of political parties in American constitutionalism by connecting unwritten party practices with commitments to constructed constitutional meanings related to majority rule and minority rights. Political actors turned to a national two-party system to bind the written and unwritten Constitution into a coherent, workable whole.[34]

CHAPTER 1

Antiparty Constitutionalism and the Tradition of Political Parties

Political parties and partyism have been disregarded and often vilified because of what they represent or, better yet, what they fail to represent. Parties, based on the self-interest inherent in human nature, tend to pursue
a narrowly defined interest, and they can be subversive to the definition
and actualization of the common good. Critics of parties accuse them of
threatening the overarching needs of the nation, undermining vital group
interests, or dividing the will of a unified populace.[1] In this view, parties
are often equated with factionalism. Experience with republican government, from ancient Greece and Rome to the Articles of Confederation,
demonstrated that factionalism based on religious, economic, social, or
political interest created political instability, often involving violence.
Madison famously recognized the danger of factionalism to political stability and social tranquility.

> A zeal for different opinions . . . have, in turn, divided mankind into
> parties, inflamed them with mutual animosity, and rendered them
> much more disposed to vex and oppress each other than to co-operate

for their common good. . . . So strong is this propensity of mankind to fall into mutual animosities, that where no substantial occasion presents itself, the most frivolous and fanciful distinctions have been sufficient to kindle their unfriendly passions and excite their most violent conflicts.[2]

It was widely believed during the founding era that parties and partyism precipitated the downfall of many republican governments. In modern terms, the aversion to parties has followed a similar position, that of finding justification for parties only if they are capable of overcoming narrow interests. "If a party is not a part capable of governing for the sake of the whole, that is, in view of a general interest," explains Giovanni Sartori, "then it does not differ from a faction. Although a party only represents a part, this part must take a *non-partial* approach to the whole."[3]

The idea of political parties, however, is not synonymous with party government. Not all governments have an institutionalized party system, and it is necessary to distinguish the idea of party from that of party government.[4] The former is long-standing; the latter emerged more recently. The idea of party is universal because politics are fundamentally based on disputable opinions, and such opinions unite and divide, creating partisans.[5] A polity without political parties is conceivable, but partisanship rarely fails to emerge when there exists a difference of opinion. Even Thomas Jefferson, who attempted to subvert party government through party conciliation, recognized the prevalence of partisanship: "Men have differed in opinion and been divided into parties by these opinions from the first origin of societies, and in all governments where they have been permitted freely to think and speak. The same political parties which now agitate the U.S. have existed through all time."[6] Partisanship and party government have not always coincided, and history is teeming with attempts to eliminate parties or at least control their effects to avoid party government. Party government, the transition from personal, partisan reflection to public, partisan policy, only came into existence when the idea of party competition became respectable and accepted.

Political parties have varied in form throughout history. However, the term "party" used to describe a particular group or subset of government negatively has been used with seeming consistency. This history of antipartyism is directed less toward any particular institutional form and more toward the use of "party" as an accusatory term. One cannot expect to find consistency when evaluating parties as an institution, but, according to Nancy Rosenblum, consistency exists in "identifiable streams of antipartism. . . . 'Party' may not have coherence, but aversions do."[7] A particular party may be bound by its historical context, but the reason it is labeled negatively as such is not. Party government did not occur naturally in politics, nor was it inevitable. History is replete with examples of individuals and societies attempting to circumvent partyism and avoid party government. The institutionalization of a party system is the result of choice, and only recently have choices been made to adopt partyism rather than to avoid it. Ideas of party and historical experience with them are central for understanding the development of party government. A brief survey of the history of political thought reveals that party government in the United States constituted a significant break from conventional antipartyism, as political actors turned to a party system as a normatively defensible component of democracy and constitutionalism.

PLATO, HOBBES, AND ROUSSEAU: ELIMINATING PARTYISM

Partyism has constituted a threat to politics since the study of politics started. In *The Republic*, written around 380 B.C., Plato recognized the dangers of political divisions that tended to create disunity within a polity. For Plato, parties—or groups based on particular interests and opinions—were dangerous to the city and the soul because they were seen not as parts of the whole but as parts against it. In the dialogue, Thrasymachus's understanding of justice is fundamentally based on a division between the ruler and the ruled. For Thrasymachus, justice was nothing more than the ruler's own selfishness and establishing laws that tended to serve his own personal benefit. In this way, the ruler served only private interests at the expense of the rest of polity, thereby subverting the whole for a part. It is the concept of justice, then, that produced factions, hatred, and disunity among society. Plato's dialogue had to refute Thrasymachus's assertion and prove that justice was beneficial for both the city and the individual soul. Or as Socrates responded, "For surely Thrasymachus, it's injustice that produces factions, hatreds, and quarrels among themselves, and justice that produces unanimity and friendship."[8] In his pursuit of justice,

Plato needed to overcome divisions in society that tended to disrupt the unity of both the city and the soul: "Have we any greater evil for a city than what splits it and makes it many instead of one? Or a greater good than what binds it together and makes it one?"[9] Overcoming partyism could only be accomplished by establishing the common good and having every individual, not just a part of society, gain fulfillment from the prosperity of the whole.

Based on the dialogue with Thrasymachus, partyism made political justice unobtainable, and Plato's hypothetical "city in speech" was intended to theoretically establish a political order capable of subverting divisions in the city and the soul and promoting unity within each. Hence Socrates's provisional definition of justice: "this—the practice of minding one's own business—when it comes into being in a certain way, is probably justice."[10] Furthermore, Socrates described the importance of each part of the city in ensuring their individual interests did not interfere with the collective good: "But a city seemed to be just when each of the three classes of natures presented in it minded its own business."[11] Plato acknowledged the division within the city and the soul and even cast the separate parts of each as natural. However, the parts, no matter how natural, needed to be subordinate to the greater good. No part could be granted political recognition without creating disunity. Parties were considered internal enemies of both the city and the soul, and no part had claim to rule over the whole; otherwise, the whole could be subverted by and to a part. Unity required that each part share the same interest rather than having separate interests.[12] Ambition was not designed to counteract ambition; ambition was to be tamed by and subordinate to the common good. For Plato, the natural divisions within the city and the soul were not simply parts of the whole that needed to be balanced by something like a mixed constitution. Rather, the parts were understood to have a tendency to work against the whole and needed constraining to achieve true unity. Constraining the parts to achieve unity in the whole was a dominant method for combating if not completely eliminating partyism in politics. Centuries later, Thomas Hobbes appropriated this method.

In *The Leviathan*, published in 1657, Hobbes depicted individuals as naturally predisposed to self-preservation and engaged in a war "where every man is enemy to every man."[13] In this natural state, violent individualism precludes the possibility of society because individuals are left as the final arbiter of what is necessary to self-preservation.[14] Any association with others is temporarily necessitated by self-preservation and gaining an individual advantage. Once the necessity had passed, individuals dis-associated because of their distrust of fellow associates. Hobbes depicted antipartyism at its most extreme, as individual self-judgment subverted any semblance of unity or the common good. Unity was central to Hobbes's political project, and he attempted to explain how to unite individuals without this unity devolving into a state of war.

Self-interested individuals maintaining sovereignty over questions of peace and necessity caused this perpetual division and insecurity. Indeed, Hobbes observed that "the disease of a commonwealth" is "that every private man is judge of good and evil actions."[15] Problems in Hobbes's state of nature and civil society arose when there was no external source to arbitrate controversies. Individuals were left to their own biased self-judgments, which resulted in definitions of right and wrong based simply on the individual's preference. This situation was indeed dire: "To this war of every man against every man, this also is consequent: that nothing can be unjust. The notions of right and wrong, justice and injustice, have there no place. Where there is no common power, there is no law; where no law, no injustice."[16] Hobbes required an external arbiter to establish law, justice, and right and thereby avoid lawlessness, injustice, and wrong. This meant that individuals no longer settled questions of right and wrong because these disputes have but one of two outcomes: "their controversie must either come to blows, or be undecided."[17] To avoid this problem, an absolute, undivided sovereign was required to establish law. For if sovereignty was divided, there would be continual disputations over governance. Matters of right and wrong would never be settled, thereby thrusting individuals back into the state of war.

To ameliorate the problem, Hobbes rejected the idea of a mixed constitution that divided sovereignty, as in England, between a king (monarchy), lords (aristocracy), and commons (democracy). A mixed constitution represented a government that was not really a government but a "division of the commonwealth into three factions, and [called] mixed monarchy, yet the truth is that it is not one independent commonwealth, but three independent factions, nor one representative person, but three."[18] Because individuals are inclined to a diversity of opinions, government must be capable of unifying these opinions so as to promote unity within the commonwealth. A mixed constitution provides opportunities for individuals to find expression of various opinions within the multiple branches of government. Hobbes's solution, then, was absolute sovereignty capable of maintaining stability of the whole by eliminating factions within the commonwealth. The executive, legislative, and judicial powers were committed to the sovereign's hands rather than divided among governmental branches. Accordingly, the Leviathan was the only means by which to establish a unified, "common power to keep [individuals] all in awe" and establish law, thereby avoiding the state of war characteristic of a society with competing parties.[19] In Hobbes, like Plato, a mixed constitution could not successfully circumscribe parties and resolve the problem of partyism. Partyism was factionalism. Recognizing the problem of partyism and self-interest, Jean-Jacques Rousseau provided a more republican solution than Hobbes's recommendation in *The Leviathan*.

Rousseau's political project in *The Social Contract* (1762) attempted to reconcile individual self-interest with duty to the state. For Rousseau, conflict between the individual and the state existed because these two entities were understood to be apart. As Rousseau phrased this dichotomy, "Man is born free, and everywhere he is in chains."[20] His project emphasized legitimizing the chains of civil society rather than freeing man from them. He, like Hobbes, endorsed submission to a civil authority as a means of overcoming divisive and dangerous self-interest within a polity. Rousseau, however, differed from Hobbes in that Rousseau's sovereign was more republican, emanating from the public's connection and identification with the public good rather than a Hobbesian external entity. In the words of Bryan Garsten, Rousseau transformed "Hobbes's external sovereign into an internalized public conscious."[21] The common good can only be created through the sovereignty and unity of citizens. Civil society's chains are only legitimate if they emanate from citizens, or what Rousseau called the "general will," and not some external ruler or assembly.

Rousseau's conception of the general will legitimized an authoritative public judgment regarding the common good. It is the general will that allows individuals to transition from private, selfish interests to participation in the establishment of a collective consciousness regarding the common good. For Rousseau, individuals, by nature, have a private will

derived from their own self-interest. This private will must be transformed by a broader interest as individuals become part of a collective
whole and pursue the will of the collective of which they are now part.
The general will and individual will become one, and laws and public
judgments will become legitimate and authoritative because they emanate from the general will, not some species of individual self-interest.
"When private interests," Rousseau concludes, "begin to make themselves felt and small societies begin to influence the large one, the common interest changes and finds opponents. . . . [T]he general will is no
longer the will of all." Furthermore, "when the social bond of unity is
broken in all hearts, then the meanest interest brazenly appropriates the
sacred name of the public good, [and] then . . . the general will is anni-
hilated or corrupted."[22] Rousseau's republicanism is predicated on unanimity; he rejected the notion of a society divided between a majority
and a minority. Parties indicate partiality, thereby fracturing the general
will and making unanimity and public judgment regarding the common
good impossible.

Like Hobbes's, Rousseau's constitutionalism did not allow for a mixed
government sustained by checks and balances that represented and
maintained divisions within society. Under a mixed form of government,
sovereignty is

> a fantastic being made of interconnected pieces. It is as if they built a
> man out of several bodies, one of which had eyes, another had arms,
> another feet, and nothing more. Japanese sleight-of-hand artists are
> said to dismember a child before the eyes of spectators, then, throw-
> ing all the parts in the air one after the other, they make the child fall
> back down alive and all in one piece. These conjuring acts of our po-
> litical theorists are more or less like these performances. After having
> taken apart the social body by means of a sleight-of-hand worthy of
> a carnival, they put the pieces back together who knows how.[23]

Mixed constitutionalism recognized parts of society and attempted
to reconstitute the various interests into a coherent whole. This reconstituted sovereignty, however, could never be a true representation of
the general will because "sovereignty is indivisible for the same reason
that it is inalienable. For either the will is general, or it is not."[24] Mixed

constitutionalism divides sovereignty, and Rousseau intended to firmly lodge sovereignty in an indivisible general population. The general will must be expressed without reference to any partial association, such as political parties, because a private or partial will cannot adequately represent the general will and does not apply to all. Without a general will, there would be no common interest or common expression to truly unite individuals within society. In other words: "Any outcome short of unanimity (and even unanimity when consensus does not correspond to the general will) is an expression of partiality. Anything less than assent by all is abhorrent."[25] Because mixed constitutionalism could not express a generalized will, it failed to provide legitimacy to the social chains that necessarily bind human freedom. Like Plato and Hobbes, Rousseau, through his conception of a general will, endeavored to completely eliminate the cause of parties or partiality in politics.

HUME: CONTROLLING THE EFFECTS OF PARTYISM

Antipartyism was understood in another distinctive form, one that is closer to the antipartyism during the early stages of political development in the United States. Plato, Hobbes, and Rousseau all understood parties as political entities that were dangerous parts of the whole, and much of their efforts aimed at eliminating their causes and effects. Under this view, the polity was intended to constitute a complete, coherent whole, and party divisions dangerously detracted from achieving this end. Parties were not only dangerous, but they were unnecessary for politics. However, social division, often manifested in party form, was not a political consequence in need of remedying. Attempting to remedy partyism by eliminating divisions in society was considered worse than the actual problem of parties. Subsequently, the constitutionalism of this antipartyism does not seek to eliminate parties from politics. This tradition remains open to the possibility that partyism may, on occasion, be necessary amid social division and demands for diversity in political representation.[26] This distinctive form of antipartyism—parties as a necessary evil—seeks to control the effects of party rather than completely eliminate them.

In discussing English constitutionalism, David Hume provided a partial defense of party politics. In so doing, he also defended a concept of a mixed constitution: a properly balanced constitution was essential for controlling parties, a view absent in Plato, Hobbes, and Rousseau. "The just balance," argued Hume, "between the republican and monarchical parts of our constitution is really, in itself, so extremely delicate and uncertain, that, when joined to men's passion and prejudices, it is impossible but different opinions must arise concerning it, even among persons of the best understanding."[27] More to the point, he argued, contrary to Plato, Hobbes, and Rousseau, "to abolish all distinctions of party may not be practicable, perhaps not desirable, in a free government."[28] Parties were likely to emerge in any regime, particularly a free one, so partyism needed to be checked rather than completely eliminated. Hume's view of a properly balanced mixed constitution was intended to temper the excessive influence of both the government's monarchical tendencies and its republican ones. Herein was a solution to partyism that did not resort to completely eliminating their political presence. Parties, particularly opposition ones, were likely to form over disputes between the competing parts of the mixed constitution, and a properly mixed constitution resolved these conflicts without tending toward the extremes of the mixed elements, thereby preserving the constitutional balance.[29] The substance—the manner in which the constitution was mixed—took precedence over the form.

Given the competing elements of the mixed constitution, Hume acknowledged the potential for moderate partyism as the disparate elements competed and compromised over matters susceptible to moderation. On this point, he made a distinction between parties of interest and parties of principle, with the former tending toward the partyism for which he advocated. Parties of interest were unpreventable, yet these were the parties most susceptible to moderation. On the other hand, parties of principle or affection were often susceptible to the "same madness and fury as in religious wars" making compromise and moderation unlikely if not impossible.[30] The dangerous parties were those that "entertain opposite views with regard to the essentials of government . . . where there is no room for compromise or accommodation, and where the controversy may appear so momentous as to justify even an opposition by arms to the pretension of antagonism."[31] It was these types of party rivalries that tended to lead to civil war and revolution. Parties of principle were preventable because individuals became attached to a constitutional principle, that of a proper mixed regime. Parties of interest, however, were unavoidable but susceptible to moderation, thereby facilitating compromise by building a "coalition of parties." Through a proper mixed constitution and moderation, "faction is at an end and Party Distinctions abolished."[32]

Many scholars have connected Hume's ideas about partyism to those of the founders of the first political party, James Madison and Thomas Jefferson.[33] Perhaps the most prominent articulation of this type of antipartyism comes from Madison when discussing factions in *The Federalist.*

> There are again two methods of removing the causes of faction: the one, by destroying the liberty which is essential to its existence; the other, by giving to every citizen the same opinions, the same passions, and the same interests. It could never be more truly said than of the first remedy, that it was worse than the disease. Liberty is to faction what air is to fire, an aliment without which it instantly expires. But it could not be a less folly to abolish liberty, which is essential to political life, because it nourishes faction, than it would be to wish the annihilation of air, which is essential to animal life, because it imparts to fire its destructive agency. The second expedient is as impracticable as the first would be unwise.[34]

Scholars have taken Madison's position to mean that the first party competition between the Federalists and the Republicans was intended to be temporary. According to the Constitution-against-parties thesis, the ratification of the Constitution is understood as an experiment testing the viability of democracy. Even though the experiment started without national political parties, the founders eschewed their aversion to partyism, turning to parties as a temporary necessity to ensure that the democratic experiment would succeed.[35] So, the thesis concludes, the first political parties and partisan competition would wither away once the mixed constitution was restored to a proper balance, as Hamilton's attempts at executive aggrandizement were replaced with principles of local self-government and the federal nature of the constitutional order was restored.[36] Our understanding of early constitutional development has long been founded on the highly influential thesis that American constitutionalism was a continuation of the antiparty tradition along the lines of Hume. Overall, partyism in the United States developed despite a long intellectual tradition of antipartyism.

THE HISTORICAL EXPERIENCE: GREAT BRITAIN

Americans were exposed to the politics, as well as the intellectual history, of Great Britain, which set a more immediate precedent for the problem of partyism and the acceptance of a legitimate opposition. Many of the influential English antiparty thinkers, like Henry Bolingbroke and Hume, developed their thought amid party development in Great Britain. American antipartyism drew on English experience with party divisions, which often resulted in political conflict, malice, and violence. Immediate experience with partyism in Great Britain established a common antiparty bias prior to the American Revolution.[37]

Toleration for limited opposition emerged in 1215 with the Magna Carta, in which the archbishop of Canterbury sought reconciliation between a group of barons and King John of England. The charter sought to limit the monarchy's power and included various clauses protecting the barons from what was deemed arbitrary rule. It also created a controversial council of twenty-five individuals elected by the barons to monitor King John's adherence to it. Four of these men were tasked with reporting any infringements to the council, and King John was given forty days to successfully rectify any grievances. If he failed to do so, all men were to take an oath that they would assist the council to control the king.[38] Although initially agreed upon, the Magna Carta could not keep peace between the barons and King John, leading to the First Barons' War. Nevertheless, it captures the idea of limiting the Crown's prerogative through recognized opposition. This development is reminiscent of the subsequent emergence of the prominent English division between "court" and "country."

English partyism emerged during the 1600s with two important periods of party development based on power struggles between Parliament and the Crown: the Long Parliament from 1640 to 1660 and the Restoration from 1660 to 1688. During the Long Parliament, a division arose between those supporting parliamentary prerogatives, the Roundheads, and those supporting the Crown, the Royalists or Cavaliers. This

division was primarily contained within Parliament because the competing groups lacked formal organizations that connected them to a base
and the larger electorate. However, when the monarchy returned to
power during the Restoration, English partyism developed further based
on this distinction between Roundheads and Cavaliers.[39] During the
Restoration, the division between Roundheads and Cavaliers evolved
into conflict between two identifiable groups, the Whigs, who supported
Parliament (country), and the Tories, who supported the Crown (court).
Although lacking many of the features of modern political parties, partyism in the eighteenth and nineteenth centuries originated with the
Whigs and Tories.[40]

The Whig/Tory division highlighted the continuing institutional
struggle between the Crown and Parliament and the political rights of
each. Coupled with religious division, extreme institutional antagonism
over governance persisted until the Glorious Revolution in 1688, when
King James II was overthrown and replaced by William III. Thereafter,
"the English Court finally abandoned the persecution of dissenters for
limited toleration, and it accepted a permanent role for Parliament in the
governance of the realm."[41] Shortly after the Glorious Revolution, Parliament passed the Bill of Rights (1689), detailing limitations to the
Crown's powers and making it more dependent on Parliament. The English government transitioned from being controlled by the monarch to
being subject to Parliament and the majority that controlled it. William,
a foreigner and a Calvinist, relied precariously on the support of both the
Whigs and the Tories. This caused him to form his ministries from both
parties in the hope that they would elicit policy support from followers
in Parliament. Ministers, therefore, were party politicians rather than
servants of the Crown. William realized the advantages of aligning with
the majority party in the House of Commons and the folly of trying to
build a cabinet with individuals from both parties. Queen Anne, William's successor, resisted selecting party leaders as ministers. But her resistance soon gave way to the reality of partyism in Parliament, and she
too selected ministers based on the outcomes of elections and party control of the House of Commons.[42] This partyism persisted in English politics, and exclusively Tory administrations formed in 1700 and 1710, with
an exclusively Whig administration intervening in 1708.[43]

During this time, the monarch still influenced the ministerial cabinet
and policy by personally presiding over meetings, despite the fact that

partyism in the Commons heavily dictated its composition. When the House of Hanover ascended to the Crown in 1714, George I, who did not speak English, no longer attended meetings, leaving an absence of leadership and direction in the cabinet. This absence allowed for the rise of Sir Robert Walpole, first lord of the treasure, who unofficially became England's first prime minister in 1721–42.[44] Walpole worked closely with the House of Commons to exert control while also maintaining favor with the Crown. This was a period of declining competition between the Whigs and the Tories. Until 1760, the Whigs dominated both the House of Lords and the House of Commons, and the Tories were unable to gain sufficient strength and voting power to seriously challenge them.[45]

Without credible competition from the Tories, the Whigs began to lose unity, and factionalism within the party emerged. Whig control of patronage and elections, specifically, the Septennial Act, which increased the length of time between general elections, also contributed to party divisions. Influence and power within the party resided with prominent families who allowed differences between them to undermine party unity. With power distributed among Whig families, Tories such as Bolingbroke criticized the Whigs for their oligarchic tendencies and for subjecting the Crown to corrupt factionalism.[46] Bolingbroke expressed deep antiparty sentiments in his two most prominent writings on parties, "A Dissertation Upon Parties" and "The Idea of a Patriot King." These works aimed to abolish prejudice and party.[47] Opposition, therefore, came from discontented Whigs who formed coalitions with the remaining Tories. Politically, opposition to Walpole's regime remained weak because it was, as the historian Bernard Bailyn explains, "composed of a heterogeneous cluster of malcontents drawn from every segment of the political spectrum—from the far left . . . as well as from the far right . . . now indistinguishable from the centrist Whigs—it only rarely approached substantial voting strength in Parliament, and only once . . . in effect defeated the government."[48] Partyism at this time was closer to factionalism than to sustainable and acceptable party competition because opposition was understood as an attempt to disrupt unity and overthrow the government.

During the first half of the 1700s, the Whigs, particularly under Walpole, created interdependence between the Crown and Parliament through the executive branch's influence on the House of Commons. The Whigs excluded Tories from influencing policy and used ministry patronage tactics to appoint members of Parliament to executive offices as a means of exerting influence over the Commons.[49] When Walpole's successor was chosen, their power was so thoroughly entrenched that they were able to ensure that George II appointed an acceptable new prime minister, Henry Pelham. Taking the throne in 1760, George III attempted to free the Crown from its dependence on Parliament and end the Whigs' dominance. The king's efforts combined with Tory electoral victories beginning in 1761 displaced the Whigs. By 1770, the Whigs found themselves out of power and in the role of the opposition.[50] As the opposition, explains Karl Loewenstein, "they used the intervening years to transform themselves into a national party in the true sense of the word," connecting the parliamentary party with the electorate through formal organization.[51] Moreover, Edmund Burke, a Whig leader, articulated a positive account of parties that emphasized the importance and necessity of legitimate opposition to the government. Although still in its infancy, by the end of the eighteenth century, the British political system was trending toward partyism and a party system, a system that continued to significantly develop with the Reform Act of 1832 and the expansion of the electorate.[52]

These general developments in British partyism provided foundational ideas and experience with parties leading up to, during, and after the creation of the U.S. Constitution. In tracing the development of the idea of party, Hofstadter connected Hamilton's view of party with Bolingbroke's antipartyism and Madison's with David Hume to demonstrate the spectrum of antiparty sentiments in the United States. Importantly, for the Constitution-against-party thesis, there was no American expression of Burke's partyism defense by any of the founders of the Constitution.[53] Burke's defense of party was an outlier because, in both England and America, the terms "party" and "faction" were used interchangeably. In Samuel Johnson's 1755 *Dictionary of the English Language*, *party* is defined as "a number of persons confederated by similarity of design or opinions in opposition to others; a faction." The definition of *faction* differed slightly: "(1) A party in a state. (2) Tumult, discord, dissention." Based on these definitions, the words were understood synonymously, but *faction* carried a more pejorative connotation.[54] Prominent American thinkers, like John Adams, Madison, Hamilton, and Washington, used *party* and *faction* interchangeably and warned against the baneful effects of partyism.[55] No real effort was made to differentiate between the two terms.

Modern political parties, and the idea and practice of a legitimate opposition, emerged only after a long tradition of antipartyism and efforts to circumscribe party practices. Scholars have traced the emergence of partyism in the United States conceptually to the early national and Jackson eras, providing a historiography of party development from the early partisan struggles between the Federalists and the Republicans to the Jacksonians and the emergence of party competition as a permanent feature in American constitutionalism. Martin Van Buren is often credited with establishing permanent party competition in the United States as he pushed for a theoretical defense of party politics while also strengthening their practical applications. He rejected the traditional antipartyism and combined the idea of party with institutional design, breaking from a long intellectual and historical tradition of attempts to circumscribe if not completely eliminate partyism.

Combining the Idea of Party and the Practice of Government

Van Buren matured politically during the contests between the Democratic-Republicans and the Federalists. He admired Thomas Jefferson as the "image of principled statecraft" and avoided numerous recruitment attempts by the Federalist Party in one of New York's predominantly Federalist counties.[56] State politics in New York had as much influence on Van Buren as the national contests. The Democratic-Republicans in New York lacked party cohesion, and Van Buren navigated local politics amid significant divisions at the state level. George Clinton and DeWitt Clinton were among the most prominent Democratic-Republicans in New York, and Van Buren initially aligned himself with their faction.[57] As Hofstadter describes it, Van Buren was "reared . . . largely in the Clintonian faction where he must had learned most of what he knew about the use of spoils, and even as late of 1812 he was still willing, with whatever misgivings, to support Clinton's bid for the presidency."[58] Van Buren, however, challenged the Clintons' claim to be true Democratic-Republicans because of their use of patronage instead of regular party mechanisms to make nominations by party majority. For him, the Clintons were no different from the elitist Federalist Party, and he believed true Democratic-Republican principles required common people to take political matters into their own hands rather than be reduced to servile reliance on political elites. Van Buren became DeWitt Clinton's leading political rival, developing a highly organized political machine in the process. Van Buren's party organization included establishing caucus control of his part of the Democratic-Republican Party, creating a party press, and creating corresponding committees. Party regularity and party organization were more than just a partisan maneuver to win elections, as Van Buren believed partyism was an indispensable principle of democracy.[59] He emerged from local New York politics committed to the fundamental principles and democratic merits of party organization. As he entered the national scene, Van Buren needed to return competition to politics because the Democratic-Republican dominance had led to party stagnation and fracturing.

Van Buren's partyism developed amid significant attempts by DeWitt Clinton, James Monroe, and John Quincy Adams to maintain the traditional antiparty constitutionalism established by their predecessors. DeWitt Clinton's style of political leadership did not reflect a commitment to party cultivation and promotion. Rather, he obtained many of his political appointments due in part to his family name. By 1812, Clinton came out in open opposition to the Democratic-Republicans and challenged President Madison in the 1812 presidential election. He did not, however, run as a Federalist despite being supported by many members of that party, particularly those in New York who considered him the lesser of two evils. Clinton lost prestige among the Democratic-Republicans as well as their support. To compensate, he forged a coalition with the supportive Federalists and soon turned his once declared Democratic-Republican partisanship into antiparty statesmanship. In so doing, Clinton conformed to the long history of antipartyism by warning against the dangers of parties: "When these contentions spread over society, they form parties; and mingling sometimes with private views and local interests, degenerate into faction, which seeks its gratification in violation of morality, and at the expense of the general good."[60] In particular, Clinton objected to Van Buren's emphasis on party regularity: "All our part and lot in the election is to be appointed on a ward committee, and to do a duty at the polls and to scour around through the cellars and groceries to buy up votes, and for what? To elect a set of young men, of whom I know but little and care less." The Democratic-Republicans were too much of an organized party, and Clinton claimed to hold to the previous ways of subverting parties: "If I can find the old Republicans again I'll join them; if I cannot, why I'll be independent and vote as I please."[61]

Like DeWitt Clinton, James Monroe and John Quincy Adams continued the tradition of antiparty statesmanship, and party discipline at the national level disintegrated under the leadership of these two presidents. Van Buren was elected to the U.S. Senate in 1820, and his arrival in Washington was marked by considerable hostility to his desire for party government and principled partisan competition. President Monroe referred to parties as the "curse of the country" and celebrated the fact that they had "cooled down or rather disappeared."[62] As president, Monroe intended to eliminate partisanship by emphasizing national unity and to push for conciliation by offering government positions to Federalists. Van Buren opposed what he called "Monroe's fusion policy,"[63] believing "that [his] policy of conciliation, by destroying the open party contest, was permitting Federalists to infiltrate the [Democratic-Republican] party and undermine the integrity of its organization."[64] After his political career, Van Buren lamented the failure in party leadership.

> In the place of two great parties arrayed against each other in a fair and open contest for the establishment of principles in the administration of Government which they respectively believed most conducive to the public interest, the country was overrun with personal factions. These, having few higher motives for the selection of their candidates or stronger incentives to action than individual preferences or antipathies, moved the bitter waters of political agitation to their lowest depths.[65]

Contrary to President Monroe's "fusion policy," Van Buren believed opposition was necessary for maintaining party unity. The Democratic-Republicans lost party unity by forging coalitions with Federalists, which resulted in compromises in the Democratic-Republicans' party principles. Van Buren advocated purging the party of Federalists and their influence to keep the Democratic-Republicans from sacrificing their foundational principles. More to the point, divisions within the party, as Van Buren witnessed in New York, allowed for an increase in Federalist influence because they provided support to particular factions within the Democratic-Republican Party. The pursuit of party conciliation and the absence of a rival party to promote solidarity fractured the Democratic-Republicans, and the ultimate result of antipartyism and party disunity was the election of 1824.

Before Monroe became president, the Democratic-Republican Party had successfully promoted a presidential successor through party regularity—the caucus system. President Monroe's antipartyism, however, fractured the Democratic-Republicans to a point where there was no consensus as to who would be the party's nominee for president. Only one candidate, William Crawford, followed party protocol by submitting his name to the party caucus and received the nomination from a minority of the Democratic-Republican congressmen in attendance. The other presidential nominees, John C. Calhoun, John Quincy Adams, Andrew Jackson, and Henry Clay, were all opponents of the caucus system. For the first time since 1800, the election of 1824 would be decided in the House of Representatives because no candidate won a majority of electoral college votes. For Van Buren, there may have been no greater need for partyism and party unity than the "corrupt bargain" that delivered the presidency to John Quincy Adams. This resulted in numerous calls to change the electoral college.

Like his predecessor, President Adams was an ardent opponent of political parties. Even before assuming office, Adams had every intention of eliminating political parties. Rehearsing the antipartyism tradition of unity, he sought to unite people under a common sentiment and destroy the remnants of prior party distinctions.[66] In his first inaugural address, Adams declared antipartyism a major theme and goal of his administration. Van Buren characterized Adams's antipartyism in the following way: "He [Adams] therefore embraced with avidity and supported with zeal the project of Mr. Monroe to obliterate the inauspicious party divisions of the past and to bury the recollection of their causes and effects in a sepulchre proposed by himself—to wit in 'the receptacle of things lost on earth.'"[67] Adams's antipartyism extended from the uniqueness of his election: he was the first president elected without the nomination and support of a political party.[68] As a result, antipartyism successfully attacked the caucus system and partisan nomination by displacing the prominent role of political parties in presidential selection. President Adams's opposition to party government, in line with the history of antipartyism, attempted to eliminate parties from politics both theoretically and institutionally.

During this time, Van Buren witnessed the dangers of antipartyism, particularly to his view of republican constitutionalism and the Democratic Party. The Democratic-Republican Party, "so long in the ascendant, and apparently so omnipotent, was literally shattered into fragments, and we had no fewer than five Republican Presidential candidates in the field." The Democratic-Republicans were split. The factionalized environment replaced open political contests over principles of administration and the public good between two competing parties. As Van Buren observed, "In the place of two great parties arrayed against each other in a fair and open contest for the establishment of principles in the administration of Government which they respectively believed most conducive to the public interest, the country was overrun with personal factions."[69] He believed Madisonian constitutionalism in the extended republic failed to control the effects of factions, and political parties, unified by political principles, in competitive electoral contests, were the cure to the violence of factionalism. A well-constructed competitive party system was needed to replace antiparty constitutionalism to achieve the common good by subjugating ambition to principles.[70]

Once elected to the Senate in 1821, Van Buren transformed his experience with local partisanship in New York into national competition by combining party organization at the state level with increased national-level participation.[71] He attempted to transform national politics in both partisan and constitutional terms.[72] By the presidential election of 1828, the Democratic-Republicans had split, and each side, the Democrats and the Republicans, ran national tickets for the presidency. As a partisan, he believed the Democratic Party benefited from strengthening party organization and coordinating efforts among those with common interests to achieve their goals. Specifically, strengthening the party would help forge a truly national party that could create an alliance between the North and the South. The Democrats emphasized existing partisan commitments, particularly an attachment to states' rights, so as to perpetuate existing coalitions between the North and the South rather than having to create those attachments anew.[73] As Van Buren described it, "If the old ones [party sentiments] are suppressed, geographical divisions founded on local interests, or what is worse, prejudices between free and slaveholding states will inevitably take their place. Party attachment in former times furnished a complete antidote for sectional prejudice by producing counteracting feelings."[74]

In contrast to this view, Van Buren relied heavily on Jeffersonian constitutional principles; however, he departed from Jeffersonian constitutionalism by eschewing partisan conciliation for partisan competition. Van Buren's constitutionalism, then, seemingly conflicted with his partisanship in that he wanted not just to strengthen the Democratic Party, but, importantly, to institute a system of party competition. The former benefited one party, his party, while the latter benefited the regime. This is to say, Van Buren recognized both the existence and the importance of parties and articulated a defense of party constitutionalism, thereby breaking with the history of antipartyism and the Constitution-against-parties tradition.

Martin Van Buren recognized that party organization and permanent party competition were a break from traditional antiparty constitutionalism. The Federalists and their successors vocalized and adhered to their suspicion of partisanship and political parties, mainly because of their fear of democratic politics and the connection between the electorate and political parties.[75] Leaders and members of the Federalist Party, argued Van Buren, mainly desired to bring the concept of partyism and party unity into disrepute with the people. Their ability to do so coincided with their success in elections.[76] Once the Federalist Party was no longer competitive in national elections, the Democratic-Republicans were not able to maintain unity and win elections. Despite general antipathy to partyism, Van Buren recognized the value of partisan competition and the role partyism played in resolving unsettled constitutional issues.

Van Buren, then, provided one of the first positive accounts of political parties that attempted to merge the idea of parties with the notion of party government. Indeed, many scholars have viewed this as a fundamental shift in the constitutional system as the new party constitutionalism replaced the original Constitution against parties.[77] Van Buren's

1836 presidential victory epitomized the conflict between the newly conceived partisan constitutionalism and the desire for nonpartisan statesmanship. The Democratic Party, fearing fragmented sectionalism, used party organization and party solidarity to capture the presidency. The Whigs, on the other hand, attacked partyism, maintaining that "party is the only source whence destruction awaits our system."[78] The Whigs ended up nominating three different candidates for the presidency each with his own sectional interests.[79] In response, the Democrats recognized the dangers of sectionalism in the Whig's "nonpartisan" nomination tactics. Sectionalism threatened the Union because it created localism and animosity. Successful partysim could not be based on geography, such as the division between the North and the South. Without a party to unify interests and overcome sectionalism, localism tended to kindle animosity and arouse angry passions.[80] Antiparty constitutionalism actually endangered the Union; partyism was intended to preserve it by subordinating politicians and sectional interests to the party. Or, as Aldrich described it, a major principle of the Democratic Party was the importance of the party over its individual members, including subordinating the ambition and strong personalities of leaders to the party. This also entailed compromise by members of the party throughout the North and the South so that one region could not dominate the other.[81] Institutionalizing parties and party government overcame individual factionalism and dangerous division both within the regime and within the individual parties. Party would be a unifying mechanism, and party competition would contribute to party unity because external pressure forced party solidarity to avoid internal disunion. Hence, for Van Buren, party politics was more than organizing an electoral machine; party competition would become an institutional norm benefiting both the individual parties and the constitutional system as a whole. However, the party system that emerged with Van Buren was the result of decades of constitutional constructions and creations that grounded parties in the context of American constitutionalism. And it is these constructions and creations—the way the idea of partyism shaped the Constitution—that conventional accounts of party development and the Constitution-against-parties thesis miss.

CHAPTER 2

Partyism prior to the Constitution

James Madison concisely described state parties prior to ratification of the U.S. Constitution. "From 1783 to 1787 there were parties in abundance," he wrote, "but being rather local than general, they are not within the present review."[1] Appearing in the *National Gazette*, Madison's essay "A Candid State of Parties" traced the development of parties in the United States and distinguished between the two emerging parties at the time, the "antirepublican party" and the "Republican party."[2] His recognition of different party periods focused on national issues—declaring independence from England, ratifying the Constitution, and determining the meaning of republican, self-government. That is, Madison's assessment of the "real state of parties" was his attempt to understand the facts of an emerging partyism that engaged political issues transcending state borders. This focus on divisive, large-scale political conflicts is underscored by the existence of party activity at the local level before the Constitution. But local political parties existed before 1783. Prior to the constitutional convention, many states were divided along economic, geographic, cultural, or religious lines, creating opposing interests within states that competed for agenda and policy control in the state legislatures. Understanding the place of partyism in the constitutional order is a product of both the ideas about political parties and practical experience with them within the separate states prior to the creation and ratification of the Constitution.

The American Revolution was more than a war for independence. A military victory was a necessary means to the desired end of the Revolution, establishing a system of self-governance within the separate colonies. As early as 1775, a year before the Declaration of Independence was promulgated, many revolutionaries viewed the establishment of independent governments in the separate colonies as the primary means of severing ties with England.[3] Many colonies began doing just that. In May 1775, Massachusetts sought advice from the Continental Congress on establishing a civil government with its own authority and power. Later in the fall, both New Hampshire and South Carolina petitioned Congress to form governments. By the end of the year, Congress recommended that these states, along with Virginia, "call a full and free representation of the people to form whatever government it thought necessary."[4] In May 1776, the Continental Congress passed two resolutions, advising all colonies to adopt new forms of government and replacing English authority with that of the people:[5] "It is necessary that the exercise of every kind of authority under the said crown should be totally suppressed, and all powers of government exerted, under the authority of the people of the colonies."[6] This newly declared political independence allowed for a period of constitutional experimentation in the larger development of American constitutionalism.

Following the Declaration of Independence, partyism within states emerged in varying degrees, with many state legislatures developing consistent alignments of legislators in two parties. Independence from Britain created political arrangements that aided in the development of partisan competition within the states. More elective offices emerged, and politics turned on more local affairs, with the states assuming all powers of government. Important issues, such as monetary and fiscal policy, divided many of the states into early parties consisting of Localists, who represented agrarian interests, and Cosmopolitans, who typically represented commercial interests.[7] The evidence from state legislatures suggests that these early parties were more than a "swirl of pluralism" producing "continuing confusion and disorder."[8] More than temporary factionalism, the partyism that emerged during the 1770s and 1780s provides evidence of a developing party system. The development and acceptance of a party system in the United States derives from the sources of partyism during the colonial period and in the separate states prior to the adoption of the Constitution.

Sources of Partyism

The English model of governance helped re-create the mixed constitution in many of the colonial governments. Decades prior to the revolution, local governments mirrored those of England. Like the House of Lords and the House of Commons, many state legislatures, with the exception of Pennsylvania, Georgia, and Vermont, were bicameral. This institutional feature developed from the need to represent diverse interests within a given state and the general acceptance of a mixed government prevalent in English public discussion.[9] The lower houses in these state legislatures often represented local, particular interests. The upper houses mirrored that of the House of Lords, designed to counter and balance the lower house. However, if the English mixed government was designed to overcome factionalism and produce public harmony, it did the opposite in the colonies. Strife and conflict between the executive and the legislature abounded in local governments, and many colonies were divided between competing parties. "There was besides this [conflict between branches]," states Bernard Bailyn, "a milling factionalism that transcended institutional boundaries and at times reduced the politics of certain colonies to an almost unchartable chaos of competing groups."[10] Various factors defined these groups, such as economic, regional, social, and personal interests. Some groups were more durable on account of their consistent organization and political activity. But disputes among all of them were often very vociferous and difficult to control. While the colonies formally mirrored England institutionally, informally they were structured very differently.[11]

Colonial governments differed from their English counterparts in three important ways related to the executive: veto power, prerogative power, and judicial power. In many of the colonies, governors were given veto power over legislative acts. Under direction and authority from England, these governors would use their vetoes to prohibit or overturn certain types of legislation pursued by colonial assemblies. Governors were also capable of utilizing "suspending clauses," which prevented legislation from being enacted until explicitly approved by England. The governors' veto power gave England direct influence over colonial assemblies. While great efforts were made to reduce the crown's prerogative power, many of the colonial governors were able to discontinue legislative sessions and dissolve houses in the assembly. Legislatures were, subsequently, at the whim of governors, who could dissolve defiant assemblies while maintaining compliant ones. Finally, governors had complete control over the judiciary; they both nominated and removed judges at all levels of the judicial system. Likewise, they could create courts without legislative statutory authorization.[12]

These differences in governmental power between England and the colonies and the governors and the legislatures created differences in opinion regarding government objectives and outcomes.[13] This political arrangement often pitted the assembly against the governor, as both institutions feared tyranny. In general, the assembly feared the governor's powers, which were unchecked by any legislative restraints; the governor opposed the sway of popular passions in the assembly capable of disrupting established political and constitutional norms.[14] In other words, colonial governments were divided between the prerogative of the crown and the demand for local, self-government. Following this division, there existed two forms of public opinion in the colonies, a "court" party that supported the governor and his prerogative and a "country" party that called for more power granted to the assembly and representatives.[15] Thomas Hutchinson, a prominent loyalist and the governor of Massachusetts, exemplified England's influence. He used his prerogative and patronage to create "a numerous and powerful party, formed under the direction of a Governor," to support England's control over the colony.[16] Of course, this partyism between governor and assembly did not produce political parties as we have come to understand them in the modern sense because there were no gubernatorial elections. The country party could not unify the interests of the two institutions because there was no way to make the executive responsive to public sentiment by electoral means—at least not until after the ratification of the Constitution.

Leading up to the American Revolution, the division between those supporting the governor and those supporting the assembly created competing alignments on fundamental principles, including independence. Those supporting the court defended England, while the country supporters became the leading opponents of England and executive power within the colonies. As in England, by 1764, the colonists were either Tories or Whigs. Subsequently, patriotic societies emerged in all the colonies. "These organizations," explains Edgar E. Robinson, "kept alive agitation; in many instances they nominated the Whig candidates. . . . It is in such nominations that we may cease to consider such organizations merely as transitory vehicles for expression of public opinion and to look upon them also as party organizations."[17] Conflict in the colonies between Whigs/Patriots and Tories/Loyalists coincides with Madison's assessment of parties during "the first period" concerning the question of supporting independence or adhering to "British claims."[18] In 1774 and 1775, when the Continental Congress was called into session, the Tory/Whig division had a significant impact on deliberations.[19]

As noted above, many colonies were divided along economic, religious, or political lines intensified by geography. Many of these divisions existed prior to the revolution, manifesting themselves primarily in colonial legislatures, as the various interests put pressure on representatives and affected voting behavior. Once independence was declared, the absence of English influence on the executive resulted in a power vacuum in the colonies. Partyism took shape in many of the state governments with new structures of power created by the state constitutions. Institutional arrangements created new competing political alignments and deepened already existing ones.[20] Legislatures were particularly influenced by the creation of state constitutions, as many states shifted power from the executive to the legislature. Eight states put the election of the governor in the hands of their legislatures. In Connecticut, Rhode Island, and New York, the people elected the governor. Massachusetts, returning to its 1691 charter, had no governor, and Pennsylvania replaced the office with the Supreme Executive Council.[21] Increased political power in the legislatures coincided with many states providing greater representation to rural areas, shifting political power away from urban areas along the coast. The increase in rural representation affected interests within the state legislatures and the pressure on representatives to vote a particular way on policy.

Prior to the Constitution, partyism within the states was the result of institutional and ideological factors. However, parties did not develop

consistently across states because of variations in institutional arrangements and heterogeneity of interests. Some states, like Pennsylvania and
New York, developed highly organized parties. In other states, like New
Hampshire, partyism existed but lacked organization. In general, state
parties before the Constitution can be understood on a spectrum, with
some states developing parties at the extremes of highly and loosely organized partyism and other states falling somewhere in between. The
remainder of this chapter summarizes the uneven development of partyism within the states prior to ratification of the Constitution.[22]

HIGHLY ORGANIZED STATE PARTYISM: PENNSYLVANIA AND NEW YORK

Pennsylvania developed highly organized political parties because of
three central issues: the state constitution of 1776, the treatment of Loyalists and neutrals during the Revolutionary War, and competition for
political power. The party division created by these three issues deepened
and solidified between 1787 and 1790, as clashes developed over proposed constitutional reforms in the state. In response to these controversies, the two parties created party names and platforms, nominated candidates, competed in campaigns and elections, and consistently voted along
party lines in the state legislature.[23] Of all the states prior to the ratification of the Constitution, Pennsylvania had the most advanced party formation and organization, one closest to our modern conception of a political party.

In 1776, the adoption of the Pennsylvania constitution created bitter
partisanship. Pennsylvania's constitution had many unique features, such
as a unicameral legislature and the Supreme Executive Council. However, one particular feature created the political arena for party competition. The constitution established a method for amendment and revision,
the Council of Censors. This council, composed of two elected members
from each county, met every seven years to determine if the Supreme
Executive Council and assembly had performed their duties without assuming unwarranted powers, if taxes had been levied and collected fairly,
and if laws had been executed faithfully. The Council of Censors was also
empowered to pass public censure, impeach, and provide the assembly

with recommendations of laws to appeal. If it determined that the constitution needed alterations, it could propose amendments and convene a convention to consider proposed alterations.[24] A two-thirds majority was necessary to call a convention.[25] In essence, every seven years, the party that controlled the Council of Censors could control the constitution.

Shortly after Pennsylvania's constitutional convention, opposition to the proposed constitution emerged. Those supporting the document were termed Radicals or Constitutionalists, and those opposed were called Republicans or Anti-Constitutionalists.[26] The constitution was largely a product of the Radicals, as Benjamin Franklin was the only convention attendee with experience in the theory and practice of government.[27] Republicans argued that the constitution lacked a sufficient check on the single-chamber legislature. There was no check on excessive or extreme legislation because there was no upper house to balance the interests of the lower house, and there was no veto power in the newly formed Supreme Executive Council or in the judicial system. For the Constitutionalists, the people were a sufficient check on the legislature, and they feared any reforms would make the constitution too aristocratic. The Constitutionalists' belief that the people provided a sufficient legislative check only fueled the Republicans' complaints that the constitution was too democratic. As such, the Republicans desired constitutional reform that included a bicameral legislature, a separate executive branch, and an independent judiciary.

Other aspects of the constitution further defined and deepened party lines. Fearing that those who were loyal to England or were neutral during the revolution would undermine the new constitution, a loyalty oath was included. Members elected to the assembly were required to profess allegiance to the state and the new constitution. Sometimes, individuals were required to profess a belief in one God and the divinity of the Bible.[28] Those refusing to take the oath were prohibited from voting and holding office and considered enemies of the state.[29] Republicans adamantly opposed the Test Oath because they felt it prohibited them from pursuing amendments and alterations to the constitution lest they be labeled as disloyal. Some Republicans in the town of Carlisle held a meeting at which they unanimously agreed not to take the oath, and a meeting in Philadelphia was held to encourage similar action. The Philadelphia meeting, chaired by John Bayard, a leader of the Philadelphia

Sons of Liberty, also adopted thirty-two resolutions detailing their opposition to the constitution.[30] During the war, they postponed their efforts at constitutional reform for fear of being labeled as Loyalists.

After the war, the oath again was a central issue and became intertwined with the treatment of Loyalists. Constitutionalists continued to support the Test Oath and also wanted to prohibit Loyalists from returning to the state. Some went further, calling for the seizure of property and expulsion from the state of anyone who aided England during the war. Outside of the legislature, those supporting the Republicans sent petitions to their representatives to repeal the Test Oath. Moreover, Republicans also sought support from those unwilling to take the oath, such as Quakers, who were considered enemies of the state and disenfranchised. During the legislative session in 1784 and 1785, Republican legislators attempted to repeal the Test Oath and improve the treatment of Loyalists and those refusing to take it. Both parties fought for control of the legislature, and political power shifted between the two. Party lines solidified as consideration of a bill to repeal the Test Oath proceeded: Republicans almost unanimously supported the bill, and only one Constitutionalist went against his party. After the fall 1785 election, Republicans found themselves in the majority and were able to unanimously pass legislation that successfully repealed the Test Oath.[31]

The Test Oath was not the only issue that led to voting along party lines in the legislature. Difference of opinion on the Bank of North America, a private bank created by merchants to help finance the debts left from the Revolutionary War, further divided and defined the competing parties. Constitutionalists opposed the bank because they believed it benefited the wealthy merchants while punishing rural farmers. The Republicans accused their opponents of opposing the bank for partisan reasons: "[The Constitutionalists] do not wish any thing to prosper which has originated and is supported by their opponents the republicans, however useful and beneficial it may be."[32] The parties also clashed over the College of Philadelphia. In 1779, the Constitutionalists revoked its charter because many who were considered neutral on the war controlled it. The Constitutionalists then reinstated the college and installed a new governing board and teachers who were ardent supporters of the Revolution.[33] After the war, the former president of the college, William Smith, pushed for the repeal of the 1779 act and reinstatement of the previous board of trustees. The quality of education was not the big issue at stake. "Instead," the historian Jackson Turner Main explains, "the significant division pitted the commercial areas and nonfarm occupations against the agrarians, Episcopalians and Quakers against Presbyterians, and most of all party against party."[34]

The division between the Constitutionalists and the Republicans resulted in drastic shifts in policy, depending on which party was in control of the legislature and the agenda. Competition between these two parties persisted through the period of Articles of Confederation and creation of the Constitution. While both parties agreed on the need to replace the Articles, the delegation to the constitutional convention consisted primarily of Republicans. Predictably, the Constitutionalists were prepared to oppose aspects of the Constitution that favored Republicans. During the ratification process, party lines were clearly drawn, as all Constitutionalist legislators opposed ratification and every Republican favored it. This same division permeated politics in the subsequent decade, as all the Constitutionalists became Jeffersonian Republicans and every Republican became a Federalist.[35]

In New York, partyism was also highly organized and resulted from two important factors. The first was institutional. Prior to the Revolutionary War, contests between the governor and the assembly emerged because of the different interests each institution represented. The governor was beholden to England, while the assembly represented the colonists' interests.[36] The second cause was political. During the 1760s and 1770s, prominent families, such as the De Lanceys, Van Rensselaers, Schuylers, and Livingstons, competed for political power in the legislature. These families and their supporters campaigned for contested assembly seats, which included circulating prepared tickets with candidates' names and posting broadsides.[37] The institutional conflict resulted in a familiar division between court and country. However, this conflict masked a larger one that emerged in the assembly after the war. The assembly was primarily composed of members of the wealthy class. Colonists' interests were only generally represented in the assembly's struggle against the governor's prerogative and executive encroachments on the legislature. Once this struggle was removed, economic interests divided the legislature, and a new political figure emerged, George Clinton, who helped define and organize the contest for governmental power.

New York's state constitution was created in 1777 by a special convention. Like many other state constitutions, New York's created a bicameral legislature, with representation in both houses determined proportionately to the population of the counties. During the 1780s, the lower house represented many of the economic, social, and cultural divisions within the state. Farmers with substantial property and tradesmen such as innkeepers and merchants occupied most of the seats in the lower house.[38] The Senate contained more representatives with large property holdings and urban elites than the lower house. Yet farmers still held two-fifths of Senate seats.[39]

As in Pennsylvania, anti-Loyalist sentiments divided the state at the conclusion of the Revolutionary War. Animosity toward Loyalists was most pronounced in areas that were under British control during the war, especially New York City. Individuals in areas not under British control felt that they had shouldered most of the financial and military burden of the war. They argued that taxes should be levied on previously occupied areas to rectify this disparity. Naturally, citizens in previously occupied areas felt the taxes were unfair, impeding their ability to fully participate in independence.[40] These circumstances heightened the sectional division in the state and contributed to partyism in the state legislature.

Individuals also contributed to the division of New York politics into two parties. George Clinton, a popular war hero, served as governor from 1777 to 1795, being reelected five times. Clinton's reelections, however, did not signify unanimous support. Those holding anti-Loyalist sentiments and strong emotional ties to the war primarily supported Clinton. Clinton was known for his anti-Loyalist actions during the war, imprisoning or banishing dangerous loyalists and confiscating their property. Although he firmly believed in the right of property, given the state's financial needs, Governor Clinton supported efforts to sell seized Loyalist property and estates to help finance the war and keep taxes low.[41] Those unenthusiastic about Clinton began supporting other prominent individuals such as Philip Schuyler, John Morin Scott, or John Jay. Coalitions in both houses of the legislature began to form, and there emerged a two-party competition between those who supported Clinton and his policies and those who did not. Voting patterns in the legislature emerged between the Clintonians and anti-Clintonians on the treatment of Loyalists, taxation, salaries of government employees, the grant of citizenship to members of the Anglican vestry of New York City, and the requirement that certain lawyers obtain a certificate of loyalty before practicing law.[42]

The division between Clintonians and anti-Clintonians extended beyond the legislative arena, and the beginnings of modern political parties can be seen during the partisan disputes of the 1780s. Once New York City was no longer under British occupation, elections took place, and partisans produced their own electoral tickets. Before the constitutional convention in Philadelphia, parties in New York never achieved organization across the entire state. However, partyism on the local level emerged, and partisanship was evident in many votes in the state legislature. The Clintonian party became identified as part of the emerging national Republican Party during the late 1780s and early 1790s. Moreover, the strength and organization of the New York Republicans developed prior to and absent any efforts by Madison and Jefferson, who are often regarded as the organizers of the first national political party.[43]

Moderately Organized State Partyism: Virginia and Massachusetts

Unlike Pennsylvania and New York, Virginia did not have serious divisions leading up to and during the Revolutionary War. Policies concerning the treatment of Loyalists created significant cleavages among individuals and legislators in many states. Virginia, however, was more unified in this regard because it had few Loyalists. Virginians agreed on most issues during the war, and there was no significant division on economic matters or the state's constitution. Shortly after the war, when there was disagreement in the legislature, delegates either acted independently or voted with other groups, albeit inconsistently. That is, initially there were no clearly defined parties, as in Pennsylvania's legislature, but several different coalitions emerged with no clear party blocs forming through consistent voting by legislators across multiple issues. Virginia's partyism is often referred to as factionalism.[44] Yet, toward the end of the 1780s, a sectional division produced more consistent political alignments and voting blocs in the legislature.

The two principal divisions in the legislature were geographic, with one centered in Virginia's Northern Neck on the western shore of Chesapeake Bay and the other based in the southern counties. These partisans were less organized than those in Pennsylvania and New York because they did not engage in similar electioneering efforts and party line voting was not as consistent. During the early 1780s, voting blocs based on this division were present in only a little over half of the legislative votes.[45] The clearest examples of Virginia's divided legislature during this time concerned tax collection and prewar debts owed to British merchants. Although the legislature lacked cohesive voting blocs, prominent men such as Patrick Henry and Richard Henry Lee were able to organize followers and were looked to as proto-leaders of the coalitions. However, from 1782 to 1784 their followers were never numerous enough to garner a majority, and no consistent voting patterns emerged based on region.[46]

Beginning in 1781, tax collectors were met with resistance and insurrection because of economic problems throughout the state. The legislature continually took up questions of potential relief measures, including granting additional time before legal actions were taken and postponing collections. Henry was considered the leader of those seeking debtor relief and encountered little opposition to these measures. Even Lee, Henry's supposed political rival in the legislature, voted for debtor relief, signifying a majority consensus supporting the provisions. Difficulty paying taxes meant difficulty paying other private debts, including those to British merchants. At the conclusion of the war, courts were once again open to British creditors seeking collection of unpaid debts. As long as debts were not paid, England retained possession of posts and forts. In a letter to James Madison, Lee "lamented" Virginia's laws impeding British debt collection. "It is much to be wished," he wrote, "that the Advocates for retaining those laws wd. no longer insist upon furnishing pretext for detaining from the U.S. possessions of such capital importance to the Union as these posts are."[47] In 1783 and 1784, three roll call votes were taken to remove restrictions on British debt collection, and large majorities rejected all three. Delegates from the Northern Neck and the lower James River counties supported the measures. Henry and many of his supporters opposed them.[48] More than regional divisions, economics played a key role in these votes. Merchants, professionals, and large property owners supported the creditors. Farmers and smaller property owners supported debtors. A similar economic division emerged in a subsequent vote in 1788 dealing with creditor-debtor relations.[49] Overall, among various roll call votes during the 1782–84 legislative sessions, voting alignments varied depending on the issues, with little correlation among them.[50]

Legislative sessions during the early 1780s lacked any coherent legislative agenda, as issues were addressed as they emerged. In fall 1785, George Washington outlined a comprehensive legislative agenda that included provisions to vest Congress with powers to regulate commerce, continue regular tax collection, and develop Virginia's ports, courts, militia, and inland navigation. He hoped the Virginia assembly would give these issues "due attention . . . which will . . . mark the present epocha [sic] for having produced able Statesmen—sound patriots—and liberally minded men."[51] At the beginning of the 1785 legislative session, partisans fought over control of the speaker's chair and Madison developed a coalition of delegates. In a letter to Thomas Jefferson, Archibald Stuart described Madison's influence:

> I entertain sanguine hopes of Placing Our friend Madison in the Chair this session. It is surely the just reward of his merit and ability. These qualifications have rendered him almost absolute in the House of Delegates. Although I am an Enemy to absolute Government generally speaking, yet I cheerfully submit to his Authority and admire him as One of the brightest Ornaments of this Country.[52]

By 1787, regional alignments had formed to a point that Madison was able to count votes and predict opposition on specific issues.[53] By the constitutional convention, conflict over economic issues and voting patterns had created a clearly discernible regional division in the Virginia legislature.[54]

The emerging partyism in the state legislature carried over to voting on ratification of the Constitution. In December 1787, Madison predicted that three different "parties" would emerge during the ratification vote based on regional divisions. Those from the "upper and lower Country" and the Northern Neck would support the Constitution. Among this group, two divisions would occur, between those willing to adopt the Constitution without amendments and those, led by George Mason, who would adopt it with "a few additional guards in favor of the Rights of the States and of the people." The "middle Country" and the "South side of James River," led by Patrick Henry, would oppose it.[55] Delegates to the state ratification convention were ultimately chosen based on their stance on the Constitution. Before the March delegate elections concluded, a relatively accurate list of delegates and their predicted vote on the Constitution emerged. Although the vote was close and hotly contested, the Federalists were predicted to carry the day and the state vote to ratify the Constitution.[56]

The debate over ratification between the Federalists and Anti-Federalists likewise created division during the first federal election. The Anti-Federalists, led by Patrick Henry, controlled the house in the Virginia Assembly when it met in fall 1788 to elect the state's two senators to Congress. With each legislator casting two votes, the Federalists hoped Madison would receive enough second votes to get elected. The Anti-Federalists, however, successfully elected two of their own: Richard Henry Lee and William Grayson. Madison came in third. Having lost the Senate seat, Madison ran for a seat in the House of Representatives. The Anti-Federalists, because they controlled the assembly, attempted to prevent his election by manipulating the northern Piedmont district to include additional Anti-Federalist counties. "By an ingenious combination of new and old tactics," explain Risjord and Den-Boer, "Madison's friends kept him informed of the sentiment in each county of the district, identified the wavering regions, and enlisted prominent members of the gentry to endorse him at strategic moments."[57] The electioneering worked, and Madison won the election by a large majority. These emerging divisions in Virginia anticipated the partyism that developed in Congress, as many of the Anti-Federalists in Virginia became Republicans.

Partyism in Massachusetts developed primarily after the Revolutionary War. A large number of individuals favored independence, and Loyalists constituted a small minority of the total population. By 1776, the number of Loyalists were so far outnumbered that there was little resistance to the war efforts and little support for England and her interests. This harmony came to an end, however, when political disagreements created sharp cleavages throughout the state during the 1780s. Economics and monetary policy divided the state, as parties competed over state and federal debts, taxation, and private debts.[58]

Many of the postwar legislative conflicts arose from economic developments and monetary policy during the war. Due to high farm prices, increased demand and scarcity, and currency inflation, commercial farm areas close to major markets benefited the most during the war and were able to pay their taxes and purchase higher-priced goods needed for production. Interior towns lacked these advantages and struggled to remain financially viable, let alone pay taxes to contribute to the war. The majority of Massachusetts's economy was concentrated in the commercial centers and surrounding agricultural areas, creating uneven economic development and significant gaps in wealth. The discrepancy in tax payments to fund war efforts led the state to rely on deficit financing, printing more paper currency, and borrowing.[59] The state also experienced a recession because of economic stagnation, heavy taxes, and the discontinued use of Continental bills, which meant reliance on gold and silver as currency.[60] Financial reform was necessary, and these reforms produced conflict and division within the legislature and throughout the state.

Reforms primarily addressed inflation problems. Money in Massachusetts had little backing, and from 1776 the value of paper money depreciated while prices sharply increased. In 1776, the state had adopted the Tender Act, which officially made Continental bills legal tender for private and public debts. This act primarily benefited poor farmers in interior towns while putting creditors at a financial disadvantage. In 1780, the state repealed the Tender Act and required debtors to pay their debts with gold and silver coins instead of near-worthless paper money. Paper money was also no longer an accepted means of paying taxes. As the House of Representatives voted on repeal of the Tender Act, support came primarily from the coastal areas and opposition from the interior of the state. Subsequent issues, such as the settlement and payment of the state's debts, produced divisions similar to those on the Tender Act vote. Voting was consistent: those who supported repeal of the act also favored these new economic provisions; those who opposed repeal voted with similar consistency. Many delegates who voted on these early issues maintained a similar voting pattern throughout the decade.[61]

Increased taxes and the repeal of the Tender Act created conflict throughout the state. The composition of the legislature changed slightly, as previously unrepresented counties in the interior sent representatives opposed to the measures taken in 1780.[62] Protests became organized and conventions were held in the interior calling for the government to issue new paper money to aid their credit condition. The legislature did not respond to these requests for relief, continuing tax collection efforts and implementing an additional excise tax on luxury goods in 1781.[63] High costs of legal fees and court litigation over debt collection compounded the matter. High taxes, economic depression, and poor yield on crops culminated in Shays' Rebellion, a product of the division within the state between creditors and debtors and merchants and subsistence farmers. This division produced two competing alignments in the state legislature.

Overall, votes taken in the legislature, the demographics of the representatives, and public sentiment throughout the state produced a continuing division in Massachusetts's legislature.[64] From 1780 to 1788, this division was manifested on every issue but especially monetary and fiscal policy. Those living in and around Boston, wealthy merchants and professional men, formed a durable voting bloc, and those living inland, poor farmers and artisans, formed the other. The two groups competed for control over the house and the senate, often resulting in vigorous campaigning.[65] Debates over ratification broke along similar lines, with those around Boston becoming associated with the Federalists and those living inland, the Anti-Federalists. Politics before the Constitution produced moderately organized partyism in that two clearly identifiable sides emerged. Toward the latter half of the 1780s, these two sides conducted rudimentary campaigns but largely lacked statewide identification and organization.[66]

LOOSELY ORGANIZED STATE PARTYISM: NEW HAMPSHIRE

No readily discernible voting patterns emerged in New Hampshire. During the 1780s, the New Hampshire House of Representatives recorded over thirty votes. Yet voting did not fall along sectional lines that created political alignments in other states. The size of New Hampshire may have contributed to the lack of uniform voting by partisan blocs. Most of the state was undeveloped. While the potential for wealth existed, especially in manufacturing, most of the land was frontier or used for subsistence farming. The composition of most towns consisted of small farmers, with very few professionals.[67] These towns mostly agreed on political, economic, and social issues, and any controversy between them created inconsistent factionalism rather than consistent partyism.

Although no consistent geographic voting blocs emerged, very small partisan alignments based on individual voting did develop. No one group was ever able to command a majority in the assembly. But of the more than seventy assembly members, around sixty individuals formed two voting blocs that voted together roughly 86 percent of the time.[68] These groups coalesced around specific individuals, with George Gains, a Portsmouth artisan, John Pickering, a lawyer from Portsmouth and Newington, John Sparhawk, a Portsmouth merchant, and Ephraim Robinson, a merchant from Exeter, on one side and Moses Leavitt, a Northampton innkeeper, Jonathan Dow, a Quaker farmer-preacher from Weare, Jonathan Gaskett, a Richmond farmer, and Stephen Powers, a Newport farmer, on the other.[69] Characteristic of other state legislatures, two voting blocs formed and competed on policy issues. The groups in New Hampshire were just smaller and less organized.

As in other states, economic development, taxes, debts, paper money, and, to a lesser extent, the treatment of Loyalists divided representatives in the assembly. Some representatives from Portsmouth and surrounding areas voted in a bloc in support of creditors, the collection of taxes (with the exception of an excise tax), and import and poll taxes. These representatives often voted in favor of the interests of towns and areas most associated with trade. The other group opposed these measures and supported policies that benefited the noncommercial communities.[70] This legislative division also carried over to ratification debates, with most representatives supporting commercial areas becoming Federalists and those supporting noncommercial areas, Anti-Federalists.

Partyism in New Hampshire remained fragmented despite two small, interest-based voting blocs in the legislature. The competing legislative groups did not pursue electioneering strategies, and no organized campaigns emerged in New Hampshire until after ratification of the Constitution. In general, New Hampshire was more representative of the antiparty sentiments attributed to the framers. Even in the annual statewide gubernatorial race, party competition attracted very little if any interest.

Voters were often encouraged to eschew partisan preferences and party spirit because these were averse to the public good.[71]

Partyism and the 1787 Constitution

The Declaration of Independence demonstrated the importance of the various states acting together for their collective interests. Hence the use of language such as "The unanimous Declaration of the thirteen united States of America" and "And for the support of this Declaration . . . we mutually pledge to each other our Lives, our Fortunes and our sacred Honor." No state alone was capable of successfully winning the war against Great Britain or successfully funding the debts accrued during the war. To facilitate cooperation, the Articles of Confederation established a "perpetual union" and a "league of friendship" among the thirteen states. Ratified in 1781, the Articles of Confederation established a central government for the newly formed nation. If the Articles' goal was collective action, the new government faced the challenge of balancing the requirements to contribute to the collective good with the independence asserted by each individual state. This created competition between the interests of the individual states and the national interest, and the entire structure of the Articles of Confederation depended on states subverting their partial interest for the good of the whole.[72]

Under the Articles of Confederation, partyism took two interrelated forms. The first form stemmed from partyism in the separate states. In the new Congress, each state was allowed no less than two and no more than seven representatives. As state legislatures selected representatives, these delegates were representative of the electing assembly. If a state maintained a particular policy interest, this interest was transferred to the delegates in Congress. Furthermore, state legislatures maintained control over their congressional delegations and replaced delegates when they acted against the state's interest. As Keith L. Dougherty explains, annual elections of congressional delegations meant that "each change in state personnel corresponded with a new election of congressional personnel. This made delegates responsive not only to their state assemblies but to current interests within their assemblies."[73] Because delegates closely mirrored the partisan preferences of their state legislature, their partisanship affected their position on issues that came before Congress. This established the second form of partyism, as the individual states became political actors within Congress. State delegate votes were not counted individually. Rather, they were counted by states based on the majority preference of the state delegation. A state's vote was not counted if the delegation could not come to a majority decision. Divisions in Congress emerged based on policy preferences, with regionally based cleavages between New England, the Middle States, and the South being the most prominent. Alliances were necessary because no one region could command a majority, and by 1786 Congress had become increasingly polarized between the North and the South.[74]

Under the Articles of Confederation, the issue of congressional powers divided the states between those who supported providing Congress with broad powers and those opposed to such measures. Many believed the ill-defined congressional powers in the Articles provided a necessary check on Congress to prevent it from assuming more power at the expense of state sovereignty and the people's liberty. Others believed Congress needed enough authority to fulfill the purpose of the Articles: common defense, security of liberty, and mutual and general welfare. Under the Articles, Congress was at the mercy of the states because financial and military contributions were essentially voluntary. Congress had no coercive power over the states and could only make requests for military personnel and funds. Alexander Hamilton believed this situation would lead the union to ruin: "The fundamental defect is a want of power in Congress. . . . [T]he confederation itself is defective and requires to be altered; it is neither fit for war, nor peace."[75] Shortly after the Articles were ratified, Madison echoed Hamilton's sentiments and proposed an amendment that vested Congress with "general and implied powers . . . to enforce and carry into effect all the articles of the said Confederation against any of the States which shall refuse or neglect to abide by such their determinations."[76] States' rights advocates eventually blocked his amendment, leaving Madison only indirect methods of expanding national power, including referring his key proposals to committees dominated by more nationally minded delegates.[77]

Division between state delegations, deficiencies in the Articles, and his inability to successfully remedy the situation pushed Madison toward a constitutional convention and criticism of what he considered factionalism under the Articles of Confederation. In April 1787, Madison prepared an analysis of the Articles of Confederation and a report titled "Vices of the Political System of the United States." He identified eleven political deficiencies needing remedy for the union to survive. Many of these deficiencies, or vices, were the product of partisanship at the national and state levels. According to Madison, there existed a "want of concert in matters where common interest requires it." But achieving common interest was frequently subverted by the "perverseness of particular States whose concurrence is necessary." At the state level, majorities continually created a "multiplicity" of unjust laws, as "selfish views [were veiled] under the profession of the public good" and "one part of the society [invaded] the rights of another."[78] In other words, factionalism sacrificed the public good for private interest and often led majorities to suppress the rights of minorities. Madison made a similar argument in Federalist No. 10.

Leading up to the constitutional convention, delegates faced various sources of division stemming from partisanship within the states and disagreements over constitutional design and principles. Similar to Madison's observations, many delegates at the convention recognized the disparity in power between Congress under the Articles and the state legislatures and the political vices resulting from granting power to the states at the expense of national authority. The convention addressed the need to revise the Articles of Confederation and remedy the problems with state governments. While many delegates agreed that change was necessary, the extent of change to the national government's power played a significant role in creating partisan divisions at the constitutional convention. Other divisions emerged over the issues of representation and slavery. The former was settled through compromise between the large states, which wanted representation based on population, and the smaller states, which wanted equal representation. The latter issue created a cleavage between the northern and southern states, with delegates reaching a compromise on the slave trade and counting slaves for representation and taxation purposes.[79]

These divisive issues failed to produce cohesive voting blocs as coalitions shifted across various issues. Analyses of voting at the convention reveal numerous shifts in coalition structures during voting as delegates debated various constitutional provisions and their perceived benefits and disadvantages to various interests. Summarizing various attempts to describe the dynamics of decision making at the convention, Hoadley explains, "It appears clear that no solid foundations for a party system were established. At most, there existed a set of shifting factions, but they certainly did not exhibit the strength, depth, or stability of parties."[80] The lack of cohesive voting blocs across multiple dimensions of conflict extended through ratification debates after the conclusion of the convention.

Conflict over ratification produced the first national, partisan campaign between the Anti-Federalists, who opposed ratification, and the Federalists, who supported ratification. However, these partisan groups did not necessarily produce cohesive national alignments. Michael Allen Gillespie describes these early parties as "little more than diffuse groups of disparate men in various states who were connected principally by the issue of the Constitution. There were also profound differences within both groups over the meaning of the Constitution."[81] Although the issue was seemingly dichotomous, to adopt the Constitution (with or without amendments) or to reject it, the coalitions that formed were more pluralistic and diverse, consisting of men of differing opinions and interests within and between states.[82]

Prior to the adoption of the Constitution, American history is replete with examples of partisan competition and political divisiveness. From colonial conflicts between local assemblies and the Crown to the development of legislative voting blocs in state legislatures, political actors involved with the creation of the Constitution were exposed to varying degrees of partyism. These political parties were not the equivalent of their modern counterparts. However, the interests, issues, and coalitions were an indication of the developing partyism that emerged shortly after ratification of the Constitution. Many of the partisan alignments within the states prior to the constitutional convention continued after ratification with the development of legislative parties in Congress. That is, the conflict over national policy, such as Hamilton's financial plan, the location of the national capital, and the Jay Treaty, reflected early partisan alignments prior to the Constitution.[83]

After ratification, political actors faced the difficulty of reconciling the prevailing partyism, particularly evident in many state legislatures, with an intellectual and political history that condemned parties. "Wherever the Americans looked," argues Richard Hofstadter, "whether to the politics of Georgian England, their own provincial capitals, or the republics of the historical past, they thought they saw in parties only a distracting and divisive force representing the claims of unbridled, self-ish, special interests." Hofstadter rightly argues that the idea of a mature, modern party system was an "immensely sophisticated idea, and it was not an idea that the [founders] found fully developed when they began their enterprise in republican constitutionalism in 1788."[84] However, this does not preclude the possibility that they recognized the beginnings of this mature party system and embarked on the completely novel enterprise, absent philosophical or historical precedent, of creating a party system around the idea of a legitimate political opposition. As partyism emerged at the national level, these political actors developed the foundations of a party system and the two-party constitution.

CHAPTER 3

Partyism and the First Amendment

Organizing Opposition and the Partisan Press

One of the early steps in constructing the two-party Constitution involved the nature and scope of the First Amendment. The First Amendment states, "Congress shall make no law . . . abridging the freedom of speech, or of the press." Yet in 1798 President John Adams signed into law the Sedition Act, which restricted the content of newspapers, particularly Republican ones. The Federalists' broadly constructed Sedition Act made individuals criminally liable for criticizing the government or governmental officials. It empowered the predominantly Federalist courts to punish opinion, without distinguishing criticism and opposition from defamation and subversion.[1]

Despite the seemingly simple guarantee of freedom of expression, the meaning of this freedom is unclear and, sometimes, unsettled. Although the First Amendment seems to protect speech, laws forbidding certain types of speech are commonplace.[2] When dealing with difficult First Amendment issues, the Supreme Court has answered freedom of speech and press questions by developing principles on a case-by-case basis rather than a general theory of free speech. This has led the Court to only superficially rely on the language of the amendment and the history of its meaning.[3] In this way, the Court has produced a "complex and conflicting body of constitutional precedent," and our legal understanding of the First Amendment is restricted to principles derived from a history of cases in which the amendment was invoked to protect what was deemed illegal action.[4] The applicability and meaning of the First Amendment, however, extends beyond this jurisprudential genealogy.

Much of our understanding of the First Amendment is based on the judicial branch's effort to establish an accepted legal norm by interpreting meaning from the inherited constitutional text by way of analysis and elaboration. This jurisprudential model relies on an authoritative judiciary to interpret the Constitution and ultimately declare what the law is. In terms of freedom of expression, many constitutional law casebooks start First Amendment examinations with the Espionage Act of 1917 and the landmark case *Schenck v. United States*.[5] In addition, the First Amendment was not applied to the states until 1925, when the Supreme Court incorporated it through the due process clause of the Fourteenth Amendment. Because of the limited number of times the Court dealt with freedom of expression, there is relatively little emphasis on Supreme Court cases prior to *Schenck*.[6] Our First Amendment understanding comes from cases decided more than a century after it was adopted. This emphasis on the legal history since 1917 has structured the way the First Amendment is understood and the extent to which it is applied to our understanding of modern politics. The amendment is traditionally understood as a protection for minorities from an overbearing majority. That is, these rights are interpreted as minority rights—those of unpopular groups or individuals to speak out in the face of a hostile majority.[7] In the modern legal context, the core purpose of the First Amendment was protection from a tyrannical majority. This meaning is largely the result of a jurisprudential model relying solely on the interpretive authority of the judicial branch. The jurisprudential model, however, provides just one of many ways in which political actors can understand and use the First Amendment and the protections it guarantees.

Another model is political. Under this model, other governing actors and institutions participate, through the political process, in resolving constitutional issues stemming from substantive and procedural issues and questions of textual meaning.[8] This political model allows for a larger breadth of constitutional meaning by incorporating the efforts of nonjudicial actors in how we understand the mechanisms by which constitutional questions are conceptualized and addressed and how these political responses redefine the types of influential actions available to political participants in their efforts to alter their political environment. Framing our constitutional understanding in the more general context of American political development can broaden and supplement the jurisprudential model, thereby enhancing our understanding of constitutional orders and the related political resources available to actors seeking political change.

One of the earliest controversies involving the First Amendment was not solely a matter of judicial interpretation. The Alien and Sedition Acts of 1798 proved that the First Amendment's meaning was unsettled and that the path to settling the meaning would be paved by political actors, in addition to the judiciary.[9] The politics of the acts helped establish the nature and scope of freedom of speech and the press as a guarantee against oppression from a congressional minority attempting to legislatively circumscribe the political participation of a rising national majority. The responses to the controversial legislation were also critical in developing an expanded theory of the protections guaranteed by the amendment beyond prior restraint to include subsequent punishment.[10]

Federalists and Republicans had competing interpretations of the First Amendment. For the Federalists, basing their understanding on English common law tradition, the amendment only protected against prior restraint. The Republicans, however, developed a broader interpretation that protected individuals from both prior restraint and subsequent punishment. However, the controversy between the competing parties extended well beyond the nature of rights guaranteed by the First Amendment. More broadly, this constitutional debate had a lasting impact on the development of political parties, as the Republicans' broader construction would allow the press to be used as a mobilizing mechanism for political parties, particularly opposition parties. The controversy between Federalists and Republicans over the meaning of the First Amendment redefined the resources available to an opposition party by legitimizing the use of the press as a means of building a majority coalition around political principles different from those accepted by the prevailing administration. Events such as President Jefferson's 1807 embargo on trade and the War of 1812 accelerated the development of the partisan press, as the Federalists founded a number of new press outlets to organize and disseminate their opposition to the Republicans.[11] The early debates over the meaning of the First Amendment established a much stronger commitment to majoritarian politics than previously understood by the jurisprudential model.[12]

The commitment to majoritarian politics that emerged in response to the Alien and Sedition Acts was central for understanding how political parties became an integral component of American democracy. Print became the primary tool used by early political parties to organize electoral efforts and disseminate political information. The Republicans' understanding and use of newspapers made political parties at that time appear more similar to their modern counterparts than once thought.[13] Compared to a modern, mass political party, early American parties were still in developmental stages because they lacked many institutional structures such as national committees, party nominating conventions, and campaign committees. However, despite their lack of formal institutional structures, early parties approximated some of the key functions of modern political parties such as organizing and mobilizing voters in elections. And newspapers, protected by the Republicans' understanding of the First Amendment, was the primary means by which an opposition party, committed to majoritarian politics, could organize an electoral challenge to those in government.

This early controversy over the meaning of the First Amendment determined the extent to which political parties, and an opposition party, would be allowed to participate in the democratic process. The partisan press was one of the primary tools in the subsequent development of the two-party system in the United States. As one scholar has written, "The many gaps left by the party system's underdevelopment were filled by networks of partisan newspapers, which provided a fabric that held the parties together between elections and conventions, connected voters and activists to the larger party, and linked the different political levels and geographic regions of the country."[14] In addition, these partisan newspapers gave party members an identity through association with others pursuing a common political cause.[15] Subsequently, subscriptions to newspapers served as a proxy for party registration, and the press was capable of connecting individuals ideologically.[16]

It should be no surprise that the development of an opposition party and the rise of the press occurred in tandem, as newspapers can easily be understood as a means by which the Republican Party could effectively disseminate their alternative political principles in an effort to win office.[17] Commenting on the development of American democracy, Alexis de Tocqueville was correct in placing so much emphasis on freedom of the press: "[The newspaper] not only has the effect of suggesting the same design to many men; it furnishes them the means of executing in common the design they themselves had already conceived," and "the newspaper has brought [individuals] nearer, and it continues to be necessary to them to keep them together."[18] Both the Federalist Party and the Republican Party were keenly aware of the influence newspapers could have on public opinion, and both used newspapers, pamphlets, and political essays to influence public opinion. In addition, both parties distributed opinions from fellow partisans collected from petitions and resolutions.[19]

However, although both parties were beginning to utilize newspapers to influence public sentiment, the constitutionality of these practices was not settled because there was no clear constitutional consensus on the rules governing the use of the press. As the party in government, the Federalists' use of the press during the Jay Treaty controversy was ultimately supportive of the government's actions, and their acceptance of the relationship between the press and public opinion extended only to these positive pronouncements of government action, not opposition politics. Early debates over the meaning and application of the First Amendment's free press clause can be understood as a step in the constitutional creation of a legitimate opposition party that facilitated larger democratic movements in the early republic.

Focusing on this early construction of the First Amendment and the development of political parties helps clarify the function of an opposition party in American politics and the two-party system's democratic and majoritarian features. The Federalists' controversial Alien and Sedition Acts have been used as evidence to substantiate claims that parties were deemed illegitimate during the early republic, that Republicans and the Federalists did not view each other as alternating parties in a two-party system, and that organized opposition parties could not sustain both freedom and social unity.[20] The Federalists viewed the Republicans as traitors; the Republicans viewed the Federalists as monarchists.

However, history has not necessarily overcome the propensity to view rival parties as embodying governing principles that are unacceptable alternatives in the two-party system. As Jefferson explained, a difference in opinion does not necessarily mean a difference in constitutional principles.[21] Rival parties can disagree without undermining the constitutional process by which parties gain electoral victories. In other words, we must understand the development of oppositional party politics apart from the perceptions each party has of the other and look at the procedural and substantive developments that facilitated the emergence of countervailing perceptions of the party in government, which creates an oppositional party in the electorate. The Sedition Act was less about suppressing political name-calling and critical opinions of governmental offices and more about prohibiting the participation of political parties and an opposition in the political arena.[22]

THE ALIEN AND SEDITION ACTS OF 1798

In 1798, amid escalating tensions between the United States and France, President John Adams placed the country in a "virtual state of undeclared war" as he increased the size of the army, established the Department of the Navy and ordered more warships, attempted to fortify the nation's harbors, authorized naval attacks on armed French ships, and nullified all treaties with France.[23] Loyal Federalists were quick to support Adams's efforts; Republicans were weary of the expanding national power. Most of Adams's and the Federalists' proposals were easily adopted because the latter controlled majorities in both the House and the Senate. Meanwhile, mounting opposition to the Federalists accused them of using an exaggerated threat of war as a vehicle to pursue their partisan agenda of strengthening the national government. Escalating political antagonism between the parties began to divide the nation.

The press became a battleground for partisan struggles and the means of attacking public officials. Benjamin Franklin Bache, Benjamin Franklin's grandson, was editor of the most prominent partisan Republican newspaper, the *Aurora*. Bache, who was uncompromising in his partisan attachments, used the paper to openly insult Federalist officials and has been credited with printing a description of Adams as "blind, bald, crippled, toothless, [and] querulous."[24] Not even George Washington was immune to his attacks. Bache claimed that the "American nation had been debauched by Washington," and once Washington stepped down from his presidential position, he was chastised for being "the source of all the misfortunes of [the] country."[25] In response, Washington believed the Republican-leaning newspaper and Bache wanted to "weaken, if not destroy, the confidence of the Public" through a "malignant industry and persevering falsehoods."[26] The *Gazette of the United States*, the most prominent of the Federalists' newspapers, responded by openly opposing the abusive and irresponsible accusations from the "worst and basest men." The *Porcupine's Gazette* labeled Bache an "abandoned liar" to be dealt with like "a Turk, a Jew, a Jacobin, or a Dog."[27] Although many of the available newspapers did not follow Bache in his partisan rhetoric and defamation of public officials, the Federalists still were concerned with the impact opposition to the government could have on representatives and public opinion.

"No character," warned Alexander Hamilton, "however upright, is a match for constantly reiterated attacks, however false[,] . . . [for] the public mind, fatigued at length with resistance to the calumnies which eternally assail it, is apt at the end to sit down with the opinion that a person so often accused cannot be entirely innocent."[28] The Federalists feared that the persistent, vehement attacks on the character of public figures would keep those most qualified for office from entering public service, leaving only those "without virtue or talents" to replace them.[29] There was truth behind the Federalists' fears. Toward the end of his administration, Washington lamented the increasing number of accusations against the government and his administration. Although Washington was rarely named, he took these attacks as indirect personal attacks against him. In a conversation with Madison, Washington cited the increasing opposition to the government as one of the primary causes driving him from public service.[30] Even the honorable George Washington was ready to leave his public position due to the indirect attacks on his character and the growing disenchantment with his administration.

The relationship between the United States, England, and France was a significant source of division in Washington's administration and the public at large. After the Revolutionary War, tensions were high because Britain continued to export goods to the United States while blocking imports through tariffs and trade restrictions, occupied northern forts despite agreeing to vacate them at the conclusion of the war, and interfered with American sailors on neutral ships, seizing military supplies. The situation escalated with the French Revolution and the outbreak of war between England and France. Foreign relations had to be addressed to avoid armed hostilities with Great Britain and maintain the country's healthy economic life, which was heavily tied to relations with England.[31] In attempting to resolve the situation, President Washington had to navigate competing policy positions from Hamilton and the Federalists and Jefferson and the Republicans. Caught between war and negotiation, Washington opted for the latter, organizing a special mission to England to negotiate a treaty. The main question remained, whom would he send? Deep partisan divisions meant that whomever Washington chose might negotiate a treaty favorable to a particular ideological preference. Much to the dismay of the Republicans, he chose John Jay, Chief Justice of the Supreme Court and a Federalist.

The United States gained very little from the Jay Treaty, which the Federalist majority in the Senate narrowly approved. Although Washington and the Federalists attempted to keep the treaty secret, a Republican senator provided a newspaper with a copy of the ratified treaty, which was disseminated, as Madison observed, "with an electric velocity to every part of the Union."[32] The historian Todd Estes described the response to the treaty: "The initial public response was outrage. As soon as the treaty's outlines began to appear, critics denounced it in acerbic terms. Jay was hanged in effigy all around the country. Loud, angry crowds turned out to hear speakers deride the treaty as a capitulation to Great Britain." Republican newspapers, especially Bache's *Aurora*, vilified the Jay Treaty and the Federalists with "condemnatory editorials and reports of mass demonstrations."[33] Federalist leaders feared the public outcry against the treaty and the influence of the Republican newspaper on public discourse and debate. Although still in early stages of development, the partisan press, used by both the Federalists and the Republicans, was a central component of the debate over the Jay Treaty, as both parties used it to try to shape public opinion in their favor.

When Adams first took office in 1797, the development of the partisan press was still nascent. The Federalist Party maintained primary influence over many of the newspapers, as most printers either supported those in office or avoided politics altogether. After the Republicans opposed the Jay Treaty in 1795, numerous new newspapers emerged, but very few were strongly Republican and opposed to the Federalist administration.[34] Republican newspapers were vastly outnumbered and presented a limited threat to the Federalists in office. Ardent Republican newspapers lacked support given the Republicans' pro-France position, especially after the XYZ Affair, a failed diplomatic mission to address political and economic relations with France. President Adams sent Elbridge Gerry, Charles Pinckney, and John Marshall to negotiate with France's foreign minister, Charles-Maurice de Talleyrand-Périgord. The envoys, arriving in October 1797, primarily met with intermediaries, Jean Conrad Hottinguer (later referred to as "X" in the commission's dispatches), Pierre Bellamy ("Y"), and Lucien Hauteval ("Z"), who stipulated, among other things, that the Americans disavow a speech by President Adams and provide a low-interest loan and bribes before they could meet and negotiate with Talleyrand.[35] No formal treaty was made, leading to the quasi-war in 1798, and the Federalists used the publication of the commission's dispatches to attack the Republicans and their pro-France position. As Jeffrey L. Pasley points out, news of the French's misconduct with American diplomats and commerce was enough to push public opinion toward an anti-French, pro-administration position.[36] The Federalists did not need to flood the newspapers with aggressive partisanship, and the Republican presses struggled to counter the Federalists' advantage.

After word spread regarding the XYZ Affair, the Federalists in Congress pursued an aggressive agenda to ensure domestic and international tranquility. With the Alien and Sedition Acts, the Federalists targeted their political adversaries in an attempt to circumscribe their political participation and suppress domestic opposition. The Alien Act targeted immigrants, particularly the French and Irish, who overwhelmingly supported the Republicans. The Federalists also increased the naturalization requirement to fourteen years and gave the president power to deport any foreign individual who he deemed a threat to the United States. The Sedition Act specifically targeted Republicans by criminalizing any form—written, printed, uttered, or published—of dissent against the United States or the laws passed by Congress. As Jefferson noted, Republicans knew the Sedition Act was designed for "the suppression of the whig presses."[37] Although few existed, the Federalists attacked the opposition press, a valuable asset available to Republicans in their organizing efforts to challenge the Federalists politically and electorally.

Importantly, the Federalists' legislation called into question the meaning of the First Amendment's guarantee of the right of expression. More broadly, the Sedition Act is an important episode in the larger development of the nature and scope of the rights guaranteed by the First Amendment. The original meaning of the freedom of speech and press clauses is highly contested. With seditious libel being part of English common law, the question is whether the First Amendment was designed to be a departure from or a continuation of this common law practice. Many constitutional scholars and judges have taken the position of departure. "I wholly disagree . . . ," argued Justice Oliver Wendell Holmes, "that the First Amendment left the common law as to seditious libel in force. History seems to me against the notion."[38] Similarly, Justice Hugo Black argued, "In the First Amendment the Founding Fathers gave the free press the protection it must have to fulfill its essential role in our democracy. . . . The Government's power to censor the press was abolished so that the press would remain forever free to censure the Government."[39] This interpretive originalism concludes that the Sedition Act was unconstitutional because the American Revolution and the First Amendment superseded and replaced English common law.[40] Other constitutional scholars and historians argue that there is insufficient evidence that the original meaning of the First Amendment supports the idea that the founding fathers intentionally overturned common law practices of seditious libel.[41] One can look in vain, concluded Leonard Levy, for meaningful statements by public men during the First Amendment's ratification debates that support the position that the freedom of press clause was intended to prohibit the practice of seditious libel.[42] According to this position, the more libertarian understanding of the First Amendment did not develop until the Sedition Act called into question the meaning of the freedom of press clause and crystallized the argument over the perpetuation of English common law. If the departure thesis is correct, the Republicans could argue the Sedition Act was unconstitutional; if the continuation thesis is correct, the Federalists could justify its constitutionality. The importance of the debate over the Sedition Act extends beyond ascertaining the First Amendment's original meaning. Within the debates is a construction of constitutional meaning and general First Amendment theory, as political actors determined the meaning of the freedom of press clause related to the use of newspapers as a political tool and the place of an opposition party in American politics.

CONSTRUCTING THE FIRST AMENDMENT: THE FEDERALISTS

The Federalists' understanding of the right of expression and its limits can be seen in the language chosen in the Sedition Act. Section 2 of the act reads:

> That if any person shall write, print, utter or publish . . . any false, scandalous, and malicious writing or writings against the government of the United States, or either house of the Congress of the United States, or the President of the United States, with intent to defame . . . or bring them, or either of them, into contempt or disrepute; or to excite against them . . . the hatred of the good people of the United States, or to stir up sedition within the Unites States . . . or to resist, oppose, or defeat any such law or act . . . then such persons . . . shall be punished by a fine not exceeding two thousand dollars, and by imprisonment not exceeding two years.[43]

The Federalists were clearly attempting to eliminate political dissent. In their view, the First Amendment did not grant absolute license to criticize the government, in either speech or print. Freedom of speech and freedom of the press were understood in a much more restricted sense. The First Amendment was understood only to prohibit prior restraint in that courts could not prevent a publisher or author from printing offensive material but could enact civil and criminal prosecutions for material deemed seditious or libelous after publication.[44] That is, the Federalists attempted to constitutionally legitimize the Sedition Act as a mechanism for overcoming what they viewed as corrupt partisan practices by silencing the opposition press.[45] The language of the Sedition Act, therefore, gave the national government jurisdiction over libel and defined the nature of free speech.[46]

The Federalists' justification for the Sedition Act connected English common law with the new written Constitution and the First Amendment.[47] Even before ratification of the First Amendment, the concept of freedom of speech and press were part of English common law. There, the government prosecuted sedition as a means of regulating the press. Like the Sedition Act, the common law defined freedom of the press as a freedom from the government placing any prior restraint on publication. In his *Commentaries on the Laws of England*, the English jurist William Blackstone explained how prosecuting seditious libel and freedom of the press could coincide: "The liberty of the press is indeed essential to the nature of a free state: but this consists in laying no *previous* restraints upon publications, and not in freedom from censure for criminal matter when published."[48] The common law did not establish a broad guarantee of rights but attempted to balance governmental and societal restraint. By prohibiting prior restraint, the government could not tyrannically prohibit individual thought or expression; by preventing seditious libel, individuals could not undermine governmental legitimacy. In general, this eighteenth-century common law meaning of a free press was understood to be conducive to liberty because it maintained law and order, while an unrestrained press was believed to produce an "intolerable indulgence in licentiousness."[49]

The Sedition Act, however, was not simply a restatement of the principle of seditious libel in common law, as the Federalists introduced three important procedural changes. The act established a fixed punishment for violation, authorized juries (rather than the judge) to determine guilt, and allowed defendants to use truth as evidence.[50] The second and third points coincide with practices in America since 1735 with the trial of John Peter Zenger, printer of the *New-York Weekly Journal*. Zenger was charged with seditious libel for printing articles and editorials that were critical of New York's governor.[51] Zenger's attorney, Andrew Hamilton, argued that the veracity of what was printed should serve as a defense and that a jury, not the judge, should determine if Zenger was guilty. It was the jury that acquitted Zenger, establishing two new procedural standards for freedom of the press. In other words, compared to the common law, the Sedition Act was far less restrictive on the freedom of press because it incorporated the common law criminalization of seditious libel with the widely accepted principles of truth as a defense and trial by jury.[52] Although the Sedition Act incorporated principles from Zenger's case, it did not replace the common law tradition of prosecuting seditious libel.

In proposing the Sedition Act, the Federalists recognized the relationship between the press, public opinion, and representative government. This relationship concerned them because they feared the press would become a pseudo-representative body. This concern was adamantly expressed by Representative John Allen, a Federalist from Connecticut, in a speech defending the Sedition Act during the Fifth Congress. In his speech, Allen accused the Republicans of using newspapers, specifically, the *Aurora*, to "persuade the people of certain facts, which a majority of this House, at least, and of the people at large, I believe, know to be unfounded."[53] Allen applied this problem to the broader question of Congress's constitutional powers and the more specific question of the constitutionality of the Sedition Act. Who decides if Congress has overstepped its limits and if the act is constitutional? For Allen, the Constitution empowers the courts to determine such constitutional questions. The "Jacobians," however, promulgated a dangerous doctrine: "Each man has the right of deciding for himself, and that as many as are of opinion that the law is unconstitutional, have a right to combine and oppose it by force." Moreover, when a portion of the people "oppose the laws, they are insurgents and rebels; they are not the people." That is, Allen feared the press could move sovereignty away from established representative institutions and toward illicit extraconstitutional actions by fragments of the population. The only safe method of opposing government was to replace "obnoxious representatives" through elections, in which the press had no part.[54]

Society, Allen reasoned, required confidence in the "bonds of union" that connected individuals, families, society, and government. Unrestrained freedom of the press and opinion, which tended to "vomit" falsehood and hatred, dissolved these salutary bonds. As an example, Allen pointed to the French Revolution: "At the commencement of the Revolution in France those loud and enthusiastic advocates for liberty and equality took special care to occupy and command all the presses in the nation." He further pointed to the press's "baneful effects" and influence over "the poor, the ignorant, the passionate, and the vicious," who became "tools of faction and ambition, [while] the virtuous, the pacific, and the rich, were their victims." Allen then stated that the purpose of the Sedition Act was to prevent a similar revolution in the United States: "[The] Jacobians of our country . . . are determined to preserve in their hands, the same weapon [the press]; it is our business to wrest it from them."[55]

The Federalists' narrow interpretation of the First Amendment corresponded with their general democratic theory and understanding of representation in the constitutional republic. "The repressive aspects of the Sedition Act," argued James P. Martin, "served democratic purposes by keeping the public deliberation a representative, not a direct process."[56] The Federalists' legislation coincided with Hamilton's assertion in the *Federalist Papers*: "The republican principle demands, that the deliberate sense of the community should govern the conduct of those to whom they intrust the management of their affairs; but it does not require an unqualified complaisance to every sudden breeze of passion, or every transient impulse which the people may receive from the arts of men, who flatter their prejudice to betray their interests."[57]

Hamilton believed the "people commonly INTENDED the PUBLIC GOOD." However, they were also susceptible to err regarding what constituted this good because they were "beset . . . by the wiles of parasites and sycophants; by the snares of the ambitious, the avaricious, the desperate; by the artifices of men who possess their confidence more than they deserve it; and of those who seek to possess, rather than deserve it."[58] The developing opposition party presented a direct challenge to the representative institutions of government because it established a separate, undemocratic political body from that already created by the people. The opposition "arrogantly pretended," reasoned Fisher Ames, "sometimes to be the people, and sometimes the guardians, the champions of the people. They affect to feel more zeal for a popular Government, and to enforce more respect for Republican principles, than the real Representatives are admitted to entertain."[59] The Republicans' efforts were a challenge to democratic politics because they sought to betray the public interest and undermine those whom the people had entrusted to manage their affairs. Statements like these from the Federalists help explain why they believed the Sedition Act was good policy. However, its constitutionality remained in question.

Although there is no explicit mention of federal jurisdiction over seditious libel, the Federalists relied on common law tradition and a textual interpretation of the necessary and proper clause to constitutionally construct a defense of the Sedition Act. During congressional debates over the Sedition Act, the Republicans argued that the First Amendment protected against laws criminalizing sedition. Allen, however, rejected these claims and connected the Sedition Act to common law and Blackstonian principles. "The freedom of the press and opinion," he argued, "was never understood to give the right of publishing falsehoods and slanders, nor of exciting sedition, insurrection, and slaughter with impunity. A man was always answerable for the malicious publication of falsehood."[60] In addition to Allen, Harrison Gray Otis, a Federalist from Massachusetts, defended the Sedition Act on grounds similar to those of Blackstone.[61] Joining Allen and Otis, South Carolina representative Robert Harper opined that freedom of press still left individuals responsible for printing material that was against the law. The law only protected printed material that was allowable, and the First Amendment did not allow for seditious libel.[62]

In addition to defending the Sedition Act using common law, the Federalists claimed that the necessary and proper clause in Article I, Section 8, granted Congress the constitutional power to legislate on sedition. Article I gives Congress authority "to make all laws which shall be necessary and proper for carrying into execution the foregoing powers, and all other powers vested by this Constitution in the government of the United States, or in any department or officer thereof."[63] Interpreted broadly, this clause allowed Congress to pass sedition legislation if the opposition press was deemed a threat to the national interest and the exercise of governmental power. During congressional debates, Federalists invoked the necessary and proper clause to constitutionally justify the Sedition Act. Given the language of the clause, the Federalists deemed the act necessary for the preservation of the Constitution and the government.[64] A more thorough explanation of the relationship between the Sedition Act and the necessary and proper clause appeared at the state level.

After its passage, the Sedition Act was opposed by Republicans in various states on the grounds that it was a violation of the First Amendment. Jefferson and Madison both worked feverishly to oppose it, and the Virginia and Kentucky Resolutions are perhaps the most prominent examples of opposition to the congressional legislation. The resolutions, discussed in more detail below, called on state legislatures to deem the Sedition Act unconstitutional. States with Federalist-controlled legislatures responded by defending the constitutionality of the Sedition Act and Congress's power to pass it. In Massachusetts, state legislators justified the Sedition Act using the necessary and proper clause. The Constitution was instituted to promote the union of the several states and foster the happiness, property, and safety of the people. The Sedition Act was both expedient and necessary because an unrestrained press, one that allowed "licentiousness in speaking and writing, that is only employed in propagating falsehood and slander," was as a threat to the overall purpose of the Constitution.[65] Similar statements were made in Connecticut and New Hampshire.[66]

Given Virginia's role in opposing the Sedition Act, the Federalist minority in the Virginia legislature issued the *Address of the Minority of the Virginia Legislature*, a detailed justification for the necessity and constitutionality of the act. After a contentious eight-day debate over the constitutionality of the act, the House of Delegates adopted the Virginia Resolutions and quickly followed with the *Address of the General Assembly to the People of the Commonwealth of Virginia*, which defended the actions taken by the Virginia legislature and was published and distributed by the state.[67] The Federalist minority moved to add the *Address of the Minority* to the *Address of the General Assembly*, but the Republican majority defeated their motion. Nonetheless, the Federalists printed and distributed it. Although it was written anonymously, many believe John Marshall was one of its principal authors.[68] The *Address of the Minority* details an interpretation of the First Amendment that coincides with other Federalist accounts that sought to combine Blackstonian and Zengerian principles and justify the Sedition Act using the necessary and proper clause.

The author of the *Address of the Minority* frames the necessity of the Sedition Act by connecting the argument of national security and federalism. The Constitution explicitly gives the federal government exclusive power over the matters of treaty, war, and commerce. The federal government should be allowed sufficient latitude to protect the Union from internal and external hostilities because national security is a national, not a state, responsibility.[69] Having established the federal government's plenary power over national security, the question posed in the *Address of the Minority* is whether the Constitution empowers Congress to pass sedition legislation. Again, the author appeals to the common law under-standing of freedom of the press: "In all the nations of the earth, where presses are known, some corrective of their licentiousness has been deemed indispensable."[70] Because of the necessary and proper clause, the government has the power to punish "actual resistance" to federal laws. Accordingly, only a flawed construction of the clause would prohibit punishment of actions "which obviously lead to and prepare resistance."[71] Moreover, Article III, Section 2, of the Constitution provides the judi-ciary with federal jurisdiction over cases involving common law. And if a judicial power exists to punish "libels against the government, as a com-mon law offence arising under the constitution," then it is understood that Congress is empowered to legislate against sedition in order for this judicial power to take effect.[72]

The argument regarding the necessary and proper clause is related to the appropriate method of constitutional interpretation, and the author of the *Address of the Minority* defends a broad reading of the Constitu-tion. The Constitution is different from a congressional statute in that the former is constructed in general expressions while the latter captures more minute details.[73] One should avoid interpreting the Constitution in the same manner as a piece of legislation because the Constitution pri-marily deals with generalities and congressional statues must be as spe-cific as possible. The Constitution, according to the Federalists' argu-ment, should be constructed in broad terms because political expediency often requires Congress to act beyond its enumerated powers to achieve other desirable political outcomes. Although the enumerated powers in Article I do not include the capacity to criminalize seditious libel, it can be justified as an implied power to successfully accomplish the purposes of the Constitution detailed in the Preamble.[74]

Once Congress's authority to pass the Sedition Act was established, the real question remained: did the act violate the First Amendment? The act could be deemed unconstitutional if the freedom of speech and press clause specifically prohibits Congress from any type of legislation regulating speech. To do so, the author of the *Address of the Minority* turns to the language of the First Amendment by comparing the clauses regarding religion and speech. The language used in the Constitution, argued the author, is purposeful and meaningful, and words and phrases are kept to their most basic forms to clearly convey meaning and intent.

Any variation in expressions indicates a clear design to provide a difference in meaning and intent.[75] Regarding religion, the First Amendment prohibits Congress from "making any law respecting a religious establishment." However, regarding expression, the term "respecting" is replaced with the term "abridging." This difference indicates that Congress is prohibited from making any laws dealing with a religious establishment but not laws relating to expression. The First Amendment does not completely remove Congress's legislative capacity regarding expression so long as its laws do not abridge this freedom.[76] The Sedition Act does not abridge the freedom of press clause because of the common law understanding, which prohibits governmental censorship and punishment prior to publication. The punishments detailed in the Sedition Act are only applicable after publication. Any interpretation beyond this understanding, the author concludes, far exceeds the rational application of the freedom of the press as a protected right.[77] Congress was well within its legislative powers to pass the Sedition Act, and it did not abridge the freedom of the press because it did not violate the dominant interpretation of the First Amendment.[78]

In addition to the constitutional ramifications, the Federalists' construction of the First Amendment had political consequences for party development. Newspapers were capable of creating networks of voters, disseminating opinion across a vast geographic area, and forging connections between local, state, and national politics.[79] The Federalists recognized that the partisan press was a central institution in the emergence of a national opposition movement. Their attempt to suppress it coincides with the Constitution-against-parties thesis by delegitimizing the idea and practice of opposition within the political system.[80] Consequently, the passage of the federal sedition law also politicized the judiciary for party purposes. The Federalists dominated the federal judiciary and were now empowered by the Sedition Act to engage in partisan prosecutions of Republican writers. "The partisan intentions of the Federalists Congress," claimed Whittington, "were understood and accepted by the judiciary, and [Associate Justice Samuel] Chase's enthusiasm for persecuting Republicans made him exemplary of the partisan judiciary as a whole."[81] It was no secret that the Federalists aimed to discredit and destroy Republican opposition. They sought to control public opinion in their favor leading into the elections of 1800 and to create a unitary party system supported by a single-party press.[82]

THE REPUBLICANS' ALTERNATIVE FIRST AMENDMENT INTERPRETATION

The Republicans constructed a dramatically different interpretation of the freedom of the press clause. In place of the common law tradition, the Republicans publicly articulated an understanding of the First Amendment in more absolute terms: it should be constructed to prohibit any federal legislation regarding the press.[83] This alternative construction of the First Amendment tied political parties to the Constitution by articulating a constitutional defense of newspapers disseminating opinion, even if it is in opposition to the government. It also tied political parties, especially the party out of office, to public opinion, with newspapers serving as a mediating institution.

Partyism was manifested in the competing constructions of the First Amendment. The Sedition Act brought the concept of parties and opposition to the forefront of politics, and competition between rival parties became defensible with the threat of using the Constitution to eliminate party practices. In the wake of the Sedition Act, the Republican press expanded and became an integral part of the Republican Party.[84] The immediate consequences of the Sedition Act benefited the Federalists because they were able to successfully prosecute and suppress the few Republican presses at the time.[85] In this way, the Sedition Act was a success. The long-term effects, however, reveal its failure; the Sedition Act actually galvanized journalists to eschew traditional nonpartisan approaches to the press. These partisan printers found a place in the growing political parties.[86]

The Republican's connection between opinion, parties, and the press was present long before the Sedition Act. At the beginning of Washington's first term, John Fenno, an entrepreneur from Boston, established the *Gazette of the United States.* Although Fenno intended his paper to be nonpartisan, he printed various columns, such as John Adams's "Discourses on Davila," that were viewed as pro-Federalist and pro-administration. In addition, many of the leading advertisers in the *Gazette* were brokerage firms involved with government securities that benefited from Hamilton's financial policies.[87] Demonstrating the growing animosity in Washington's administration between Hamilton and Jefferson, the latter described the *Gazette* as "a paper of pure Toryism, disseminating the doctrines of monarchy, aristocracy, and the exclusion of the influence of the people."[88] In response, Jefferson envisioned a national paper capable of reaching the national public to counter the antirepublicanism of the *Gazette*. Along with Madison, Jefferson devised a plan to establish a newspaper capable of shaping public opinion against the Federalist administration. With the help of Madison's college friend and roommate, Philip Freneau, Jefferson and Madison established the *National Gazette,* and both assisted in creating a base of subscribers to the new Republican-based paper.

Jefferson's and Madison's intentional turn to the press as an organ of opposition introduced partyism as an alternative means of affecting the political landscape. During his first year in Congress, Madison experienced great legislative success, particularly with the Bill of Rights. However, at the hands of the Federalists' congressional majority, Madison suffered defeat in policy debates related to Hamilton's financial plan, including the assumption of the states' war debts and the creation of a national bank. Madison could have accepted these policy losses as part of the designed process of congressional deliberation and separation of powers. Yet he and Jefferson deliberately opted for an extraconstitutional alternative involving the creation of an opposition party.[89] In so doing, they would have to defend the concept of a legitimate opposition, which would become inextricably tied to the partisan press and the First Amendment. In the course of founding the first opposition party, Madison also connected partyism to the constitution by constructing an understanding of the freedom of the press clause that would allow for dissenting opinion, his dissenting opinion, to shape public opinion. That is, even though the turn to partyism was extraconstitutional, Madison attempted to make it constitutional. He used his essays in the *National Gazette* to provide the public with foundational principles to help them distinguish between "republicans" and the "anti-republican" Federalists.

Appearing in October 1791, the Philadelphia-based *National Gazette* avoided overtly partisan publications. However, by spring 1792, the partisan tone of the paper increased, and essays appeared denouncing the Federalists' antirepublican tendencies and aristocratic fiscal policy. Amid these intense partisan debates, Madison began his contributions to the *National Gazette*, providing foundational principles for the newly emerging opposition party. Madison's contributions, Lance Banning explains, should not be overlooked because the *National Gazette* was the national mouthpiece of a rapidly emerging opposition party that developed and disseminated a coherent ideology to challenge that of the Federalists.[90] Madison's views of parties and the press expressed in his *National Gazette* writings help explain why he would later develop a more libertarian understanding of the First Amendment in response to the Sedition Act.[91] Madison recognized that newspapers were powerful tools for a party because they have the capability to connect otherwise disconnected readers. In other words, his early essays in the *National Gazette* demonstrate that he understood that the press can connect public opinion with a political party.

Madison's turn to public opinion reveals a tension in the scholarship on both Madison and political parties in general. For some scholars, Madison's appeal to public opinion was a significant departure from his position on public opinion in *The Federalist*.[92] In this view, later in his career Madison became more democratic both in his political theory and in his political practice. Other scholars, however, argue that Madison was consistent in his political thought and commitment to democracy.[93] For many of these scholars, Federalist No. 49 represents the clearest example of this tension in Madison's thought, as he criticized Jefferson's proposal for more frequent constitutional conventions to refer constitutional issues back to the people.[94] For those who attempt to provide a consistent account, Madison's democratic attachments are framed in terms of state's rights within the federal system. And in the case of the national government abusing its constitutional powers, Madison's consistent position was one in which the state legislatures "sound[ed] the alarm to the people, and . . . exert[ed] their local influence in effecting a change of federal representatives" to "annul the acts of the usurpers."[95] Key to this explanation is the difference between Madison's proposed electoral solution and a reoccurring constitutional convention. Rather than follow Jefferson's suggestion that the people consider constitutional issues in constitutional conventions, Madison recommended that they should do so by means of elections, replacing representatives who overstepped their constitutional boundaries. Colleen A. Sheehan connects Madison's position in Federalist No. 44 with his propositions in the Virginia Resolutions.[96] As Sheehan points out, Madison combined a discussion of how the Sedition Act violated the Constitution with his own constitutional interpretation.[97] Madison's use and defense of the partisan press did not culminate with the 1798 Virginia Resolutions; the partisan press was an effective tool in the election of 1800, as the Republicans used public opinion and majoritarian elections to settle the constitutional construction of the First Amendment by removing the Federalists from office. Madison's openness to an opposition press did not waiver during his presidency and the War of 1812. Even in wartime, Madison did not impose limitations on the freedom of the press, and Federalist newspapers were free to openly oppose his administration.[98]

Madison's turn to the partisan press was grounded in his commitment to majority rule, which the extended republic both assisted and restricted. The extended republic assisted in constructing a national majority free from factional dominance because it would "enlarge the sphere" of politics and "divide the community into so great a number of interests and parties, that in the first place a majority will not be likely . . . to have a common interest separate from that of the whole or of the minority."[99] The press could overcome these geographic distances, guide and unify public opinion, and construct a national majority. The importance of the First Amendment's protection of speech and print allowed Madison and the Republicans to combine the "voice" and "sense" of the "millions of people" to facilitate "acting together" in a national, opposition majority.[100] Madison used the partisan newspaper as a means of settling, or "fixing," public opinion. In general, his essays in the *National Gazette* can be separated into two categories: general, theoretical principles of republicanism and specific opposition to Federalist policies.[101]

In December 1791, Madison published another essay in the *National Gazette*. In this essay, "Consolidation," he introduced general themes that would unify subsequent essays and create a Republican ideology based on self-government and republicanism. He underlined the importance of state governments serving as a check on the concentration of power in the national government. Without state legislatures, the "splendor and number" of the executive's prerogatives would increase, as Congress would inevitably transfer more power to the executive due to its inability to "regulate all the various objects belonging to the local governments."[102] These "local organs," or governments, acting together could ensure that national representatives would faithfully execute their responsibilities, thereby preventing an "undue growth of executive power." Madison's argument, however, does not simply rely on state legislatures providing a check on the national government. The fundamental check is the "mutual confidence and affection of all parts of the Union," and the state legislatures are a possible means to this end. The "greater the concord and confidence throughout the great body of the people," explains Madison, "the more readily must they sympathize with each other, the more seasonably can they interpose a common manifestation of their sentiments, the more certainly they will take the alarm at usurpation or oppression."[103] Self-government and a republican constitution require the vigilance of the people. In this early essay, Madison is making a distinction between the Federalists and the emerging opposition by drawing attention to the foundational principles of his opposition party: limited government and the sovereignty of public opinion.

Building on the general themes in "Consolidation," Madison addressed the importance of public opinion in a republican government in an essay titled "Public Opinion." Every government, argues Madison, is restrained by public opinion, especially in a republican government where it is the true sovereign.[104] A republican government must obey public opinion when it is fixed. If public opinion is not fixed or cannot be determined, then the government can influence the direction of public opinion and take a self-directed course. Madison assumes that "real opinion" can be discovered. Measuring public opinion is difficult in a large country, however, increasing the ease with which public sentiment may be counterfeited. This situation, according to Madison, is dangerous to liberty.[105] This is not an argument about the importance of the separation of powers and checks and balances in preserving liberty and a republican form of government. Rather, the people and public opinion defend constitutional rights and keep the government within its proper constitutional limits. But the increased geographic distances between individuals and multiplied interests had to be overcome. To do so, Madison made clear that "whatever facilitates general intercourse of sentiments," including "good roads," a "free press," and "a circulation of newspapers through the entire body of the people," is equivalent to a contraction of territorial limits and is favorable to liberty."[106] Madison's position echoed Jefferson's view of the relationship between public opinion and newspapers: "The way to prevent these irregular interpositions of the people is to give them full information of their affairs thro' the channel of the public papers, & to contrive that those papers should penetrate the whole mass of the people. The basis of our governments being the opinion of the people, the very first object should be to keep that right."[107] The proliferation of newspapers could overcome geographic distances in the extended republic to fix public opinion, even if the force with which it would direct government was in opposition to the current administration.

Madison's commitment to democratic and republican principles revealed a sobering and challenging electoral reality. In the great debate over governmental administration, Madison realized he was at a significant disadvantage. His preferred electoral outcome relied heavily on the "general coalition of sentiments."[108] If republican principles were to guide the administration of government, candidates needed to unify a national majority in support of these principles. However, "the antirepublican party," while "weaker in point of numbers," could take "advantage of all prejudices, local, political, and occupational," thereby "preventing or disturbing the general coalition of sentiments."[109] Although Madison believed his position was backed by national public opinion, "experience shews that in politics as in war, stratagem is often an overmatch for numbers."[110] This became pertinent as many of the important decisions structuring the character of the government were made in Congress. If the Federalists were able to secure a majority, their "antirepublican" principles would find little legislative opposition, particularly if the legislature and executive were united in their policy preferences. By the Second Congress (1791–93), most members could already be identified as either Federalist or Republican, and in the Third Congress (1793–95), party affiliation substantially influenced voting because significant party voting blocs began to form.[111] Far from denouncing the activity of party politics, Madison needed to make his party "a check on the other, so far as the existence of parties cannot be prevented, nor their views accommodated. If this is not the language of reason, it is that of republicanism."[112] He could not prevent the emergence of a Hamilton-led party. Nor could he accommodate the competing views on governmental administration. The solution was to develop a constitutional construction of the First Amendment to counter that of the Federalists' and to embrace an opposition party as a guardian and enforcer of republican principles. Importantly, Madison's view of partyism, particularly the importance of an opposition party for checking the party in government, anticipated Martin Van Buren's promotion of partyism and party competition. Contrary to the Constitution-against-parties thesis, there is continuity in the development of the idea of party competition from Madison to Van Buren, and the institutionalization of partyism during the 1820s was not a break from early constitutional practices.

The need to organize and unify public opinion reveals Madison's view of the freedom of speech and the press. While the Federalists appealed to the common law understanding of these rights, he constructed a more expansive view of their application. In his later *Report on the Virginia Resolutions*, Madison related the First Amendment to the electoral process. Confirming that the right of electing popular officials is "the essence of a free and responsible government," to properly exercise this right there must be organized opposition capable of evaluating those in office. "The value and efficacy of this right," explains Madison, "depends on the knowledge of the comparative merits and demerits of the candidates for public trust, and on the equal freedom, consequently, of examining and discussing these merits and demerits of the candidates."[113] The Sedition Act made electoral competition unequal because the Federalists were protected from censure while leaving the opposition "exposed to the contempt and hatred of the people without a violation of the act."[114] The language of the act specifically protected the president while remaining silent on the vice president, thereby subjecting Vice President Jefferson to malicious and seditious statements. People were "not free" because they were "compelled to make their election between competitors whose pretensions they are not permitted by the act equally to examine, to discuss, and to ascertain." Furthermore, "those in power derive an undue advantage for continuing themselves in it, which, by impairing the right of election, endangers the blessings of the Government."[115] The purpose of the rights guaranteed in the First Amendment was not necessarily to endow individuals with substantive protections from the government or popular majorities. Rather, as Akhil Amar argued, "the genius of the Bill of Rights was not to downplay organizational structure but to deploy it, not to impede popular majorities but to empower them."[116] Madison's interpretation of freedom of speech and the press served an electoral function by permitting an opposition to procedurally unify public opinion into a majority and have a substantive electoral impact without necessarily disadvantaging the rival party.

Both the Federalists and the Republicans took interest in newspapers as a means of influencing public opinion, and as animosity between Hamilton and Jefferson escalated, both were convinced that newspapers were vital to their causes. The Federalists turned to the *Gazette of the United States*; the Republicans, to the *National Gazette*.[117] The turn to public opinion, particularly for Madison and the Republicans, became a key feature in electoral competition and the proliferation of partisan newspapers increased exponentially, particularly following the Sedition Act.

The Republicans used the Alien and Sedition Acts as a catalyst for their opposition to the Federalists. Even the Federalists recognized the growing discontent with their controversial legislation and the electoral danger of an organized opposition. While serving as an ambassador in London, Rufus King received a report from a fellow Federalist who described the situation in the 1798 legislative session: "Much Clamor has been made about the Alien and Sedition Bill, & a Vigorous Attack in the course of the Session, supported by all the Virginia faction, will be made on it, in order to alarm the Public Mind & prepare the way for their success, in the Ensuing election in April next."[118] Scholars attribute the eventual Federalist defeat to the discontent aroused by the Alien and Sedition Acts, as the protests and mobilization leading up to the election of 1800 provided the Republicans with the ideology, organization, and momentum to strip the Federalists of their power at the national and state levels.[119] Newspapers were at the center of organizing this political opposition. The *National Gazette* was the flagship newspaper for developing and distributing a coherent ideology for the Republicans, and they utilized it as an organizational tool for their rapidly developing party.[120]

Evidence of newspapers as a tool of partisan organization can be found throughout many of the states. For example, in 1798, the *Kentucky Gazette* helped organize opposition by advocating for meetings, committees of correspondence, and a general mobilization against the Federalists and their legislation.[121] In New Jersey, Daniel Dodge and Aaron Pennington used Newark's *Centinel of Freedom* to organize opposition against the Alien and Sedition Acts in a predominantly Federalist state. The *Centinel of Freedom* urged "real republicans" in the state of New Jersey to convene "together in either township or county meeting, as convenience may dictate, and there request your public agents by way of remonstrance to repeal the Alien and Sedition Laws, which have been enacted in open violation of the Constitution."[122] William Duane, a staunch Republican, an Irish immigrant, and editor of the *Aurora*, used his newspaper to organize and disseminate petitions from Irish immigrants opposed to the unconstitutional acts. States lacking a Republican newspaper, like New Hampshire, struggled to organize opposition to the Federalists. In a letter to Madison, Jefferson described this difficulty:

> I have however seen letters from New Hampshire from which it appears that the public sentiment there is no longer progressive in any direction, but that at present it is dead water. that during the whole of their late session not a word has been heard of Jacobinism, disorganization & no reproach of any kind cast on the republicans. that there has been a general complaint among the members that they could hear but one side of the question, and a great anxiety to obtain a paper or papers which would put them in possession of both sides.[123]

Newspapers gave Republicans throughout the states the ability to promote a coherent narrative in opposition to the Federalists. "Americans, both men and women," Andrew W. Robertson has written, "constructed new identities that arose more from partisan loyalties than from attachment to national institutions. Their primary frame of reference was the parties—and the ideologies and personalities associated with them."[124] It is for this reason that Tocqueville observed, "Newspapers make associations, and associations make newspapers."[125]

Newspapers were the primary partisan tool used by parties in their effort to expand their voting base and connect voters and activists to the party's larger identity. The Federalists' construction of the First Amendment challenged this by criminalizing the expression of oppositional opinion. The Republicans needed to successfully counter the Federalists by constructing a more expansive understanding of the freedom of press. As Jefferson wrote to Madison:

> We are willing to view with indulgence, to wait with patience until passions and delusions shall have passed over which the federal government have artfully and successfully excited to cover its own abuses and to conceal its designs; fully confident that the good sense of the

American people and their attachment to those very rights which we are now vindicating will, before it shall be too late, rally with us round the true principles of our federal compact.[126]

Jefferson expressed his concern over the appropriate response to the Sedition Act as well as the Republicans' ability to organize a formidable coalition of states (and interests) supporting their cause against Federalists.[127] They could not defeat the Federalists by force. "Anything like force," he wrote to Edmund Pendleton, "would check the progress of the public opinion and rally them around the government. This is not the kind of opposition the American people will permit. But, keep away all show of force, and they will bear down the evil propensities of the government, by the constitutional means of elections and petitions."[128] They had to work within the limits of the Constitution and the established electoral process. They needed the press to accomplish their goals in the upcoming elections of 1800, so the use of the press to disseminate oppositional opinion also needed to be constitutional. Consequently, the Republicans needed to develop a broader interpretation of the First Amendment by prohibiting prior restraint and protecting against subsequent punishment.[129] In other words, the Republicans provided a major evolution in the meaning of the First Amendment by rejecting the common law understanding and connecting the freedom of speech and the press with oppositional politics and partyism. Importantly, this electoral strategy involving party competition built on a constitutional understanding of the First Amendment was a more viable challenge to the Federalists than an alternative strategy of nullification involving state legislatures.

The Kentucky and Virginia Resolutions: Support for the Republicans' Broad Interpretation of the First Amendment

In June 1798, Jefferson left Philadelphia and returned to Virginia. At the time of his departure, congressional discussion on the Alien and Sedition Acts was still under way. Despite his opposition to the acts, Jefferson's presence could do little to prevent the Federalists from passing their legislation. Opposition to the controversial legislation would have to come from another organ of government. Jefferson returned to Virginia to pursue a course of action that would involve state legislatures. According to Jefferson, the state governments were "the true barriers of our liberty in this country."[130] Madison shared a similar view of the role states could play in checking the national government. In Federalist No. 51 Madison had argued that "a double security arises to the rights of the people"; that is, the Constitution fosters a check between the national government and the state government, and these "different governments will control each other, at the same time that each will be controlled by itself."[131] This line of thinking was not unique to the Republicans. Hamilton, in Federalist No. 28, expressed a similar understanding of the role of the states in the American system. The genius of America's federal system allowed the states to "at once adopt a regular plan of opposition, in which they can combine all the resources of the community. They can readily communicate with each other in the different states: and unite their common forces for the protection of their common liberty."[132] As Madison had previously argued in his newspaper articles, if the national government posed a danger to liberty through the Alien and Sedition Acts, then the appropriate organ was unified opposition from the separate states. Coordination and unification of opinion, however, was a significant obstacle that the Republicans would have to overcome. With the Federalists passing the Alien and Sedition Acts, the political stage was set for the Republicans to utilize their alternative understanding of the First Amendment.

Jefferson's and Madison's preliminary courses of action resulted in the Kentucky Resolutions and the Virginia Resolutions, with Jefferson secretly penning the former and Madison authoring the latter. Random protests and petitions to the national government would not suffice, as they believed only a coordinated effort in the state legislatures would accomplish their political objectives. Jefferson and Madison undertook to challenge the Federalists' legislation by penning resolutions to oppose the federal acts and encourage other states to join in a unified opposition. These resolutions were intended to disseminate an understanding of constitutional principles to counter those that the Federalist used to justify the Alien and Sedition Acts. That is, the resolutions expressed the developing constitutionalism of the authors and the Republicans.[133] Both resolutions aimed to unify opposition to the Alien and Sedition Acts based on a constitutional argument centered on the nature and scope of delegated powers, an argument at odds with the Federalists' endorsement of implied powers.

For Jefferson and Madison, the difference between an absolute and a limited government was delegated powers to the national government. The enumerated powers in the Constitution were vital to recognizing when authority had been exceeded and understanding the delicate and difficult division of governmental powers between the national government and local units. This division was a major concern during the ratification debates as opponents of the Constitution feared they were exchanging the Articles of Confederation, which secured state sovereignty, with a dangerously ambiguous document giving "the new government free access to our pockets, and ample command of our persons."[134] In the Virginia ratifying convention, Madison explained that "the powers of the federal government are enumerated; it can only operate in certain cases; it has legislative powers on defined and limited objects, beyond which it cannot extend its jurisdiction."[135] Building on Madison's point, Frances Corbin of North Carolina stated, "The internal administration of government is left to the state legislatures, who exclusively retain such powers as will give the states the advantage of small republics, without the danger commonly attendant on the weakness of such governments."[136] Consistent with these observations, in the Kentucky Resolutions, Jefferson affirmed the limited power of the national government, as it was only "delegated . . . certain definite powers."[137] Similarly, Madison insisted that federal powers were "limited by the plain sense and intention of the instrument constituting that compact; as no farther valid than they are authorised by the grants enumerated in that compact."[138] Because of the limiting enumerated powers, Jefferson and Madison were able to make the claim that the national government had exceeded its authority in the Alien and Sedition Acts.

After identifying the political problem, Jefferson and Madison explained the danger of the national government exercising inappropriate implied powers. According to Jefferson, the assumption of "undelegated powers" destroys all prescribed limits, thereby reducing the sovereignty of the states to "the absolute dominion of one man" and the "barriers of the Constitution [are] thus swept away."[139] Likewise, Madison expressed "deep regret, that a spirit, has, in sundry instances, been manifested by the federal government, to enlarge its powers by forced constructions of the constitutional charter which defines them," resulting in a consolidation of the federal republic "into one sovereignty[,] . . . into an absolute, or at best a mixed monarchy."[140] The very notions of self-government and federalism were in danger because the Alien and Sedition Acts were founded on principles of "undelegated" and "unlimited" powers. These principles confirmed the Anti-Federalists' initial fear that the Constitution allowed a consolidated government to swallow state sovereignty. Following this reasoning, the Alien and Sedition Acts were unconstitutional because the national government would be assuming an inherent power that undermined federalism and distorted the constitutional order.

The national government's inappropriate assumption of inherent powers was not the only constitutional issue at hand. The meaning of the First Amendment was also at stake. As a supplement to the Kentucky and Virginia Resolutions, Madison agreed to offer an explanation and defense of the Virginia Resolutions. In January 1800, the *Report on the Virginia Resolutions* was adopted by the Virginia legislature. The historian Ralph Ketchum characterized the *Report* as serving "both as a culmination of Madison's long attention to states' rights and freedom of expression and as a Republican manifesto for the election of 1800."[141] Combining the issues of federalism and implied powers with the First Amendment provided the Republicans with a coherent platform with which they could challenge the Federalists.

For Madison, the Federalists had incorrectly interpreted the First Amendment and the freedom of the press clause by assuming that its meaning was derived from English common law and that it only protected freedom of expression from prior restraint. The common law tradition was intended to protect the people and their rights from encroachments by the executive magistrate. Common law, argued Madison, did not apply to the English Parliament because it sufficiently protected its constituents' rights, as it "is unlimited in its power, or in their own language, is omnipotent." According to British constitutionalism, it was the executive, and only the executive, that was constrained by all the common law "ramparts" protecting the people's rights.[142] The Constitution significantly deviated from this common law understanding; it states that Congress is the direct subject of the First Amendment and the people are considered sovereign. American constitutionalism recognized that the people's rights are also in danger of encroachment by the legislature, not just the "royal prerogative." The only way to assert the people's sovereignty and secure their rights was having constitutions paramount to laws. This understanding conflicted with the English case in which rights were secured by laws paramount to magisterial prerogative. This "security of the freedom of the press," he further argued, "requires that it should be exempt, not only from previous restraint by the executive, as in Great Britain; but from legislative restraint also; and this exemption, to be effectual, must be an exemption, not only from the previous inspection of licensers, but from the subsequent penalty of laws."[143]

In addition to the constitutional differences between the United States and Great Britain, Madison referenced the ratification of the Constitution and Bill of Rights as further evidence of the unconstitutionality of the Federalists' broad understanding of congressional power and narrow interpretation of the First Amendment. To substantiate this point, he referred to ratification debates in which apprehension was expressed regarding the absence of "some positive exception from the powers delegated, of certain, rights, and of the freedom of the press particularly, [which] might expose them to the danger of being drawn by construction within some of the powers vested in Congress."[144] More specifically, many feared the necessary and proper clause could be used to justify congressional encroachment on political rights. The Constitution ratified by the separate states was not one in which the national government was capable of invoking broad implied powers. According to Madison, "the arguments now employed [by the Federalists] in behalf of the sedition act, are at variance with the reasoning which then justified the constitution, and invited its ratification."[145] As an alternative to the Federalists' reliance on English common law to understand the Constitution, Madison developed a broader understanding of the First Amendment based on the ratification process as an authoritative source for constructing constitutional meaning.[146]

The responses to the Kentucky and Virginia Resolutions demonstrate that the Republicans' broad interpretation of the First Amendment was more widely accepted than originally thought. Most accounts of the Resolutions contend that they were not widely supported and that states were openly opposed to such radical propositions.[147] The lack of state support implied that there was also a lack of support for the Republicans' broader construction of the First Amendment. However, the historical record is not as hostile to the Resolutions as was once thought. As Wendell Bird found, only half of the states actually responded negatively to the resolutions, and only four opposed them on First Amendment grounds. Moreover, opposition to the resolutions was fundamentally based on partisanship, as the states opposing them were primarily New England states where Federalists were dominant.[148] This broader acceptance, Bird explains, "implies that the principles of freedom of speech and press expressed in the Virginia and Kentucky Resolutions to condemn the Sedition Act were less novel and more widely accepted, and that the narrow Blackstonian principles challenged in the resolutions were less entrenched and less generally accepted."[149] President Jefferson used his first inaugural address to state that his electoral victory settled the meaning of the First Amendment in favor of the Republicans' broader interpretation.

> During the contest of opinion through which we have passed the animation of discussion and of exertions has sometimes worn an aspect which might impose on strangers unused to think freely and to speak and to write what they think; but this being now decided by the voice of the nation, announced according to the rules of the Constitution, all will, of course, arrange themselves under the will of the law, and unite in common efforts for the common good. All, too, will bear in mind this sacred principle, that though the will of the majority is in all cases to prevail, that will to be rightful must be reasonable; that the minority possess their equal rights, which equal law must protect, and to violate would be oppression.[150]

Despite constructing a new understanding of the First Amendment, the Republicans remained faithful to the Constitution by challenging the Alien and Sedition Acts by constitutional means. The electoral path to settling the meaning of the First Amendment also meant that the Federalists, now the new minority party, would enjoy the same constitutional rights. This more libertarian understanding of the First Amendment did not immediately and absolutely prevent the party in office from attempting to thwart the opposition's efforts to utilize the press as a tool for party organization. The Jefferson administration largely reverted to the common law understanding of seditious libel despite initial declarations of adherence to a broader construction.[151] Yet after Jefferson's election, both Federalists and Republicans contributed to the creation of newspapers that circulated throughout the growing country.[152] After Jefferson's presidency, Madison adhered to the broader construction by not preventing the Federalists from utilizing the press to oppose his policies and the War of 1812. That is, the Federalists appropriated the Republicans' strategy of using the press as an organizational tool for an opposition party.

The events surrounding the Alien and Sedition Acts resulted in a constitutional construction of the First Amendment that gave rise to the exercise of an opposition political party. In attempting to proscribe freedom of speech and the press, the Federalists constructed a narrow interpretation of the First Amendment aimed at protecting the Union from unnecessary political dissent. The Republicans responded with essentially two political alternatives to challenge the Federalists, nullification or electoral opposition. Underlining each of these alternatives was a broadly constructed view of the First Amendment that relied on public opinion and recognized the function of evaluating the merits of public officials. This turn to public opinion and evaluating public officials coincided with views regarding the importance of newspapers as a means of disseminating information to overcome geographic limitations. Republicans who sought to discredit the Sedition Act were required to construct an understanding of the First Amendment that broke with the common law tradition of criminalizing seditious libel. It was within the controversy of the Sedition Act that the ambiguities of the First Amendment emerged, as the American Revolution and ratification of the Constitution did little to authoritatively reject the common law view of freedom of speech and the press. Anticipating the pro-party arguments of Van Buren, by rejecting the Sedition Act, the Republicans defended partyism and the importance of one party being a check on the other. Newspapers allowed Republicans to simplify complex political, financial, and constitutional issues for their readers by organizing the conflict between two distinct identities and ideologies, Republican and Federalist.

Procedurally, the Republicans' response to the narrow, disadvantaging Sedition Act aimed at allowing for an opposition to the party in government no matter which party it was. While the Federalists aimed at disadvantaging the Republicans, the broad construction of the First Amendment granted the Federalists the same rights if they found themselves no longer in office, thereby creating a foundation for a constitutional opposition party, not just a Republican one.

In addition to these procedural developments, the Republicans' response to the Sedition Act constructed substantive improvements to the electoral procedures in the United States. Madison recognized the importance of an opposition for democracy's fundamental feature of popularly electing members to governmental offices. The Republicans' concern about the oppressive legislation was more comprehensive than immediate electoral outcomes; they constructed new democratic principles to also govern the future. To achieve normatively better elections, the Republicans needed to liberate the press, a vital organ for ensuring that governmental opposition has the capacity to make substantive electoral impacts and overcome the difficulties of the extended republic. The use of newspapers allowed a single thought to be deposited in the minds of thousands of people, which created a bond and a unity among individuals that was not possible absent a free press.[153] Overall, the Republicans constructed a constitutionally based opposition capable of effectively challenging the Federalists, thereby enhancing American political practice and further influencing the development of political parties. The conflict between the Federalists and the Republicans over freedom of the press and the First Amendment preceded the growth of the partisan press and newspaper politics central to the reconstruction of the party system during the Jacksonian era.[154]

CHAPTER 4

Partyism and the Presidential Selection System

The Twelfth Amendment and Political Opposition

While an opposition party was given a political voice through a constitutional construction of the First Amendment, two-party competition in presidential elections could not fully emerge until the presidential selection system of 1787 was corrected. Under the original system, each member of the electoral college cast two votes, and the candidate receiving the highest number of votes and a majority of electors elected the president. The runner-up was vice president. However, if no candidate received a majority of votes, then the House, where each state had one vote, selected a winner from the top five candidates receiving votes. No constitutional provision existed requiring electors to vote for a particular candidate, and neither was Congress required to vote for a specific individual other than choosing from the top five candidates. Constituted this way, the system was intended to allow for independent judgment on the part of both the electors and Congress in choosing a president.[1]

With political parties forming and George Washington retiring, the 1787 system proved to be problematic because it produced undesirable electoral outcomes. In 1796, the system resulted in political adversaries from rival parties sharing the executive office, as Federalist John Adams was elected president and Democratic-Republican Thomas Jefferson was elected vice president. Just four years later, the system produced a contentious election between Jefferson and Aaron Burr, with the two Democratic-Republican candidates receiving the same number of electoral college votes. Without a majority winner, the House selected Jefferson. As a result, the 1787 mode of presidential selection detached the executive from the public, failing to provide presidential leadership with, as Hamilton argued, "a sense of the people."[2] Even if an opposition party was capable of forming an electoral majority, the election rules did not necessarily guarantee that this new majority could elect a president who reflected their political principles and preferences. If the First Amendment allowed for an opposition to form a majority, then the Twelfth Amendment allowed this new majority to elect a president who reflected their collective voice.

Current accounts of the Twelfth Amendment recognize its relationship to political parties and correctly argue that it was as an attempt to remedy a flaw in an original constitutional design that did not account for political parties.[3] In other words, the Twelfth Amendment was a temporary means of overcoming the Aaron Burr problem, a tie in the electoral college. Once resolved, under President Jefferson's leadership, political parties, while recognized, would no longer be useful. This account, however, obscures important political and constitutional developments by overstating President Jefferson's attempt at consolidation and unanimity. Jefferson's oft-quoted statement from his 1801 inaugural address, "We are all Republicans, we are all Federalists," is used as evidence of his intent to produce a single-party system, and the Twelfth Amendment was the means of creating a "party to end all parties" by ensuring the Democratic-Republicans could rally around a unified executive office.[4] Most accounts of the Twelfth Amendment understand Jefferson and his politics as a continuation of the Constitution-against-parties thesis. Shifting the emphasis from Jefferson, however, reveals a different story and purpose for the amendment. To understand its importance to America's political and constitutional development, we must understand what the framers intended, especially in regard to political parties and the mode of presidential selection.

Framing the Twelfth Amendment in terms of the presidential selection system raises an important question: if we accept the claim that the framers recognized the emergence of parties and maintained their antagonism to them, then why did they design a constitutional amendment that strengthened their role in the electoral process? In *Presidential Selection*, James W. Ceaser argues that the framers of the original presidential selection system meant for the presidency to be the result of a nonpartisan election process, reflecting their view of nonpartisan presidential power. The original intent of the Constitution and presidential selection was contingent on the nonpartisanship of the public and the president. Otherwise, presidential politics would be susceptible to the framers' biggest fear, demagoguery. Consequently, the changes in the selection process in 1800 were not the product of a conscious plan to create a new electoral system. Partisans, responding to political events, changed the system to win elections and further ideological goals. Under this view, political actors in 1800 did not frame the question of the Twelfth Amendment in terms of partisan disputes rather than institutional design.[5] This leads Ceaser to argue that although the political actors involved with the amendment recognized the emergence of political parties, under Jefferson's leadership, the Democratic-Republicans' victory sought to establish a constitutional regime that would eliminate the need for a national opposition party. Ceaser's account concludes with a difficulty prevalent in early party literature: the Twelfth Amendment "seemed to require parties—or a party—to perform the task of concentrating national support behind a candidate"; however, this "powerful new justification for recreating parties" was inadvertent.[6] Although the Twelfth Amendment required party organization, because the amendment's framers maintained their antagonism to institutionalizing partisan competition, any developments regarding a two-party system or a legitimate opposition were unintentional.

Congressional debates in *The Annals of Congress*, however, demonstrate that the currently accepted scholarly account of parties and the Twelfth Amendment is incomplete. For the relationship between the amendment and parties to remain unintentional, debates during the amendment process would have to demonstrate that the framers of the amendment viewed any changes to the constitutional mode of presidential selection as a means of ensuring Thomas Jefferson's victory in 1804 and the end of

partisan competition. At the very least, claiming that strengthening political parties was an unintended consequence of the amendment at-
tributes to the framers a position of neutrality toward parties, which
challenges the claim that they were actually antagonistic to them. If this
antagonism thesis is correct, then the amendment should work against an
opposition party and reduce the likelihood of an opposition party gaining
political recognition and access to the electoral process. Returning to the
congressional debates, the amendment's framers intended something entirely different from the standard scholarly accounts. While partisanship
did animate debate in both the House and the Senate, the amendment
was not adopted with the sole intent of securing a Democratic-Republican
electoral victory in 1804. Although the Democratic-Republicans held
majorities to unilaterally pass the resolution, they designed a proposition
accounting for an opposition party's role in the political process. In framing the amendment, the Democratic-Republicans recognized they would
not always be in the majority and adopted rules that would not disadvantage them in future elections. Thus both Federalists and Democratic-
Republicans recognized the fluidity of party politics and agreed on a system that would help ensure majoritarian election outcomes without
disadvantaging a competitive opposition party.

Early Electoral Strategies and Outcomes: The Need for Change

Writing during the ratification process, Alexander Hamilton described
the mode of presidential selection prescribed in the Constitution as "perfect" or "at least excellent."[7] However, this system quickly revealed glaring
flaws. In retrospect, the deficiencies of the presidential electoral process
were somewhat overshadowed by George Washington's popularity and
the overwhelming consensus that he would be elected president. Yet his
unanimous selection was not guaranteed, and ensuring that Washington
was not elected vice president rather than president required significant
organization. According to the constitutional mechanism for executive
election, the states were given power to determine the selection of electors
equivalent to the sum of their congressional representatives. Each elector
would then cast two votes for his top presidential choices, at least one of

which was to be given to an out-of-state candidate. These votes were then certified and delivered to Congress, with the two top candidates named president and vice president. In 1789, while the clear election outcome was Washington as president and John Adams as vice president, there was no prescribed way to indicate the vote as such. Nothing in the Constitution indicated that electors were supposed to designate their votes for either president or vice president. If all electors had voted for Washington and Adams, they would have emerged with identical vote totals, thereby indicating no real preference between a President Washington and a President Adams in the minds of the electors.

Recognizing the problem of an electoral tie, Hamilton undermined the selection process by attempting to organize the electoral vote to ensure that Washington received more votes than Adams, thereby indicating a clear electoral preference. To accomplish this, votes needed to be organized and diverted from Adams to other candidates. For example, in a letter to Hamilton, Jeremiah Wadsworth informed him that Connecticut's electoral votes "were given agreeably to your wishes—Washington, 7; Adams, 5; Governor Huntington, 2."[8] This election strategy ultimately succeeded: Washington was unanimously elected president by the 69 appointed electors, and Adams was elected vice president with 34 votes. The remaining 35 votes were strategically allocated to other candidates. While these results indicated that Washington was the clear choice for president, the strategic allocation of votes violated the spirit of the presidential election system created in Philadelphia.[9] More to the point, Hamilton's electioneering clearly violated the spirit of the Constitution and his own explanation that Article II established a system in which presidential selection would be made by a "small number of persons" who were "most likely to possess the information and discernment requisite to so complicated an investigation" without being "tampered with beforehand to prostitute their votes" or influenced by a "sinister bias."[10] Although the election produced the desired outcome, the organization of blocs of electors and efforts to strategically allocate votes undermined the original electoral college design and revealed the imperfections of the system.

Initial presidential elections made it clear that the election system and the electoral college needed to be addressed. The 1796 election resulted in the election of John Adams, a Federalist, as president and Thomas Jefferson, a Democratic-Republican, as vice president. Not only was this the first contested presidential election, it would be the only time in history that a president and vice president were elected from opposing tickets. Many of the proposed solutions for presidential elections wrestled with the nature and scope of political opposition in the constitutional system and the emergence and success of not just the Democratic-Republicans, but political parties in general. The 1796 election was truly transformative, indicating a transition from the anticipated mode of presidential selection based on political elites and presidential electors acting independent of any partisan ties to a more experimental democratic system based on party competition.[11] American constitutionalism took further developmental steps toward a two-party system once the constitutional design for selecting the president became intertwined with the reality of politics.

Debates recorded in *The Annals of Congress* offer differing solutions to remedy the problem of disputed presidential elections. Of particular importance in these debates was the recognition of an opposition in the political arena and how this political opposition was influencing election results. These debates offer valuable insight regarding the desirability and promotion of a political opposition, something typically not attributed until the 1820s and 1830s.[12] Some propositions sought to minimize an opposition's influence by creating measures that aimed solely to disadvantage the minority, thereby circumscribing political opposition.[13] Like Madison's acceptance of party competition implied in his *National Gazette* essays, other propositions embraced the concept of opposition and suggested rules that would remedy electoral shortcomings while permitting political opposition and political party competition. The Twelfth Amendment became central to incorporating a political opposition into the constitutional system because it acknowledged the existence of political parties and resolved electoral uncertainty without disadvantaging a minority party with competing principles of governance.

The Absence of Washington and the Consequences of Preventing an Electoral Tie: 1796

The presidential selection system greatly benefited from George Washington's prominence, as he was unanimously elected in the first two elections.

Washington's unanimous selection masked a significant flaw in the election process, a flaw the election of 1796 ultimately revealed. Deep electoral and political division, not unanimity, characterized the first election without Washington, and the growing opposition to the Federalists' political agenda gained significant electoral outcomes, as the Democratic-Republican candidate, Thomas Jefferson, was eventually elected vice president. This outcome was due to the difficulty of finding a suitable presidential successor who most electors would support in the double-ballot system established by the Constitution. In the first two presidential elections, Washington functioned as an electoral heuristic in that voters readily recognized his name. An election without a candidate of his prominence and popularity was substantially more difficult because there were few others capable of captivating the electorate. Madison recognized this problem when consulting with Washington as he considered retirement after his first term. Thomas Jefferson, John Adams, and John Jay were identified as the only potentially viable candidates to succeed Washington. According to Madison's calculations, Jefferson's candidacy was questionable because he had an "extreme repugnance to public life & anxiety to exchange it for his farm & his philosophy." Furthermore, even if Jefferson could be persuaded to take up public life, "local prejudices in the Northern States" could potentially become a "bar to his appointment." Adams's candidacy was to be feared if not highly improbable given his undeniable "monarchical principles," and he would be "disliked" by "republicans every where, & particularly in the Southern States." Finally, Jay's election "would be extremely dissatisfactory" because he entertained "the same obnoxious principles with Mr. Adams" and was susceptible to "propagating them." Likewise, "a pretty numerous class ... disliked & distrusted him," viewing him "as their most dangerous enemy."[14] Madison based his calculations of electoral support for the potential candidates on sectional and partisan divisions. Thus, without the prestige of Washington's name carrying a national majority of electors, the probability of the election being thrown to the House was extremely high, which opened the possibility of electing a president who was agreeable to only a fraction of the country.

As the election approached, the Federalists suffered most from Washington's absence as a geographic division split their ballot. Given his status as Washington's vice president, John Adams was chosen by a Federalist congressional caucus. Because Adams was a Northerner, the caucus also supported a Southerner, Thomas Pinckney, to produce a balanced ticket. This balanced ticket, however, posed serious problems for the Federalists. While Adams was considered their first choice for president, many northern Federalists did not necessarily view Pinckney as the appropriate second choice. Northern candidates such as Samuel Adams or Oliver Ellsworth were preferred over Pinckney. There was also no guarantee that all southern Federalists would support Adams at the top of the ticket rather than Pinckney. This division between northern and southern Federalists could have led to various intraparty intrigues and an inverted Federalist ticket. For example, as had been done in previous elections, to ensure that Adams clearly won the election, the Federalists would have to divert some votes from Pinckney. However, the southern Federalists, to compensate for these diverted votes and to ensure a Pinckney victory, could choose to ultimately divert votes from Adams, leaving his election as president in doubt. Without a clear presidential choice like Washington, the Federalists were subjected to various undesirable electoral outcomes.

These intraparty issues were only exacerbated by the potential problems from interparty conflict. The Democratic-Republicans could also vote in ways that would upset the Federalists' ticket. Like the Federalists, the Democratic-Republicans supported a balanced ticket, with the Southerner Jefferson leading the nomination and the Northerner Aaron Burr a distant second. If, however, the Democratic-Republicans predicted an electoral defeat, they could cast their votes for Pinckney, which would invert the Federalists' desired ticket. To counter this tactic, the Federalists would then have to further divert votes from Pinckney to ensure Adams's election as president. If the Federalists employed this counterstrategy, they risked diverting too many votes from Pinckney, thereby creating space for the Democratic-Republicans to move their preferred candidate ahead of him. With so much uncertainty, the Federalists' hope of an Adams-Pinckney victory was replaced by the undesirable reality of suboptimal options like an electoral defeat, an inverted ticket, or a divided executive administration.

Both the Federalists and the Democratic-Republicans waited with uncertainty for the election results to come in. Neither party could confidently predict the results. With so many possible outcomes, both parties waited with anticipation to see if they had captured the presidency, vice presidency, both, or neither. Even with many of the electors pledging support for Jefferson or Adams, the election hinged on how electors cast their second vote. As results came in, both Adams and Jefferson were disheartened. Adams lost a significant number of votes to Pinckney and was dismayed by the lack of support from many of the Federalists and Hamilton. Jefferson found himself trailing both Adams and Pinckney, losing votes in both the North and the upper South. As more electoral college votes were reported, Adams maintained his lead, but Jefferson moved to second place behind a swell of support from the West and the South. These two regions maintained the most cohesive party "ticket," giving almost all their votes to Democratic-Republicans. The final results gave Adams a narrow victory over Jefferson, and rival parties would now occupy the presidency and vice presidency.[15]

At the conclusion of the 1796 election, the Federalists tasted electoral defeat despite retaining the presidency. Without Washington's reputation to bridge the geographic division within the Federalist Party, the diverted votes from the northern Federalists provided Jefferson and the Democratic-Republicans with the opportunity to secure the vice presidency. The Federalists' narrow electoral victory could have easily been a defeat had it not been for the lone votes Adams received in North Carolina and Virginia. Far from enjoying Washington's electoral support, Adams's presidency was a struggle between the waning Federalist support and mounting Democratic-Republican opposition. The election of 1796 was the first of many presidential elections organized around partisan competition between politically divergent parties. Recognizing the difficulty of an executive office divided between rival parties, even Jefferson expressed his preference for the vice presidency: "This is certainly not a moment to covet the helm."[16] Bolstered by his electoral victory, Vice President Jefferson was confident in the eventual acceptance of the Democratic-Republicans' principles and his ability to persuade President Adams to execute the government according to it's true principles.[17] Although from separate parties, Jefferson believed he and Adams could coexist and cooperate, assuming he could influence Adams. Alexander Hamilton, however, did not express confidence in much cooperation between the political rivals.

Our Jacobins say they are well pleased and that the *Lion* & the *Lamb* are to lie down together. Mr. Adams *personal* friends talk a little in the same way. Mr. *Jefferson* is not half so ill a man as we have been accustomed to think him. There is to be a united and vigorous administration. Sceptics like me quietly look forward to the event—willing to hope but not prepared to believe.[18]

Perceiving the impossibility of cooperation, Hamilton's comment revealed the disjunction between the executive office and the mode of presidential selection within the 1787 constitutional design. In practice, this mode of presidential selection undermined what Hamilton viewed as the first ingredient for executive energy, unity.

The Crisis of Executive Unity
and Good Government: 1796

In Federalist No. 70, Hamilton responded to the accusation that a "vigorous executive" was contrary to "the genius of republican government." He addressed this accusation by comparing an energetic executive to a feeble one. According to Hamilton, "Energy in the Executive is a leading character in the definition of good government."[19] Good government required a vigorous executive during times of emergency and regular political life to provide protection from external dangers and internal threats. To illustrate this point, Hamilton made reference to the Roman republic and how, out of necessity, it would transfer absolute power to a single man to provide safety from external invasion and the internal "intrigues of ambitious individuals who aspired to the tyranny, and the seditions of whole classes of the community whose conduct threatened the existence of all government."[20] During these times, a vigorous executive was required to secure the government; a "feeble Executive" entailed a "feeble execution of the government." In other words, a feeble executive cannot protect from external forces and internal intrigues and fails to fulfill its function and execute good government. And "a government ill executed, whatever it may be in theory, must be, in practice, a bad government."[21] Hamilton intended to convince those supporting a republican government to also accept the necessity of a vigorous executive despite any theoretical apprehensions to the contrary.

While "all men of sense" would easily accept the argument for a vigorous executive, Hamilton needed to explain the necessary ingredients conducive to executive energy. A vigorous executive required "unity, duration, an adequate provision for its support, and competent powers." Of these ingredients, Hamilton identified unity as the first, rejecting the notion of a plural executive because "decision, activity, secrecy, and dispatch will generally characterize the proceedings of one man . . . and in proportion as the number is increased, these qualities will be diminished." Unity is destroyed by vesting executive power in "two or more magistrates of equal dignity and authority" or by vesting it in "one man, subject, in whole or in part, to the control and cooperation of others, in capacity of the counselors to him."[22] Simply put, the executive was severely weakened if his every decision and action were undermined by a co-president or executive council disclosing confidential information or assisting an opposition in response to a controversial policy.

Hamilton's theoretical position regarding the weakening of executive unity became a reality for President Adams. Once in office, Adams chose to retain many of Washington's appointees, and his vice president happened to be the leader of the growing political opposition. Adams could hardly expect executive unity from the Federalists in the administration, whose allegiance was questionable, or from his Democratic-Republican political rival. Given Hamilton's prescription for a vigorous executive, Adams's presidency seemed destined for executive feebleness and bad government, a situation Vice President Jefferson would want to avoid as he made his presidential bid in 1800.

The Consequences of an Electoral Tie: 1800

In an effort to avoid the problem of a divided executive, the Democratic-Republicans faced the issue of averting an electoral tie. As the 1800 presidential election neared, Democratic-Republicans made substantial efforts to avoid the Federalists' 1796 electoral strategy that secured John Adams's presidential election at the expense of Pinckney's vice presidential selection. Democratic-Republicans were hesitant to expect or encourage electors to ensure Jefferson's presidential selection by diverting votes from Jefferson's running mate, Aaron Burr. They faced the same undesirable electoral outcomes the Federalists experienced in 1796 if they unsuccessfully coordinated electoral votes. Moreover, if "the electors voted 'fairly,' a term which contemporaries began to use in 1800 to mean 'faithfully' and in accordance with the expectations of those who had appointed them," explains Tadahisa Kuroda, then the Democratic-Republicans would have to consider the very real possibility of the election ending in a tie.[23]

On February 11, 1801, the electoral college votes revealed that the election did in fact end in a tie. The Democratic-Republicans had uniformly supported their candidates, with Jefferson and Burr both receiving 73 votes. The Federalists, in a losing effort, demonstrated their mastery of the 1787 presidential selection system and diverting votes to create a clear party winner. John Adams received one more vote (65) than his running mate, Charles Pinckney (64). Had the Federalists succeeded with this strategy in 1796, Jefferson would not have been elected vice president. The electoral tie, however, was not unforeseen by the framers of the 1787 Constitution. The Constitution empowers the House of Representatives to break the electoral tie so that it would be a closer reflection of the people. As a compromise between the large and small states, each state cast one vote in the contingency election to prevent the larger states from dominating the process. The procedure for a House contingency, however, did not provide the means of determining elector intent. In other words, because the system did not require electors to designate their vote for president and vice president, each vote for Jefferson and Burr was viewed as a vote for president. Even if the Democratic-Republicans had intended Jefferson to be president, the Constitution did not recognize this, and there was no guarantee the House would either. Even though they intended Jefferson to win the presidency, the House could still frustrate the Democratic-Republicans' electoral strategy by choosing Burr over Jefferson.

The inverted ticket was not the only concern for the Democratic-Republicans. The 1787 constitutional procedures further complicated the issue because (1) the "lame duck" House elected in 1798 would be voting, (2) each state had one vote, and (3) the House would make its choice from the candidates with the five highest vote totals. In the Fifth Congress, although the Federalists held a numerical majority, neither party could guarantee and command a majority of the separate states. Because each state had one vote, a president could not be chosen without substantial agreement within state delegations and among individual states.[24] Each party could prevent the election of an undesirable candidate, yet they could not ensure the selection of the desired candidate. The Federalists also maintained a procedural advantage over the Democratic-Republicans given the constitutional provision allowing the House to choose from five candidates. Because the Federalists had given one vote to John Jay, they had three candidates on the ballot, and the House would choose between Jefferson, Burr, Adams, Pinckney, and Jay. While improbable but still constitutional, the House could elect Jay, the candidate who received just one vote, president. Like the Federalists in 1796, the Democratic-Republicans faced the prospect of their electoral strategies and preferences being frustrated. At the time of the contingency election, the Federalists still dominated the House, and Burr refused to back down and accept the vice presidency. After thirty-six ballots and Hamilton's intervention, the House finally made Jefferson president rather than Burr. The Democratic-Republicans fared much better than their rivals because they were able to secure, under extreme difficulty, their desired outcome.

Given these unusual circumstances, the 1796 and 1800 elections resulted in significant constitutional and political developments. Given the mounting political discord between the Federalists and the Democratic-Republicans, out of both principle and necessity, new election laws needed to be devised. Other constitutional rules, such as the previously discussed First Amendment developments, had recognized the existence of a political opposition. Now the presidential selection system had to accommodate these changes. Would the changes in election law support or undermine the opposition party's political role and electoral access?

THE TWELFTH AMENDMENT

Partisan disputes between the Federalists and the Democratic-Republicans continued after the Democratic-Republicans took control of the executive and Congress. The Democratic-Republicans also faced problems of avoiding factional disputes within their own party, something the Federalists recognized and exploited. Looking ahead to the 1804 presidential election, retaining party control of the presidency and vice presidency was a matter of strategic calculation. If the Democratic-Republicans chose to fully support Vice President Burr for reelection, they risked a few Federalists voting for Burr and elevating him to the presidency. Under the

pre–Twelfth Amendment system, the only way for a majority party to ensure that the minority party did not use the vice presidency as leverage
was to nominate a vice president who was even more partisan and less
acceptable to the minority party than the president.[25] Once President
Jefferson was inaugurated on March 4, 1801, both parties went to work
preparing for the next election by pursuing constitutional amendments
aimed at correcting the mode of presidential selection.

In New York, Assemblyman Jedediah Peck moved for the adoption of
a constitutional amendment that required designation of votes for president and vice president. Peck was an outspoken critic of the Federalist
Party and was arrested by a Federalist judge for circulating petitions in
opposition to President Adams and the Alien and Sedition Acts. On the
same day, Governor John Jay submitted a resolution for another constitutional amendment that required selection of presidential electors by districts. In the previous election, the New York legislature selected all of the
state's presidential electors, all of whom were Democratic-Republicans,
and Thomas Jefferson received all twelve of New York's electoral college
votes. Selecting electors by districts would allow the Federalists to influence presidential elections by providing them with electoral college votes
in districts where they were the majority. Hamilton believed the proposed amendment was good policy and beneficial to the Federalist Party.
In particular, he recognized that selecting electors by districts would
minimize the role of state legislatures, of which many were controlled by
the Democratic-Republicans and their "burning zeal."[26] That is, selecting electors by districts provided the Federalists with proportional representation in the electoral college.[27]

In anticipation of the election of 1804, the Democratic-Republicans
also took an interest in elector selection. Treasury Secretary Albert Gallatin paid particular attention to how his party would choose both electors and candidates for vice president. Assuming President Jefferson
would run for reelection, Gallatin attempted to eliminate the Aaron
Burr problem by recommending the party screen vice presidential candidates. Burr was losing support within the party and would likely be replaced as Jefferson's running mate in the next election. However, Gallatin did not have a viable alternative. Madison was the obvious choice, but
the Constitution prevented electors from voting for candidates from the
same state. Jefferson's running mate would have to come from outside

Virginia. Recognizing the impending partyism in the election, Gallatin claimed there were two options:

> [Our choices are] either to support Burr once more, or to give only one vote for President, scattering our votes for the other person to be voted for. If we do the first, we run, on the one hand, the risk of the federal party making B[urr] president; and we seem, on the other, to give him an additional pledge of being eventually supported hereafter by the republicans for that office. If we embrace the last party, we not only lose the Vice President, but pave the way for the federal successful candidate to that office to become President.[28]

To solve this problem, Gallatin supported an amendment that (1) distinguished votes for president and vice president, so Burr could not be elected president on account of the Federalists; and (2) to select electors by districts to fragment Burr's support. President Jefferson believed this was a "remedy to a certain degree."[29] He also offered a plan that eliminated electors altogether: the candidate receiving a plurality of votes in the state would receive all of the state's electoral college votes. This too removed the chances of a minority party casting votes for a candidate that was not supported by a state. In general, there were various ways in which the mode of presidential election could be altered to achieve the desired outcome. As the debate over an amendment went to Congress, Democratic-Republicans sought to eliminate uncertainty and the prospect of the Federalists disrupting their electoral plans in the upcoming presidential election.

As Congress convened in October 1803, two important issues were on the agenda, the acquisition of Louisiana and amending the presidential selection system. For the Democratic-Republicans, fixing the electoral college was important to prevent a recurrence of the election crisis of 1801. The undesirable possibility of a Democratic-Republican president and a Federalist vice president also remained. In previous elections when George Washington won uncontested victories, electors assumed that their first vote for Washington was a vote for the president and their second vote was a vote for the vice president. As the election of 1800 proved, the 1787 mode of presidential selection did not recognize votes for vice president. To fix the electoral college, the Constitution needed amending to include a mechanism by which electors could distinguish their votes for president and vice president and avoid a presidency divided along party lines.

Amending the Constitution to include candidate designation was the Democratic-Republicans' first step in correcting the presidential selection system. On October 17, Representative John Dawson (DR-VA) introduced an amendment that added the designation of votes between president and vice president.[30] According to Senator James Hillhouse (F-CT), Jefferson's election was fraught with ambiguity: "You are told that, at the last election, one was intended by the people for President, and the other for Vice President; but the Constitution knows no vote for Vice President."[31] If Hamilton was correct that presidential selection was an indication of the "sense of the people" so as to "afford as little opportunity as possible to tumult and disorder," then the election of 1800 demonstrated that a sense of the people could not be ascertained without designating votes between the president and vice president.[32] Even though the Democratic-Republicans intended to elect Jefferson president, there was no constitutional mechanism by which they could express this preference. By receiving the same number of votes as Jefferson, Burr had just as much constitutional claim to the Oval Office as his running mate.[33]

Distinguishing between a vote for president and a vote for vice president, however, was not the only debated topic during the congressional proceedings. A central point of contention was the contingency election in the House. Specifically, if the election was thrown to the House, what was the appropriate number of candidates from which the House would choose? This matter was further complicated by the difference in voting procedures between the general election and election by the House. Each state having one vote in the House contingency election shifted presidential selection from an election by state population to an election by state equality. In the eventual House election, the people would nominate five candidates and the states would choose the winner.[34] This electoral procedure harkened back to compromises made during the constitutional convention as delegates confronted the tension between large states and small states. The 1787 mode of presidential selection was one of these compromises. The large states' advantage in the electoral college was balanced against the small states' advantage in the House because each state was granted only one vote. To further structure the House election process, Article II states, "From the five highest on the List the said

House shall in like Manner chuse the President." This structuring added to the small states' advantage in presidential elections. For example, in 1800, Thomas Jefferson (73 votes), Aaron Burr (73), John Adams (65), Charles Pinckney (64), and John Jay (1) were on the House's ballot. As the House considered the candidates, there was a possibility that neither Jefferson nor Burr would be selected president. In the election, the Federalists' candidates carried six states: Vermont, New Hampshire, Massachusetts, Connecticut, New Jersey, and Delaware. The electors in Maryland, North Carolina, and Pennsylvania distributed their votes among both parties. Maryland electors distributed their votes equally between parties, with Jefferson, Burr, Adams, and Pinckney each receiving 5 votes; in North Carolina, Jefferson and Burr each received 8 votes and Adams and Pinckney received only 4 each; and in Pennsylvania, Jefferson and Burr each received 8 votes and Adams and Pinckney received 7. Because each state had only one vote and a candidate only needed a majority of state votes for election, the Federalists could potentially elect Adams, Pinckney, or Jay if the three states dividing their votes joined with the six states supporting Federalist candidates. As a result, the 1787 constitutional provisions for presidential selection could result in the state election of a candidate supported by an electoral minority. The number of candidates on the House ballot needed to be reduced to minimize the possibility of a presidential selection by a minority of states representing only a fraction of the voting population, thereby reducing the chances of the "one vote" winner.[35]

The solution to the mode of presidential selection had implications for partyism and an opposition party. Most scholars have understood the Twelfth Amendment in terms of solving the 1800 Aaron Burr problem in strictly partisan terms.[36] Others have tried to elucidate the political significance of the amendment by focusing on the framers' intent in constructing it.[37] Regarding the latter approach, designation and the number of candidates on the House ballot would determine the extent to which a political party could unify and effectively win a presidential election. Designation would allow for an opposition party to ensure a unified electoral ticket and secure a vigorous executive capable of pursuing alternative policies and principles. Reducing the number of candidates would also guarantee that the newly elected executive would reflect the will of the people, thereby providing the new opposition party leader with a mandate to pursue an alternative political platform. Reducing the number of candidates would reduce the risk of the new minority party electing a candidate from its displaced party. The genius of the Twelfth Amendment is that it solves the presidential selection problem without disadvantaging an opposition party's political efforts. Thus in a time when most scholars believed political parties should have disappeared, the authors of the Twelfth Amendment intentionally and constitutionally grounded party politics and allowed an opposition continued political access.

The House's Amendment

On October 19, Representative Dawson introduced the need to amend the Constitution to include the designation principle.[38] The real substantive debate, however, began once the designation principle was understood in relation to the remaining constitutional text establishing the procedure for a contingency election in the House. The number of names available to the House from which they were to choose a president would structure much of the debate on the proposed amendment. Representative Joseph H. Nicholson (DR-MD) moved to amend Dawson's proposition to maintain the 1787 constitutional provision establishing five as the designated number of candidates from which the House would choose a president. In response, Representative John Clopton (DR-VA), representing one of the larger states, urged that the number be changed from five to two so as to be "more conformable to the principles of a representative Government."[39] Clopton proceeded to provide an important definition of representative government in the context of presidential selection: the "ultimate election of President and Vice President" is to provide a sense of "the will of the people," and the "electoral votes are to be considered as their expression of the public will."[40] He affirmed that the executive office would be representative of the general population and not the several states. Although states would still have one vote in the contingency election, reducing the number of candidates in the House election from five to two would prevent small states from choosing a candidate contrary to the will of people.

There was, however, another political element to this debate. In addition to their state allegiances, representatives had partisan attachments, and these attachments influenced the debate and subsequent propositions. Designation and the number of candidates in the House contingency election determined whether an opposition party would be disadvantaged in the selection process. The same concern that small states would elect an unrepresentative president applied to candidates from an opposition party. A supplanted party would want to maintain as much influence in this process as possible to have the potential of frustrating the new majority party's electoral victory. In this regard, Federalists had every incentive to keep the number of candidates in the House election high to increase the probability that a Federalist candidate would make the list from which the House would choose. On the other hand, the Democratic-Republicans, sure of their candidates receiving the most votes, would want to reduce this number to ensure that the House decision more accurately reflected the results of the electoral college.[41]

On October 28, the House voted 88–39 to approve the resolution and send it to the Senate. However, before the vote was taken, Gaylord Griswold (F-NY) and Benjamin Huger (F-SC) made closing arguments as to why the House should vote against the resolution. Griswold, despite representing a large state, opposed the resolution based on a structural interpretation of the compromises that formed the constitutional text. The original text was a compromise between the large states and the small states, and any provision that undermined this compromise deviated too far from the ratified text. Similarly, Huger argued designation would reduce state influence and the probability of a contingency election in the House. He reminded the House that the Constitution was a union of states and not of the people, and by having elections decided in the House by the separate states, the mode of presidential selection would reflect the will of those for whom the Union was created.

In addition to the constitutional arguments, the Federalists attempted to hinder passage of the amendment by drawing attention to the partisan nature of the resolution. Specifically, Seth Hastings (F-MA) believed "the present resolution . . . [grew] out of an overweening anxiety to secure, at all hazards, the re-election of the present Chief Magistrate." No changes to the election process should be made while it could benefit the incumbent president. Moreover, he coupled this accusation with another regarding the three-fifths clause. Hastings reasoned that as long as the Democratic-Republicans were trying to make constitutional revisions to a flawed electoral process, attention should be given to the issue of how the three-fifths clause substantially affected the number and distribution of presidential electors.[42] The more pressing constitutional amendment should be one that created equal representation among free citizens, and only free citizens. "One part of the Union," he argued, "has obtained a great, and in my opinion, unjust advantage over other parts of the Union." "The Southern States," he continued, "have gained a very considerable increase of representatives and Electors, founded solely upon their numerous black population."[43] Supporting Hastings, Samuel Thatcher (F-MA) calculated, based on reapportionment, that the three-fifths clause caused a "peculiar inequality" by adding "eighteen Electors of President and Vice President at the next election."[44] The Democratic-Republicans greatly benefited from the three-fifths clause in presidential elections. Southern states received additional representation in the House based on their slave population, which also meant they received an increase in electoral college votes. Despite final efforts to challenge the proposal, the Federalists were unable to dissuade or delay the Democratic-Republican majority.

The Senate's Amendment

Before the House passed its version of the resolution, the Senate already began discussing a designation resolution. DeWitt Clinton (DR-NY) crafted his own version of an amendment outlining designation. Given the Democratic-Republican majority in the Senate, he hoped proceedings would be swift. Clinton's proposition, however, was carelessly composed. Fellow Democratic-Republicans drew attention to problems with language in the resolution. For example, Stephen R. Bradley (DR-VT) noted that the section reading, "if there be more than one who have such majority, and have an equal number of votes," was impossible with designation. Recognizing the error, Clinton himself seconded Bradley's motion to have this language removed from the resolution.[45] Moreover, Clinton's proposal had a significant omission in the section pertaining to the procedures for a contingency election in the House: "if no person have a majority, then from the ___ highest on the list, the said House shall, in like manner, choose the president."[46] If the House debates were any indication, determining the number of candidates in the contingency election would be no small ordeal. Any hopes of an expedited process would be hindered by much-needed alterations to poorly constructed propositions and agreements on additions.

In addition to these issues, the Federalists voiced substantial opposition to the resolution. On October 22, as the Senate began reviewing Clinton's proposition, Jonathan Dayton (F-NJ) successfully moved that the proceeding be shifted to a select committee. Two days after the committee was formed, he seized control of the debates by drawing attention to the implications of the proposition, specifically, for the vice president. Dayton reasoned that designation reduced, if it did not completely eliminate, the purpose of the office of vice president because the vice president would no longer be the individual with the second most votes. The 1787 Constitution ennobled the vice president with the prestige of being the nation's second choice for president; designation debased the office by emphasizing the election of one candidate for president and stripping the vice presidency of its constitutional dignity. In this case, the Constitution should be amended to eliminate the office of the vice president, which would also eliminate any need for designation. While Uriah Tracy (F-CT) seconded Dayton's motion to remove reference to the vice president, Senator Clinton accused Dayton of trying to "put off or get rid of the main question" to "stave off the question till the Legislatures of the States of Tennessee and Vermont are out of session."[47] In an effort to expedite the amendment process, Clinton wanted to send the resolution to the states for a vote while state legislatures, like Tennessee and Vermont, were in session. Dayton's devised delay, however, would carry more weight than Clinton's expediency for even some Democratic-Republicans now believed they "had not had sufficient time to make up [their] mind" on such an important amendment. Wilson Nicholas (DR-VA) reminded Clinton that "two-thirds or three-quarters of the State Legislatures would be in session in two or three months," and "it was impossible to act upon, or pass the amendment . . . with a full view of all its bearings at this time."[48] Dayton succeeded in delaying debate when the Senate narrowly voted (16–15) to postpone the proceedings. His postponement tactics, however, would be more successful than originally anticipated and the Democratic-Republicans would have to wait substantially longer to resume discussion of the resolution.

The Senate would briefly return to the designation resolution before ultimately postponing discussion yet again due to an unexpected announcement from Clinton. The previous day's exchange between Dayton and Clinton proved to be highly contentious, with accusations of "rudeness and indecency of language" culminating in Dayton challenging Clinton to a duel.[49] Before discussion on the resolution could resume, the Senate was informed that "Mr. Clinton was obliged to go home" and was "now gone," and voting on the proposition would be "postponed accordingly."[50] This postponement lasted for nearly a month due to other circumstances, including debate on the Louisiana Purchase, structural problems with the ceiling in the Senate chambers, and numerous members of Congress going to the racetrack.[51] The Senate would not return to the amendment until November 23.

As the Senate resumed discussion in November, arguments were clearly based on partisanship. Democratic-Republicans and Federalists now offered differing political principles animating their respective positions. John Taylor (DR-VA) provided one of the most straightforward articulations of the Democratic-Republicans' preference that the presidential selection reflect public will. Preserving America's constitutionalism required facilitating majority rule, even if the new majority was an opposition party. Otherwise, "the minority may be through corruption made to govern." Therefore, regarding the question of the number of candidates in the contingency election, reducing the number to three was more conducive to uniting public will.[52] All the Democratic-Republicans were not of the same mind on this point. Pierce Butler (DR-SC) opposed reducing the number in favor of the original constitutional design of five. His opposition mirrored the Federalists continued reliance on the debate between large and small states as he feared allowing "four of the large States the perpetual choice of President." Butler also made the point that while out of power the Democratic-Republicans reprimanded the Federalists for being motivated by partisanship in their attempt to secure electoral victories.[53] More to the point, he clearly identified the partyism underlining the Twelfth Amendment: "But, sir, there are motives operating in this body, and promoting this amendment, which though not prominent are powerful; it is said if you do not alter the Constitution, the people called Federalists will send a Vice President into that chair and this, in truth is the pivot upon which the whole turns."[54] Despite not having complete unity within the party, the Democratic-Republicans believed they had the public on their side and their attempt to secure electoral victories reflected popular will. Their commitment was to majority rule despite the accusations of partisanship and the larger states overwhelming the small ones.

The arguments for protection of the small states from the large states were analogous to a concern about the dynamics between a majority party and a minority party. At the heart of the Federalists' insistence on maintaining the appropriate relationship between states was anxiety over the seemingly new form of party politics and if the larger party would now consume the smaller. Put differently, if the Twelfth Amendment disrupted the balance of power between large states and small states, would it also aim to eliminate the existence of a political opposition? Addressing this concern, Senator William Cocke (DR-TN) recognized a change in perceptions with regard to an opposition and assured the Federalists the new rules would not disadvantage them in their political access amid the development of a new form of opposition politics:

> Gentlemen would not a few years ago listen to any advice or even complaints of a minority; they think now, as they said then, that there was no talents or virtue in the country but that they possess and they now tell us that minorities should govern. While [Federalists] stood in that House [they] would never submit to be governed by a minority, especially a minority which, when a part of the majority, declared the then minority deserved a dungeon. We shall not treat them in that way; they shall experience no persecution; we will even endeavor to make their situation comfortable for them; but they must not expect our aid to set aside majorities, or to depart from the principles of the Constitution.[55]

Far from persecuting the new minority, the Democratic-Republicans adopted a more tolerant position regarding an opposition, recognizing that nothing in the proposed changes to the electoral system would eliminate their participation in the process.[56]

Cocke's sentiments indicate a view of party government that would accommodate an opposition party, and the Democratic-Republicans were not the only ones who recognized the enduring presence of political parties and a system of opposition politics. Senator Samuel White (F-DE) connected political parties with the Twelfth Amendment's designation principle and declared, "The United States are now divided, and will probably continue so, into two great political parties; whenever, under this amendment, a Presidential election shall come round, and the four rival candidates be proposed, two of them only will be voted for as

President—one of these two must be the man." Consequently, he feared the amendment would "more than double" the probability of parties relying on "intrigue, bribery, and corruption" to ensure their candidate was chosen over the alternative.[57] James Hillhouse was perhaps the most vocal regarding the partyism of the Twelfth Amendment. He recognized that ambitious politicians would use political parties to get elected and that competition between the two parties, absent the proposed amendment, would be salutary for politics: "There may be degrees of party spirit—more or less asperity—but there never will come a time when party spirit will not exist; never will come a time when there will be no ambitious men aspiring to power. In the present time, gentlemen are perfectly able to place two persons of their own opinions in the two great offices. The minority cannot do it."[58] Retaining the original mode of presidential selection would permit each of the two parties to hold a principal office in the government, providing a check on each other.[59] Hillhouse, like many Federalists, recognized the principles of partyism underlying the Twelfth Amendment and how the designating principle would allow for a party-unified executive.

In response to the claims of partyism inherent in the Twelfth Amendment, Senator Cocke defended the amendment by acknowledging that it, along with the designating principle, would indeed benefit his party. However, Cocke believed his overt partyism was justified by again framing the argument in terms of facilitating majority rule. The Federalists accused the Democratic-Republicans of pushing the amendment as a means of preventing a Federalist from being elected vice president. Cocke acknowledged he personally did not want to see a split-party executive office. But his reasoning went beyond partisanship; he did not want to see anyone, no matter the party, elected who was not supported by a majority.[60] The amendment's purpose, he reasoned, was to "put in the power of the people to choose those whom they think most entitled to confidence and respect. If we furnish an amendment which they do not approve they will send it back to us."[61] Senator Taylor made a similar argument:

This brings precisely to the question of the amendment. It is the intention of the Constitution that the popular principle shall operate in the election of a President and Vice President. It is also the intention of the Constitution that the popular principle, in discharging the functions committed to it by the Constitution, should operate by a majority and not by a minority. That the majority of the people should be driven, by an unforeseen state of parties, to the necessity of relinquishing their will in the election of one or the other of these officers, or that the principle of majority, in a function confided to the popular will, should to the popular will, should be deprived of half its rights, and be laid under a necessity of violating its duty to preserve the other half, is not the intention of the Constitution.[62]

The Democratic-Republicans believed that they were clearly in the majority, and the results of the presidential election should reflect majority sentiment, especially in the case of electing the vice president.

With the Twelfth Amendment allowing for a party-unified executive, Hillhouse, recognizing that the Constitution did not work against parties, articulated an understanding of party politics and the consequences of the constitutional system:

But no party can long hold an ascendancy in power; they will ill treat each other—or some of them will disagree, and from the fragments new parties will arise, who will gain power and forget themselves, and again disagree, to make way for new parties. The Constitution was predicated upon the existence of parties; they will always exist, and names will not be wanting to rally under, and difference of interests will not be wanting for pretexts.[63]

In retrospect, Hillhouse's comments were even more perceptive than he realized for they anticipated much of the modern scholarship on the political development of party politics.[64] Opposition had an electoral role in American politics, and, far from creating constitutional provisions that worked against political opposition, the authors of the Twelfth Amendment understood their work as facilitating majority rule without disadvantaging the minority, as both parties understood they would not always be in the majority.

After tedious debates over designation, the number of candidates on the House ballot, constitutional design, and original intent, the Democratic-Republicans in the Senate were able to secure the requisite two-thirds majority (22-10) to pass the proposed amendment. To do so, the Senate had agreed to the designation principle, in addition to reducing the number of candidates in the House election from five to three. The House, then, would have to approve the Senate's alterations to the amendment before it would go to the states for final ratification. As in the Senate debates, the Democratic-Republicans were able to organize just enough support to accept the Senate's reduction from five to three in the House contingency election, approving the amendment by a bare two-thirds majority (84-42).[65]

After Congress had approved the would-be Twelfth Amendment, all that was left was for the states to ratify it. Ratification was important for President Thomas Jefferson and his party because the electoral tie with Aaron Burr cast doubt on his claim to popular support. The designation principle was intended to correct this and vindicate President Jefferson and the Democratic-Republicans. Jefferson himself described the Twelfth Amendment in the following way:

> I am a friend to the discrimination principle; and for a reason more than others have, inasmuch as the discriminated vote of my constituents will express unequivocally the verdict they wish to pass on my conduct. The abominable slanders of my political enemies have obliged me to call for that verdict from my country in the only way it can be obtained, and if obtained it will be my sufficient voucher to the rest of the world & to posterity and leave me free to see, at a definite time, the repose I sincerely wished to have retired to now.[66]

But the amendment would have to be ratified in the upcoming 1804 presidential election. In Tadahisa Kuroda's words, "The President's insistence on adoption made ratification a matter of party principle and personal loyalty."[67] Consequently, the proposed amendment was quickly ratified in North Carolina, Kentucky, Ohio, Virginia, Maryland, and Pennsylvania with little to no debate.[68] The Federalists, however, attempted to deny ratification in states where they still carried influence.

This was a difficult task for the Federalists because they had promoted a similar amendment in 1796, which included the designation principle. The Federalists knew the designation principle would benefit the majority party, and their previous support of the proposed amendment was based on their attempt to deny Jefferson the vice presidency during the Adams administration. Both the Federalists and the Democratic-Republicans knew what was as stake. "That great opposition," Jefferson explained, "is and will be made by federalists to this amendment is certain. They know that if it prevails, neither a Presidt or Vice President can ever be made but by the fair vote of the majority of the nation, of which they are not. That either their opposition to the principle of discrimination now, or their advocation of it formerly was on party, not moral motives, they cannot deny."[69] The designation principle had bipartisan support, as both parties (at one point) recognized that it would allow the voice of the majority to truly prevail in presidential elections without necessarily infringing on the rights of the minority.[70]

Tennessee was the final state needed for ratification, which was done in July 1804. On September 24, 1804, Secretary of State James Madison officially declared that the Twelfth Amendment had been ratified and would take effect in the upcoming presidential election. This meant that the Federalists, with their waning electoral support, would not influence the outcome of the upcoming presidential election because the Democratic-Republican ticket now allowed electors to distinguish their vote for incumbent Thomas Jefferson for president from George Clinton for vice president.[71] The Federalists unified their ticket behind Charles C. Pinckney for president and Rufus King for vice president. The Twelfth Amendment ensured a single-party executive.

At a time when many people believed the need for national political parties had passed, the Twelfth Amendment solidified their place in American politics. George Washington's retirement from politics demonstrated the deficiencies in the original constitutional mechanism for presidential selection. The two subsequent elections were fraught with difficulty, as the presidential elections of 1796 and 1800 produced less than desirable electoral outcomes. The Twelfth Amendment intentionally altered the presidential selection system by allowing electors to submit a completely separate ballot for vice president, thereby unifying a party ticket. This change legitimized party competition in presidential elections and validated a party's claim to office by establishing unity in the executive and connecting the executive to the public will.

The Twelfth Amendment also influenced our understanding of presidential leadership by ensuring that the "sense of the people" was expressed in electoral outcomes. The amendment and the designation principle provide evidence for the theory of presidential mandates.[72] Building on this development, the amendment also created and legitimized opposition leadership.[73] It required presidents to represent the majority popular sentiment by ensuring that elections were decided by the electorate and not the House. Moreover, reducing the number of candidates in a contingency from five to no more than three was an attempt to ensure that if the House was called on to decide an election, its choice would reflect popular will by significantly reducing the possibility of selecting a minority candidate. This detail legitimized majoritarian partyism electorally for two reasons. First, there was an increased likelihood of a congressional presidential election without designation, and this situation could include a minority of states mischievously selecting a president contrary to popular will. Second, retaining five candidates in the contingency election would have increased the probability that the elected president represented only a fraction of the population. Neither situation would allow for a party leader, particularly an opposition party leader, to claim that a new policy direction was supported by popular sentiment. This change to the presidential selection system left little room to doubt the legitimacy of a presidential election, even if the president represented an opposition party.

According to current scholarship, after Thomas Jefferson's presidential election, parties and partyism were supposed to wither away. The Twelfth Amendment, however, constitutionalized party politics by creating a party-unified executive office. Understanding the 1787 constitutional method of presidential selection would weaken party cohesion, the Democratic-Republicans proposed the Twelfth Amendment to ensure that a party, supported by popular will, would win both the presidency and the vice presidency. The authors of the amendment recognized they were changing the electoral system to accommodate parties in competitive elections for popular support. Because they recognized they would not always be in the majority, the Democratic-Republicans accepted the durability of this new form of party politics by acknowledging the continual existence of a political opposition in competitive elections. The Twelfth Amendment was a crucial step in developing a legitimate party system. It ensured that a party—either an opposition party or a party in government—could claim a unified executive and use popular will as a vindication for their electoral victory.

Regarding the constitutional incorporation of partyism, an understanding of the development and adoption of the Twelfth Amendment is necessary for explaining the manner in which political parties gained constitutional status through the system of presidential selection; it is not, however, sufficient. We cannot understand the lawmakers' purpose in unifying a presidential ballot without also understanding the development of electoral college vote distribution. During the debates, Seth Hastings's connection between the proposition that would become the Twelfth Amendment and the three-fifths clause was more important than the Democratic-Republicans recognized. Hastings alluded to the electoral benefits conferred on the South by the clause and the inflated support they received from a nonvoting population. Consequently, the benefits of the Twelfth Amendment could only be achieved if the electoral rules regarding the method of choosing presidential electors and electoral college vote allocation also reflected the public's general sentiment.

CHAPTER 5

Partyism and Organized Opposition in Elections

For many scholars, Thomas Jefferson's presidential election in 1800 was a revolution. Some saw it as a revolution of presidential power.[1] For others, it was revolutionary because the Federalists willingly and peacefully turned over governing control to their rivals, the Democratic-Republicans.[2] This singular electoral event, however, was part of a much larger revolution in which political parties began to assume a critical role in American politics. Just because the Federalists were out of office did not mean they were out of electoral politics. Once the majority, they now had to adjust to being the minority party. As the Federalists assumed the role of opposition party, they were privy to the same political resources as the Democratic-Republicans, such as the newly articulated broad interpretation of the First Amendment, which allowed the Federalists to use the newspapers as a means of politically uniting and organizing, and the Twelfth Amendment, which allowed them to run a unified presidential ticket. Once the Federalists became the minority, they could avail themselves of political and electoral resources to once again ascend to power.

The Federalists' success as an opposition party was predicated on their acceptance and utilization of these rules and practices. Despite the demoralizing defeat, the Federalist Party had the electoral and constitutional means of mounting a successful opposition campaign. They were in a position to reconstruct their party and their electoral future. After the election of 1800, Elkins and McKitrick explain, it is conceivable to imagine the emergence of a reconstituted Federalist Party, having gained electoral experience and proceeding under leadership capable of adapting to the new partisan environment. While the Federalists "had become a party—a party and yet not a party," the potential for adaptation and rearticulation remained as the Democratic-Republicans had opened the door for party competition—a door that would not be closed.[3] Some Federalists, particularly Alexander Hamilton, attempted to reinvent the Federalist Party by accepting and adhering to the new party institutions and principles that the Democratic-Republicans had established. Hamilton's death, however, was also the death of the Federalist Party's reform, and the party pursued nonelectoral means of challenging their partisan opponents. As an opposition party, the Federalists failed to follow the accepted constitutional means of opposing the party-in-government. Their demise was a result of their own inability to successfully appropriate the accepted regime norms governing party practices, not because political parties were deemed illegitimate.

PARTY INSTITUTIONS AND PRINCIPLES: THE DEMOCRATIC-REPUBLICAN PARTY

The Federalist Party had maintained its dominance for more than a decade after the ratification of the Constitution. After George Washington's retirement, John Adams was the final Federalist president, and he only served a single term. During the Fifth Congress (1797–99), the Federalists controlled both the House (56:49) and the Senate (22:9). By the beginning of the Eighth Congress (1803–5), they had lost their majorities in the House (26:113) and the Senate (9:22), and President Jefferson won reelection by a landslide in 1804. As an opposition party, the Democratic-Republicans' electoral efforts began as early as 1796, during the presidential election between Thomas Jefferson and incumbent John Adams. During this election, the Democratic-Republican Party's electoral strategies demonstrated the vulnerability of the Federalist Party and their political principles as Jefferson successfully captured the vice presidency—nearly winning the presidency. The Democratic-Republicans' party efforts were further refined leading up to the "revolution of 1800" in which the transition in party dominance was completed.

During the 1796 presidential election, the Democratic-Republicans recognized the importance of key states to their party's success and focused their efforts to coordinate during the election and navigate various state election laws. Pennsylvania was a key state despite predominantly supporting the Federalists.[4] The state was divided between those who supported, in varying degrees, the current administration and those who were upset with the administration's policies during the previous four years. It also had the broadest suffrage laws, and it was one of only two states that elected presidential electors by a popular statewide vote. Pennsylvania also had some of the most highly organized political parties before the Constitution. Very little had changed, because the state contained numerous party leaders willing to organize what can be considered the first real presidential campaign. Finally, Philadelphia, the state's and the country's largest city, was diverse and had the most active group of democratic activists.[5]

Prior to the election, the Federalists, who controlled the state legislature, did not make it easy for the Democratic-Republicans. As the Federalists crafted the law establishing the method for selecting presidential electors, both parties tried to anticipate public opinion across the state. The Federalists, perceiving their party would be in the majority, established a statewide method to capitalize on their advantage. They also included various other election laws to proscribe the opposition's efforts. Presidential elector selection was scheduled after state elections. Commercial towns, including Philadelphia, typically voted Federalists, while rural, inland towns supported the Democratic-Republicans. Separating the selection of presidential electors from the state elections meant that there was a second electoral contest in which most individuals were not accustomed to participate. In addition, it was difficult for rural, inland voters to participate in elections given the cost and the distance they needed to travel. Having a separate election for presidential electors increased the difficulty for these voters, mainly Democratic-Republican supporters, to participate in two separate elections in one month. The Federalists also prohibited the use of preprinted election tickets, requiring presidential elector voters to use a handwritten ballot with the names of all fifteen presidential electors they wanted to support. This measure again targeted the Democratic-Republican supporters, who often had limited access to information and lower literacy skills. With these electoral rules, the Federalists aimed at holding an election for presidential electors with low voter turnout and at making it more likely for those with wealth, access to information, and access to a ballot box, typically Federalists, to participate in voting. Even the Democratic-Republicans recognized these electoral rules put them at a disadvantage and hoped the district method was adopted to avoid losing all presidential electors in the statewide contest. They turned their disadvantage into an advantage, however, by galvanizing and mobilizing their more numerous working-class supporters throughout the state. Despite trying to hinder their opponents' electoral competitiveness, the Federalists provided the Democratic-Republicans with the method for selecting presidential electors that they needed to secure a victory for Jefferson.[6]

To win Pennsylvania, John Beckley, Benjamin Franklin Bache, Michael Leib, and Major John Smith executed a sophisticated statewide campaign in relation to the electorally significant selection of presidential electors.[7] Beckley organized a state caucus in which the Democratic-Republicans chose presidential electors from as many prominent partisan names as possible, relying on name recognition to educate and guide voters. Once this list was compiled, Beckley kept it secret so the Federalists could not vilify those selected or replicate the Democratic-Republicans' strategy.[8] Major Smith and other Democratic-Republicans traveled throughout the state holding local meetings to rouse voters in favor of "the Republican Jefferson." As the election neared and it would be too late for the Federalists either to imitate or to impede the plan, the Democratic-Republicans provided voters with important voting heuristics by distributing handbills in every district with the prominent names of the Democratic-Republican electors. They took advantage of Pennsylvania election law that allowed for parties to distribute their own ballots as long as they were handwritten. A week before the election, a Democratic-Republican campaign committee successfully distributed fifty thousand of these handwritten ballots to local partisans.[9] As a result of these efforts, the Democratic-Republicans overwhelmingly captured fourteen of Pennsylvania's fifteen electoral college votes, a significant loss to the

Federalists considering they received all of Pennsylvania's votes in the 1792 presidential election.[10]

As the election of 1800 approached, the Democratic-Republicans' further refined their electoral machinery, developing more effective strategies to challenge the incumbent Federalists. The Democratic-Republicans looked to Vice President Jefferson as the official party leader, and, as one Federalist described it, he became "the 'rallying point,' the head quarters, the everything" for the rising opposition party.[11] Utilizing their successful experience with Pennsylvania in 1796, the Democratic-Republicans began to organize a campaign strategy with the goal of winning the presidency. To secure Jefferson's support from Virginia, Maryland, and New Jersey, they organized elaborate local committees and created networks of correspondence.[12] With organization from the 1796 election already established in Pennsylvania, local committees took on the responsibility of directing campaign efforts in local counties as well as creating and distributing Democratic-Republican ballots for the 1800 contest. Just as Pennsylvania was crucial for Jefferson's success in 1796, the Democratic-Republicans needed to win New York if they were going to capture the presidency. Recognizing this, Aaron Burr, a native New Yorker, oversaw a sophisticated and effective electioneering campaign in Manhattan.[13] Under New York election law, the state legislature appointed presidential electors, and New York would be holding its legislative election in the April before the presidential election. Winning control of the state legislature was key for determining the mode of choosing presidential electors most advantageous to the party. Recognizing this, Jefferson explained to Madison, "If the *city* election of N York is in favor of the Republican ticket, the issue will be republican."[14] This is to say, the outcome of the New York legislative races would determine the allocation of the state's electoral college votes and, potentially, the outcome of the presidential election.

The Democratic-Republicans, aided by Burr, succeeded with their campaign strategy, capturing control of the New York legislature and, eventually, the presidency. The party's success in New York was largely due to Burr's electioneering. Months before the legislative election, Burr made considerable efforts to personally visit his partisan contacts in New York City. In addition, he opened his home for "entertainment, meals, and even sleeping quarters" to those working on the campaign.[15]

To further organize efforts, Burr held regular party meetings at Abraham Martling's Tavern. With the help of his friend Matthew L. Dickenson, Burr implemented the Pennsylvania strategy in New York City by creating a Democratic-Republican legislative ticket with prominent partisan names in the hope that these distinguished and influential figures would contribute to the party's electoral success. And, as in 1796, this list was largely kept secret, and the Federalists failed to implement a similar strategy or impede their opponents'. As the April election day approached, the Democratic-Republicans coordinated by creating various party committees, including a citywide general committee and a committee for each of New York's seven wards. Burr, with the help of other local party leaders, feverishly distributed handbills and addressed as many assemblies of voters as possible.[16] Burr's efforts yielded the desired results. The Democratic-Republicans captured New York's legislature with an overwhelming victory in New York City and a narrow victory in the rest of the state. Commenting on the campaign and election outcomes, James Nicolson praised Burr: "That business has been conducted and brought to issue in so miraculous a manner that I cannot account for it but from the intervention of a Supreme Being and our friend Burr the agent."[17] Burr's success was demoralizing to Alexander Hamilton. After losing the legislative election, Hamilton pleaded with Governor John Jay to hold a special legislative session before the Democratic-Republicans took office to revise the election laws so that New York's presidential electors would be selected by district rather than by the state legislature. Governor Jay never responded to Hamilton's request. The Federalists had lost control of the New York legislature, and, because of the Democratic-Republicans' effective campaign, the Federalists soon lost control of the presidency.

For the Democratic-Republicans, the election of 1800 took on particular significance. It was one in which the Federalists' constitutional interpretation and governing actions were retrospectively evaluated and the future of the constitutional regime prospectively determined. The Democratic-Republicans gave the electorate substantive alternatives to the Federalists' governing principles, and these new "republican" principles determined the nature of the constitutional order for the foreseeable future. The competition for the presidency in 1800 was a competition between party leaders and their principles of constitutionalism. Jefferson and Madison developed competing principles of governance to those of

Hamilton, who, as early as 1791, Jefferson had identified as the leader of the Federalist Party and the architect of the Federalists' ideology and theory of constitutionalism. In August 1791, after a conversation with Hamilton, Jefferson believed Hamilton was of the opinion that "the present government is not that which will answer the ends of society, by giving stability and protection to it's [*sic*] rights, and that it will probably be found expedient to go into the British form."[18] According to Jefferson, the measures taken by Hamilton as secretary of the treasury—the assumption of state debt, the bank bill, and his financial program—were all methods aimed at mirroring English constitutionalism. In other words, Hamilton was "preaching up and pouting after an English constitution of kings, lords, and commons" in which there was "a kind of symbiosis—a link of influence, patronage, and personal relationships—between the king's ministers and the two houses of parliament."[19] Jefferson also believed Hamilton was corrupting Congress, turning it into a "legislature legislating for their own interests in opposition to those of the people." Jefferson's and Madison's characterization of the Federalists as the "anti-republican" party was tied to their perception of the Federalist Party as a party of "paper men," or "bank directors and stock-jobbers" in Congress who had an individual interest in ensuring that Hamilton and his fiscal policies were successful.[20] They would lead a party dedicated to true "republican" principles.

Leading up to the election of 1800, the Democratic-Republicans had plenty to oppose given the preceding years of a Federalist-controlled government. As Jefferson took office, he declared the new principles of government that would guide his administration. Madison had already used newspapers as a means of promoting republican values by opposing what he saw as the consolidation of states into one government, as well as Hamilton's and the Federalists' broad interpretation of executive power used to justify Washington's Neutrality Proclamation of 1793. The Federalists further added to the opposition's fervor by signing the Jay Treaty in 1796, bringing the United States to the brink of war with France, using a failed diplomatic mission—the XYZ Affair—as justification for strengthening the military, and passing the controversial Alien and Sedition Acts.[21] According to the Democratic-Republicans, all these measures aimed at one goal, subverting the republican government designed by the Constitution, a major theme of the Kentucky and Virginia Resolutions.

Jefferson used his first inaugural address to declare the "essential principles" of government, those that guided the Democratic-Republicans to office and "those which ought to shape its administration."[22] This declaration of principles served as their party's platform and as a way to evaluate elected officials' performance in office. As a direct alternative to Federalist principles, Jefferson stated his administration would seek "peace, commerce, and honest friendship with all nations, entangling alliances with none"; provide "support of the State governments in all their rights, as the most competent administrations for our domestic concerns and the surest bulwarks against antirepublican tendencies"; pursue "economy in the public expenses, that labor may be lightly burdened"; and dedicate itself to "the honest payment of our debts and sacred preservation of the public faith," the "encouragement of agriculture; and of commerce as its handmaid," and "the diffusion of information and arraignment of all abuses at the bar of the public reason." Furthermore, settling the controversy over the Alien and Sedition Acts, Jefferson eschewed the Federalists' constitutional interpretations and secured, at least at the national level, the "freedom of religion; freedom of the press, and freedom of person under the protection of the habeas corpus, and trial by juries impartially selected."[23] Although Jefferson claimed conciliation between the parties, the principles guiding his administration were distinctly Democratic-Republican. In the electoral struggle over constitutional principles, the Democratic-Republicans had provided the electorate with a substantively different mode of governance than that of the Federalists. From their perspective, the people had spoken. The Democratic-Republicans established partyism through competitive elections as the accepted norm for challenging the party in government. Importantly, they did not preclude the possibility of a Federalist challenge, as the same strategies they had used to capture governing power were available to the Federalist Party.

ADAPTING TO PARTY INSTITUTIONS AND PRINCIPLES: THE FEDERALIST PARTY

The task of successfully adapting to the new partyism norms was not easy for the Federalists. They were affiliated with a set of political commitments that had, in the course of events and elections, been deemed failed or insufficient responses to the political problems of the time. A political party in this situation has the difficult choice of maintaining its current ideological commitments and policy positions, thereby remaining associated with the political failures of the recent past, or transforming itself to reflect the newly established ideological commitments, thereby risking alienation from both its own political identity and its own natural base and allies. Adding to the difficulty, the Federalists faced a leadership crisis after Alexander Hamilton effectively removed John Adams from the party, and shortly after that Aaron Burr ended Hamilton's life in a duel. The Federalists would have to rally around a new leader, capable of articulating and executing a political strategy to match that of Jefferson's Democratic-Republicans.

When considering the importance of the election of 1800, the Democratic-Republicans' victory rather than the Federalist's defeat is often emphasized. In this view, Jefferson's election united "fellow-citizens" with "one heart and one mind" and "[restored] to social intercourse that harmony and affection without which liberty and even life itself are but dreary things."[24] This leads to the assumption that the decline in the Federalist Party was primarily driven by antiparty sentiments and Jefferson's attempt at reconciliation. The Federalists, however, were not necessarily condemned by antiparty sentiments. For, as Jefferson claimed, the election had settled a "sacred principle, that though the will of the majority is in all cases to prevail, that will to be rightful must be reasonable; that the minority possess their equal rights, which equal law must protect, and to violate would be oppression."[25] Although the Federalists now found themselves in the minority, antiparty sentiments would not necessarily translate into laws prohibiting them from partisan organization and participation. And as the Alien and Sedition Acts were set to expire (and President Jefferson allowed them to expire), the Federalists benefited from a broader interpretation of the First Amendment than they had established during the Adams administration. Moreover, the Democratic-Republicans' electoral strategy had proved to be successful, and nothing would legally or politically prohibit the Federalists from duplicating their rival's campaigning effectiveness. In other words, the Constitution would not work against the Federalists, and antiparty sentiments were not a sufficient explanation for their collapse. In order to understand the demise of the Federalist Party, more attention must be given to the Federalists' efforts to fulfill the role as a competitive, opposition party. As we will see, the Federalists' inability to be effective electorally and their lack of unity contributed to their collapse as an electorally viable party.

Partyism and Interparty Strife

Shortly after Adams was inaugurated, he assembled Congress and recommended that immediate defense measures be taken given the escalating conflicts in Europe. He recommended that officers be commissioned and arrangements for recruitment of a provisional army be made. What he did not request was the establishment of a large professional army. If Adams was going to war, he was going to rely heavily on the navy because an army was not a good instrument of defense or foreign policy.[26] President Adams's view, however, did not coincide with that of many of the Federalists, both in and out of Congress. They were convinced that a large professional army was necessary for defense against both foreign attack and internal dissent. They particularly feared internal dissent from the southern Democratic-Republicans. President Adams soon found himself in direct conflict with members of his own party and administration, thereby alienating the president from the party that he was supposed to lead. John Quincy Adams later described the result of this conflict: "The army was the first decisive symptom of a schism in the Federalist party itself, which accomplished its final overthrow and that of the administration."[27]

George Washington's death further compounded the problems for the Federalist Party. Although Hamilton drove much of the Federalists' platform and policy, Washington was the face of the party, and his presence, according to Hamilton, maintained party unity and discipline. Without Washington to unite them, the Federalist coalition was electorally vulnerable. In a letter to Rufus King, Hamilton lamented that "the irreparable loss of an inestimable man removes a control which was felt, and was very salutary." He also noted that without Washington, Adams had become perverse and capricious in his policy decisions.[28] As the election of 1800 approached, the Federalist Party lost their most valuable asset, a party leader who had unanimously won two presidential elections and provided stability to the Federalist Party and, importantly, to the country. After his death, the *Pennsylvania Gazette* wrote,

"When WASHINGTON lived, we had one common mind—one common head—one common heart—we were united—we were safe."[29] The Federalist Party experienced an identity crisis entering the election of 1800, as Adams and Hamilton competed to fill the void left by Washington's death.

Prior to the election of 1800, there was no apparent animosity between Hamilton and Adams. Both served in Washington's administration and their contact was rather limited. After Washington decided not to run for a third term, Adams was the next logical candidate, having served as vice president for two terms. During the election of 1796, Hamilton supported both Adams and Thomas Pinckney to keep Jefferson from winning. However, Hamilton preferred Pinckney as president. On numerous occasions, he wrote that "Mr. P[inckney] ought to be our man."[30] Hamilton knew that Pinckney did not have the support of all Federalists. "The attachment of our Eastern friends to Mr. Adams may prevent their voting for *Pinckney* likewise, & that some irregularity or accident may deprive us of *Adams* & let in Jefferson," he wrote in a letter to Jeremiah Wadsworth.[31] Hamilton's fear was realized, but it was Pinckney, not Adams, who was left out of office.

Adams was aware of Hamilton's expressed preference for Pinckney as president and his attempts to prevent his (Adams's) election. In a letter to his wife, Adams referred to Hamilton as a "proud Spirited, conceited, aspiring Mortal always pretending to Morality, with as debauched Morals as old Franklin who is more his Model than any one I know. As great an Hypocrite as any in the U.S." He also condemned Hamilton's electioneering and planned to avoid him: "His Intrigues in the Election I despise. That he has Talents I admit but I dread none of them. I shall take no notice of his Puppy head but retain the same Opinion of him I always had and maintain the same Conduct towards him I always did, that is keep him at a distance."[32] After winning the presidency, avoiding Hamilton was difficult. Although not formally part of Adams's administration, Hamilton was close with many of Adams's cabinet members and corresponded with them frequently about policy issues.[33] Adams sought to purge his cabinet of Hamilton's influence and those who were willing to follow Hamilton rather than himself. He requested that James McHenry, his secretary of war, and Timothy Pickering, his secretary of state, resign from their positions. Initially, Pickering was unwilling "to accept this insidious favour." He then promptly received a "peremptory discharge," after which he "quitted the office."[34]

Adding to the animosity between the two, Adams refused to appoint Hamilton as lieutenant general and commander in chief of all the armies, a position held by Washington until his death. Hamilton was the ranking major general and anticipated the appointment. Adams, however, left the position vacant. Even Hamilton's associates recognized this move was a source of contention between Hamilton and Adams. John Rutledge wrote to Hamilton, "Your opposition to Mr. A[dams] has its source in private pique—if you had been appointed Commander in chief on the death of Genl W[ashington] you would have continued one of Mr. A[dams]'s partizans."[35] Looking toward the election of 1800, Hamilton was less than pleased with the "Perverseness and capriciousness" of Adams.[36] Despite his growing animosity, Hamilton found himself in a difficult position. Personally, he did not want to support Adams, especially as Adams prepared for reelection. He also knew, however, that withholding his support for Adams would be costly to the party, and he expressed this sentiment to his colleague Theodore Sedgwick: "[Although] *most* of the *most influential men* of that party consider him as a very *unfit* and *incapable* character," supporting Adams was "a notable expedient for keeping the Foederal Party together" and would prevent the government from falling into the "fangs of *Jefferson.*"[37]

In May 1800, a Federalist congressional caucus determined the candidates for the presidential election, giving equal support to Adams and Pinckney. Hamilton quickly made his preference for Pinckney over Adams known. By July, he actively supported Pinkney, believing it was "essential to inform the most discreet of this description of the facts which denote unfitness in Mr. Adams." The Federalists' schism intensified as Hamilton recognized Adams and his supporters were devising their own plans to undermine Pinckney: "[Adams's] friends are industrious in propagating the idea to defeat the efforts to unite for Pinckney."[38] Completely dissatisfied with Adams, Hamilton expressed his desire to withdraw support from him, even if it led to the election of his rival, Jefferson. "If we must have an enemy at the head of the government," he reasoned, "let it be one whom we can oppose, and for whom we are not responsible."[39] Hamilton's position vis-à-vis Jefferson's opposition party was clearly not as severe as his distaste for Adams. For Hamilton, it would be easier for the Federalists to battle Jefferson on partisan grounds with a Federalist Party united behind leadership dedicated to Federalist principles. If, however, the Federalist Party was willing to eschew their principles in support of a "weak and perverse man," then Hamilton would "withdraw from the party."[40] In August, just a few months before the presidential election, he decided to sacrifice party unity for his personal belief that Adams was an incompetent leader and that leaders in the Federalist Party should no longer support him.[41] He went to work writing his *Letter . . . Concerning the Public Conduct and Character of John Adams, Esq. President of the United States.*[42] In the long run, strengthening the Federalist Party, and perhaps saving it, required a consolidation of leadership under what Hamilton deemed "true" Federalist principles.

It is unclear if Hamilton's purpose in writing the *Letter* was to strengthen the Federalists' electoral chances or to merely condemn Adams. In his conclusion, Hamilton wrote what he thought his *Letter* accomplished: "To promote this co-operation [between supporters of both Adams and Pinckney], to defend my own character, to vindicate those friends, who with myself have been unkindly answered, are the inducements for writing this letter."[43] The *Letter*, however, did not mention Pinckney or try to explain why he should be preferred over Adams for the presidency. Only briefly did Hamilton explain his actions in defense of his character. There was no genuine attempt to reconcile differences between the Adams and Pinckney factions within the party. His support of Adams had an undertone of insincerity and dissatisfaction. He claimed he would not openly campaign against Adams in order to promote Federalist unity. Yet he made it clear the Federalists needed to unite around a leader with fewer character flaws and more administrative capabilities. The overwhelming majority of the *Letter* consisted of his critical review of Adams's actions and decisions as president. If anything, Hamilton tried to raise doubts among fellow Federalists that another four years with Adams at the helm was desirable.

Despite their shared animosity toward Adams, many of Hamilton's Federalist colleagues did not support his decision to publicly denounce Adams. James A. Bayard counseled Hamilton not to publish the *Letter* because he recognized the negative effects Hamilton's plan would have on the Federalist Party's chances in the upcoming election. According to Bayard's vote calculations, Adams potentially had enough support to win the presidential election, and the Democratic-Republicans would "beget a system of miserable intrigue between the members of the same Party whose efforts can not be united." Bayard believed that Hamilton's anti-Adams pamphlet undermined the Federalists' "mutual confidence" and that the party's "united efforts are absolutely necessary to maintain their ground against their adversaries."[44] Contrary to Hamilton, Bayard felt that winning the election with an undesirable candidate was more important than sacrificing electoral victory for party principle. He refused to make his disdain for Adams public for fear of further alienating members of the party who supported him.[45] Fisher Ames echoed Bayard's sentiments that an Adams victory was technically better than a Federalist defeat, stating that it was "indispensably necessary" to support Adams's "inauspicious" reelection. Most Federalists, reasoned Ames, preferred Adams to Jefferson. The opinion of the many within the party mattered more than the opinion of a few, including Hamilton. Ames also feared that in denouncing Adams, Hamilton would incur the wrath of the party because he would be blamed for Jefferson's victory. Unlike Bayard, Ames questioned Adams's and the Federalists' electoral chances, and his advice to Hamilton was based more on the party's future than the immediate election: "The federalists would be defeated which is bad, and disjointed and enraged against one another which wd. be worse. Now it seems to me that the great object and duty and prudence is to keep the party strong by it's [sic] union and spirit."[46] Both Bayard and Ames believed Hamilton's vendetta against Adams was more personal than political, and if Jefferson and the Democratic-Republicans were to win the upcoming presidential election, the Federalists needed to be united so as to function as a strong opposition. Those opposed to Hamilton printing his pamphlet made a case for strengthening parties, particularly the Federalist Party. In both instances, members of the party urged party unification for the purpose of having a strong opposition once the Democratic-Republicans could no longer sustain their party discipline. Put differently, the Federalists, as a party, needed to remain united in case the Democratic-Republicans suffered the same fate as the Federalist Party, a loss of party cohesion.

Hamilton, nevertheless, did not follow the advice of his fellow Federalists. He published his *Letter*, which berated Adams and led to the strengthening of Jefferson's campaign against the Federalists and the weakening of Hamilton's position within the party. In the *Letter*, however, his stance toward Adams was less divisive. He adopted a position closer to Bayard and Ames in that despite Adams's "disgusting egoism" and "vanity," Hamilton half-heartedly claimed Adams should be supported to maintain party unity.[47] His plan to distribute the *Letter* only to Federalists, however, was undermined for it was quickly leaked to the press. The *Aurora* in Philadelphia and the *New London Bee* in Connecticut first printed selections from it, then published the entire pamphlet. Both Federalists and Democratic-Republicans responded to Hamilton's piece. George Cabot, a Federalist from Massachusetts, accused Hamilton of having the same character flaws he had attributed to Adams.[48] Noah Webster, a Federalist from Connecticut, wrote a public letter in which he accused Hamilton, just as Ames had warned, of allowing Jefferson to win the election because he had divided the Federalist Party.[49] Even Madison recognized the damage Hamilton's letter had done to himself and his party: "Added to these causes [of Adams's demise] is the pamphlet of H[amilton] which, tho' its recoil has perhaps more deeply wounded the author, than the object it was discharged at, has contributed not a little to overthrow the latter staggering as he before was in the public esteem."[50] Adams shared Madison's evaluation of the *Letter* and Hamilton: "[The] pamphlet I regret more on the account of its author, than on my own, because I am confident, it will do him more harm than me. I am not his enemy & never was. I have not adored him, like his idolators, & have had great cause to disapprove of some of his politicks."[51] Even if, as Fisher Ames had predicted, Jefferson's election was inevitable, their internal division and lack of leadership diminished the Federalists' prospects of organizing an opposition capable of challenging Jefferson. Both Adams and Hamilton had lost or were losing credibility in the Federalist Party.

Partyism and Public Sentiment

Within two years after President Adams's failed reelection campaign, the Federalists lost their majorities in the House and the Senate. The Democratic-Republicans' victory, while enthusiastically hailed as a victory of true political principle, was actually a triumph of party principles. The electoral success of 1800 was the culmination of the Democratic-Republicans' arduous efforts to create and organize a party capable of running and maintaining an extensive political campaign.

Prior to their electoral victory in 1800, the Democratic-Republicans served as the first opposition party, and their campaign strategy set a precedent for future attempts to challenge the party in government by electoral means. Although the Federalist Party never fully recovered from its loss in 1800, it nevertheless served as the new opposition party. All the electoral rules and strategies developed by and available to the Democratic-Republicans were now at the Federalists' disposal. More important, the Federalists recognized they could utilize the same party strategies as the Democratic-Republicans. Rather than accepting defeat and conciliation, the Federalists began revising their electoral strategies in an attempt to fulfill the role of an effective opposition party. The operation of political parties became an organizing feature in American electoral politics.

Leaders of the Federalist Party understood that if they were going to challenge the Democratic-Republicans, they needed to alter their electoral strategies, particularly their understanding of and relationship to public opinion. The Federalists' response to their electoral defeat "must not begin," recognized Fisher Ames, "with an impression on the popular mind that we are a disgraced if we are a disappointed party. We must court popular favor, we must study public opinion, and accommodate measures to what it is and still more to what it ought to be."[52] Bayard agreed: "We shall probably pay more attention to public opinion than we have heretofore done, and take more pains, not merely to do right things, but to do them in an acceptable manner."[53] Even Hamilton recognized that the Federalists neglected the role of public opinion while their opponents mastered it. By capturing the public's sentiment, the Democratic-Republicans had gained a significant electoral advantage that would not be easily overcome. "Unless we can," reasoned Hamilton, "contrive to take hold of, and carry along with us some strong feelings of the mind, we shall in vain calculate upon any substantial or durable results."[54] If President Jefferson claimed to embody the public sentiment, then the Federalists needed to court public opinion so as to shape it if they were going to have any success in challenging the Democratic-Republicans. Public opinion was the key to facilitating a legitimate force capable of checking political power. If the Federalists were going to legitimately challenge President Jefferson and the Democratic-Republicans, they would have to do it through majoritarian means and public sentiment.

In the battle for public sentiment, the Democratic-Republicans also recognized the possibility of the Federalists' return to power. Importantly, they understood that the Federalists' electoral failures were attributed to three main causes: intraparty conflicts, lack of leadership, and want of public support. All three of these issues were resolvable, and the Federalists could challenge the Democratic-Republicans' majority status. While the Federalists were down, they were definitely not out of politics. The Democratic-Republicans needed to prepare for the possibility that the Federalists would reorganize and become more competitive behind a stronger leader than John Adams. Moreover, even if they could not necessarily capture the presidency, they could still capture enough seats in Congress to challenge the Democratic-Republicans' majority and make it difficult to enact policy. To secure their party's position, the Democratic-Republicans had to maintain their unified and energized majority coalition while taking into consideration the positive role the opposition Federalists would have in being a check on the Democratic-Republicans. The Federalists knew this too. As Fisher Ames articulated, the Federalists needed to be a "champion who never flinches, a watchman who never sleeps," and recognized as being "deeply alarmed for the public good; that [the Federalists] are identified with the public."[55] Gouverneur Morris similarly argued, "Let the chair of office be filled by whomsoever it may, opposition will act as an outward conscience, and prevent the abuse of power."[56] This competition for public support produced a more responsive and responsible government, a central component of a two-party system.[57] But to be successful, the Federalists had to develop an effective and responsible strategy for their new role as the opposition party.

Aware of the need to develop a new political strategy, Hamilton began to organize efforts to capture and shape public opinion, including utilizing the press. The Federalists needed to avoid an opposition that could be deemed "revolutionary." For Hamilton, the "present Constitution is the standard to which [the Federalists] are to cling," and one of the major changes to the "present" Constitution was the recently settled constitutional understanding of the First Amendment. He worried the Federalist Party would never recover from their recent displacement from office unless they could "contrive to take hold of & carry along with us some strong feelings of the mind," and they would need to, in some degree, employ "the weapons which have been employed against [them]."[58]

He had newspapers in mind. In addition, Hamilton wanted to build a Federalist association at the local, state, and national levels in order to make them more competitive in elections. To accomplish this, he proposed a "Christian Constitutional Society" as a political association to strengthen the Federalist Party.

Modern political parties are commonly defined as an organized group that nominates candidates in an attempt to win political office electorally to promote specific public policies, and parties are described as having three interacting parts: the "party organization," the "party in government," and the "party in the electorate."[59] Hamilton's Christian Constitutional Society captured many of these features. He proposed an organization that included a hierarchical leadership structure at both the national and state levels with a "direct council consisting of a President & 12 Members, of whom 4 & the President to be a quorum."[60] Each would also have "a sub-directing council in each State consisting of a Vice-President &12 Members." After describing the general organization, Hamilton explained the three-part mission of the society. First, the Federalists would reestablish general support for their policy preferences by solidifying their party organization. This included "the diffusion of information" by means of "newspapers" and "pamphlets." Moreover, to support the Federalists' use of the press, "a fund must be created" with each member contributing "5 dollars annually for 8 years." And "clubs should be formed to meet once a week, read the newspapers & prepare essays paragraphs &ct." Second, in addition to an active press, the Federalists needed to make preparations to "use . . . all lawful means in concert to promote the election of *fit men*." To this end, the separate societies within the states would need to maintain "lively correspondence" to secure consensus on candidates and coordinate voting efforts and maximize electoral results. Through this effort, Hamilton aimed to strengthen their presence in the party in government. Third, to compete with the Democratic-Republicans, the Federalists would need to build and increase their party's base. To do so, he promoted "institutions of a charitable & useful nature in the management of Foederalists [*sic*]." And, as an electoral strategy, he placed additional emphasis on Federalists' efforts in "populous cities." Perhaps most important, Hamilton began to devise a strategy "for the relief of Emigrants." Prior to the Federalists' fall from political power, the Alien and Sedition Acts aimed to minimize the political influence of immigrants because they largely supported the Democratic-Republicans. Now this demographic was crucial for increasing the cumulative effect of the Federalist party in the electorate. Far from conceding to antiparty sentiments, the Hamilton-led Federalist Party was not going to accept President Jefferson's efforts at conciliation. Under his leadership, they would attempt to fulfill the role of a constitutional, responsible, and effective opposition, a role once occupied by the Democratic-Republicans.[61]

Hamilton's strategy, however, never came to fruition. Other Federalists rejected the idea because they were unwilling to court public opinion and imitate the Democratic-Republicans. More to the point, the Federalists were divided on the strategy of courting public opinion, but they were united in their desire to strengthen their party to function as effective opposition. Bayard, with whom Hamilton first shared his plan, rejected Hamilton's strategy because he did not believe the Federalists needed to court public opinion. Specifically, he believed that the Democratic-Republicans' success would be only temporary. "Without any exertion upon [the Federalists'] part," he explained, "in the course of two or three years [the Democratic-Republicans] will render every honest man in the country our Proselyte." He also believed the Democratic-Republicans' public support was dwindling, as "The Presidents Party in Congress is much weaker than you would be led to judge" and "the spirit which existed at the beginning of the [congressional] Session is entirely dissipated."[62] Time was the Federalists' greatest asset, not public opinion.

Bayard rejected the notion of using public opinion as the basis for the Federalist Party because it was "impossible to fix public opinion," as "a degree of agitation & vibration of opinion must forever prevail under a government so free as that of the U States." Rather than public opinion, the Federalists needed to rely on their own political fortunes and prominent members. He believed that the Federalists had superior "political Calculators" and that the Democratic-Republicans were "political fanaticks."[63] The Federalists, however, were running short on notable names, and they refused to promote candidates beyond their strongholds in New England. As they approached the first presidential election as an opposition party, they put themselves at a serious disadvantage in their ability to challenge the popular incumbent, Jefferson, because of their division over public opinion, not their aversion to partyism.

The Federalist Party ultimately lacked electoral effectiveness because they could not agree on the question of whether to court public opinion, and they did little to secure electoral outcomes outside of New England. Their lack of notable names outside of New England was a major hindrance. Because political parties were still in their infancy, the prestige of the candidate and not the party label served as a heuristic for voters. In prior elections, the Federalists had national success because they were associated with figures such as George Washington and John Adams, heroes of the American Revolution. Their candidate in 1804, Charles C. Pinckney, hardly had the same prestige and national renown. Moreover, the Federalist Party was still associated with the failures of the previous administration. Commenting on the first political parties in America, Tocqueville made a similar observation:

In 1801, the Republicans finally took possession of the government. Thomas Jefferson was named president; he brought them the support of a celebrated name, a great talent, and an immense popularity. The Federalists had never maintained themselves except by artificial means and with the aid of temporary resources; it was the virtue or talents of their chiefs as well as fortunate circumstances that had carried them to power. When the Republicans arrived in their turn, the opposing party was as if enveloped in the midst of a sudden flood. An immense majority declared itself against it, and right away it saw itself in so small a minority that it immediately despaired of itself. Since that moment, the Republican or Democratic Party has advanced from conquest to conquest, and has taken possession of society as a whole. The Federalists, feeling themselves defeated, without resources, and seeing themselves isolated in the midst of the nation, became divided; some joined the victors, others laid down their banner and changed their name. It has already been a fairly large number of years since they ceased entirely to exist as a party.[64]

If the Federalists were going to challenge the Democratic-Republicans, they would have to find a name equal to that of Jefferson to place on their ticket, and one whose prominence could overcome the unpopularity of their party. Many of the more notable Federalists were prominent only in New England, and they refused to enter the fray of electoral politics.

For example, Fisher Ames, who had been dedicating himself to the Federalists' cause, finally declared in 1803 that he would "not be a Tom Paine on the federal side," renouncing "the wrangling world of politics, and [devoting himself] in future to pigs & poultry."[65] Even with adoption of the Twelfth Amendment, the Federalists were unable to reap the benefits of running a party-unified presidential ticket. Indicative of this lack of notable leadership capable of garnering national support, by 1812, the Federalists failed to run a member of their own party in the presidential election.

In 1812, the presidential election was between the incumbent, James Madison, and DeWitt Clinton from New York. Clinton was a dissident Democratic-Republican, and the Federalists chose him as their presidential candidate rather than nominating someone from their own party organization and leadership. In 1816, Rufus King was the last Federalist on the presidential ticket; in 1820, Democratic-Republican James Monroe ran unopposed.

In addition, the Federalists' decision to pursue other political means, such as secession, to challenge the Democratic-Republicans further diminished their electoral effectiveness. In late 1803, in place of Hamilton's proposed electoral strategy, Timothy Pickering organized and led a Federalist plot to create a "northern confederacy" around their political party that would "unite congenial characters, and present a fairer prospect of public happiness." He predicted that this separation would be beneficial to the northern and southern states because "mutual wants would render a friendly and commercial intercourse inevitable."[66] The southern states, he reasoned, required the northern states' naval protection; for commerce and navigation, the northern states required the products of the southern states. Numerous Federalist members of Congress joined Pickering, and efforts in the upcoming elections were focused on Federalists' winning key congressional seats in New England rather than the presidency. The Federalists also believed that for their plan to be successful, they would need New York to be the center of their northern confederacy. Pickering calculated that Massachusetts, Connecticut, and New Hampshire would be welcome participants. But if New York joined, so would Vermont, New Jersey, and Rhode Island. To capture New York, Vice President Aaron Burr, who knew he would be dropped as Jefferson's running mate in the upcoming election, joined the Federalists and contended for New York's gubernatorial seat. If elected, Burr would lead New York and other New England legislatures in dissolving the current union that was corrupted by Jefferson and his Democratic-Republican followers. The Federalists sowed the seeds of secession based on regional party organization, and many members of the Federalist Party ultimately abandoned their efforts to challenge the Democratic-Republicans by winning elections in favor of this divisive alternative.

In 1804, the Federalists' efforts to create a northern confederacy proved futile. Their inefficiency as an opposition party resulted in a landslide reelection for President Jefferson. Pickering had greatly overestimated support in New England. The Federalists lost in many of the state legislative races, which placed Democratic-Republicans in the majority.[67] Adding to the failure, Aaron Burr lost the New York gubernatorial race and any chances at New York leading the secession effort. After losing the New York election, Burr returned to serve the remainder of his term as vice president only to have Jefferson and the Democratic-Republicans distance themselves from him. Subsequently, the ineffective Federalists fared even worse in the presidential election, as their nominee, Charles Pinckney, would carry only two states and 14 electoral college votes. On the other hand, President Jefferson received 162 electoral college votes, including a majority from the New England states. In other words, because the Federalists were ineffective as an opposition, the Democratic-Republicans convincingly won elections at both the state and national levels and further solidified their control over national policy.

The Federalists' ineffective campaign efforts and failed attempt at a northern confederacy in 1804 further strengthened the Democratic-Republicans position as the party in government. With little to no opposition during the election, President Jefferson interpreted his convincing victory as a validation of both his principles declared in his first inaugural address and his actions during his first term.[68] He used the occasion to solidify the place of public sentiment in a constitutional democracy. Jefferson's approach to the presidency provided an early method of checking executive power. During his 1804 reelection bid, Jefferson opened space for the public to assess his performance as president, particularly the Louisiana Purchase. A political opposition could have reprimanded Jefferson for his use of presidential prerogative and settled the constitutionality of the Louisiana Purchase differently. The Twelfth Amendment was a crucial development in this process because the Federalists taking control of the vice presidency would not have provided the necessary check on Jefferson's executive power. The only legitimate check on executive power would have been if the opposition, supported by majority will, had been able to capture the executive branch. An effective party opposition can provide a check on the presidency, especially when the courts or congressional opposition led by legislative elites are unable to do so.[69] The Federalists did not rely on established electoral means to challenge the Democratic-Republicans and provide a potentially salutary check on executive power. With the Democratic-Republicans making the president more democratic, the Federalists were further disadvantaged in elections if they did not, as Hamilton had previously advocated, pay attention to public opinion. Given this development, party competition became even more important for politics.[70]

Partyism and the Federalists' Competing Principles

With little prospect of winning an election outside of their diminishing New England strongholds, the Federalists never again became an effective opposition party. The final stage of their demise came at the conclusion of the War of 1812. The politics of 1812 offered the Federalists an opportunity to establish a responsible opposition by opposing the Democratic-Republicans' war with England, which was criticized by groups across the nation other than the Federalists.[71] Because of this opposition to the war, the Federalists managed to incrementally strengthen their numbers in the state legislatures and almost double their representation in Congress.[72] Importantly, the Federalists regained control of Massachusetts's gubernatorial seat and the state legislature, which they had lost to the Democratic-Republicans in 1806. Once war was declared, the newly elected Massachusetts governor, Caleb Strong, became an outspoken opponent of President Madison and the war. Governor Strong, along with Governors Roger Griswold of Connecticut and William Jones of Rhode Island, declined to fulfill the Democratic-Republicans requisition of New England's militia. The three governors justified their refusal on constitutional grounds: the national government could not call on the state militias unless the country had been invaded or if invasion was imminent.

According to the governors, neither situation existed.[73] The Federalists, and those opposed to the war, began to unify around antiwar principles. As long as the Democratic-Republicans continued their war efforts, the Federalists maintained a position as an opposition party with alternative principles of governance, even if they would not be able to immediately be effective in national elections. However, their decision to hold the Hartford Convention ultimately hindered any further prospects of electoral effectiveness.

Instead of using their success opposing the War of 1812 to make electoral progress, the Federalists organized the Hartford Convention, an extralegal convention that further alienated the Federalists from the electorate. Some of those who attended the convention viewed it as part of the Federalists' continued efforts to create a northern confederacy through secession.[74] Others went with the intention of protecting New England's place in the Union by proposing constitutional amendments.[75] The Hartford Convention, and the direction the Federalists decided to take, determined the future of the Federalist Party. Many in attendance viewed the meeting as a way for their leadership to avoid extremism and the false perception that they were secessionists.[76] In other words, many Federalists worried about the public's perception of the meeting and how that perception would affect the party. The Federalists' efforts as an opposition party were linked to the public's perception of the convention, which would determine their future electoral viability. They would potentially suffer in upcoming national elections if the public perceived it as the means to secede from the Union. Although Federalists in New England, including numerous New England newspapers, praised the convention for its moderate proposal and its "high character of wisdom, fairness, and dignity," people outside of New England did not view it as such.[77] Outside of New England, the convention was seen for its secession purposes when a joint committee in the Massachusetts legislature led by Harrison Gray Otis proposed it, a radical reform to the accepted understanding of the national compact. Even if the Federalists were attempting to formulate a more moderate, nonsecessionist response to the War of 1812, the public perceived it as an extralegal attempt to undermine the national government and the Union.[78] Overall, the Federalists attempted to use the convention to organize their party, not criticize the Democratic-Republicans and President Jefferson for being pro-party.

Shortly after the Hartford Convention, the United States negotiated peace with Great Britain. The end of the war ended the Federalists' means of being a viable opposition party. The loss of their antiwar position and of their ability to oppose the Democratic-Republicans on policy grounds made the Federalists a feeble opposition party that eventually disappeared from the political scene. Having created a report of the Hartford Convention, including essential constitutional amendments, Governor Strong arranged for a three-person committee composed of Harrison Gray Otis, Thomas H. Perkins, and William Sullivan to provide President Madison with a summary of the convention's proposals. On February 16, however, days after the committee arrived in Washington, the Senate unanimously ratified the Treaty of Ghent, thereby ending the war. With the majority of the grievances expressed in the Hartford Convention report being related to the war, the Federalists lost the central piece of their opposition to the Democratic-Republicans' governing principles and policies. Commenting on the events, Joseph Story claimed that the war's termination signaled a "glorious opportunity for the Republican party to place themselves permanently in power."[79] Had the war persisted, Otis believed, the Federalists would have succeeded: "I believe however we should have succeeded and that the little Pigmy [President Madison] shook in his shoes at our approach."[80] Making matters worse for the floundering opposition, the New England Federalists had spent the war trying to undermine the Democratic-Republicans' war efforts. Their demands to end the war essentially favored England, which New England merchants had been trading with throughout the war. This further alienated their political base. The end of the Federalists as a political party was a result of the public's discontent with them and not general antiparty sentiments. The Federalists' failed efforts to become a successful opposition party resulted in one-party politics until the Democratic-Republicans experienced a party fracture in the 1830s and a new opposition eventually arose and created competition for the party in government.

The history of the Democratic-Republicans and the Federalists is rarely used to understand modern political parties. Modern political parties are considered too far removed from these early parties to render any useful information directly applicable to modern party principles and organization. At best, scholars maintain that early party practices were a necessary albeit temporary evil. This stands in contrast to modern political parties, which are seen as perpetually helping make democracy viable. Reassessing the ways in which party practices became accepted, however, brings the Democratic-Republicans and Federalists closer to their modern counterparts and farther from the antipartyism used to explain this first party era.

During the first party era, the Democratic-Republicans and the Federalists followed a similar trajectory in their preliminary efforts to act as an opposition party in competitive elections. It was the Federalists' inability to adhere to the evolving political norms and accepted methods of partyism that hastened their exit from the political arena. As outspoken members of the opposition, both Thomas Jefferson and Timothy Pickering advocated secession as a preliminary response to a growing national government—although Jefferson never politically endorsed secession. Similarly, both the Democratic-Republicans and the Federalists also considered challenging the party in government by means of state conventions. As an opposition party, the Democratic-Republicans distinguished themselves from the Federalists in that the former followed developed acceptable electoral alternatives when their preliminary plans were perceived as illegitimate and extraconstitutional. By remaining committed to illegitimate political strategies, the Federalists failed to replicate the Democratic-Republicans' success. They never became an electorally viable opposition party because they never embraced the electoral strategy that allowed the Democratic-Republicans to take office. Early in the party era, the Federalists benefited from the notoriety of their leadership. With George Washington winning presidential elections unanimously, the Federalists enjoyed the electoral advantage of prominent names carrying their electoral tickets. But they were left with no prominent name to match the rising popularity of Jefferson once Hamilton removed John Adams from the party and Washington and Hamilton died. Exacerbating the problem was the War of 1812 in that all notable war heroes, including Andrew Jackson, came from the Democratic-Republicans. The Federalists were unable to capitalize on the development of party practices and norms that, in the end, brought the Democratic-Republicans repeated electoral success.

At the end of the day, the Democratic-Republicans established party norms for challenging the party in government effectively in elections. Once out of office, the Federalists, despite efforts by key members, failed to successfully adapt their party to these established norms. The Democratic-Republicans' early party building efforts further altered the political landscape by making it more likely that future parties would appropriate their electoral strategies. This was not a time of antipartyism, as political parties and partyism, particularly in elections, were becoming well established within the constitutional order. And, as the next chapter demonstrates, the advantages political parties gained from the Twelfth Amendment could not be fully realized until parties took account of the methods for selecting presidential electors to ensure presidential candidates received the full slate of electoral college votes.

CHAPTER 6

Partyism and the Electoral College

Completing the Twelfth Amendment

Previous scholarship has rightly linked the Twelfth Amendment to the emergence and development of political parties.[1] However, a history of the amendment is incomplete without connecting it to the electoral college and the method of selecting electors and allocating their votes. The framers of the Twelfth Amendment intended it to ensure that the results of the House contingency election reflected popular will. But the Twelfth Amendment alone could not ensure this result because the construction of the public will was still a product of the electoral college's election procedure. The House could still select a candidate who did not receive the greatest number of electoral college votes. The development of party politics was intertwined with the development of the rules determining elector selection because the victor in a competitive party system could claim legitimacy only if his ascent to power was in accordance with popular will.

The electoral college is usually identified as one of the undemocratic features of the Constitution.[2] Article II, Section 1, of the Constitution gives states the power to select presidential electors. However, with no clear indication of how to exercise this power, states were left to determine the most appropriate method for choosing electors and allocating votes to presidential candidates. Not until 1832 did the general ticket method, or awarding all electoral college votes to the winner of the state popular vote, become the main method of selecting electors. From the 1790s to the 1830s, two heavily disputed questions regarding the selection of presidential electors emerged: whether states should retain plenary power over the method of selecting electors and whether the district or general ticket method was the best way to select electors. Some of the most prominent founders eventually supported the district system because they believed it was the best way to facilitate majority rule while also recognizing the votes of minorities. The district method was more in keeping with the expectations regarding presidential selection at the constitutional convention. After the convention, many political actors, including Madison, supported constitutional amendments to circum-scribe state authority over elector selection and establish a uniform mode of elector selection by requiring the district system. For example, in 1817, an amendment was proposed requiring the district election of presiden-tial electors as a way to eliminate the variation in selection based on po-litical expediency. Proponents of the amendment believed it was more democratic; opponents, however, claimed the district system would re-sult in undemocratic gerrymandering.

This relationship between the electoral college and majority rule be-came a central issue in 1824 when the House selected John Quincy Adams over Andrew Jackson in the contingency election even though Jackson received more electoral college votes. Supporters of Jackson, who believed he had won the election, proposed a constitutional amendment in 1826 requiring states to adopt a uniform method of selecting presi-dential electors by districts.[3] The nature and construction of a national majority was a central point during the congressional debates as partici-pants struggled with the meaning and place of democracy in a constitu-tional republic. The debates provide an important political construction of constitutional meaning related to presidential elections, which pro-duced norms needed to govern political institutions related to the elec-tion process.[4] The participants in the debates infused the discussion of presidential selection with political principles and social concerns that framed and constrained future debates on the merits of the accepted mode of selecting presidential electors.

In 1826, Congress ultimately rejected the proposed constitutional amendment that would have required all states to uniformly adopt the district method for selecting presidential electors. In so doing, Congress reaffirmed the states' constitutional authority over elector selection and ensured the continuation of the "federal" aspect of the founding design by which states could experiment with alternative systems of selecting presidential electors.[5] In addition, during the 1820s, the general ticket system acquired a new principled defense based on the grounds that it, not the district method, best represented state majorities in the presidential selection process. Despite the early preferences for the district system and the expectation that it would be the dominant mode for elector selection, states eventually adopted the general ticket method to ensure that presidential votes were allocated according to the majorities and partisan preferences of each state. With the continued development of political parties, the general ticket system became the preferred method for parties to exert their full influence in presidential elections, thereby further entrenching party practices in the constitutional order.

While the 1824 election is studied because of the role the popular vote assumed in the presidential election, democratic movements and mobilizing the mass electorate were parts of American political life during the Jeffersonian era. A strong electoral connection between voters and politicians already existed prior to 1824.[6] The important arguments in 1824 focused on the role of political parties as a means of organizing and facilitating these democratic movements. Partyism declined after the partisan competition between the Federalists and Democratic-Republicans withered in 1815. In its wake emerged differences of opinion over the role of parties in the political process and whether they contributed to or hindered democracy. For example, the use of a caucus among elected representatives as a means of selecting presidential candidates was both challenged as an aristocratic deprivation of the people's ability to choose a president and defended as a democratic method for compromising on the party's preferred nominee.[7] The two-party system further developed as political actors defended partyism by combining its practice with constitutional text.

THE FOUNDERS AND THE ELECTORAL COLLEGE

Delegates at the constitutional convention set out to resolve deficiencies in the Articles of Confederation. The "league of friendship" created by the mutual association of independent states failed to provide a governing system capable of addressing "exigencies of Government and the preservation of the Union."[8] Many delegates argued that a national government capable of providing "security of liberty and general welfare" was ultimately necessary.[9] Yet they also knew that many states, jealous of their sovereignty, would not accept a strong national government at the expense of state power. Throughout the convention, there was little opposition to the proposed framework of a national government consisting of a legislature, executive, and judiciary. However, as substantive decisions involving procedures such as methods for selecting officers and powers had to be made, the relationship between the national government and the states became a, if not the, fundamental issue. The distribution of power was a central component in determining the mode of presidential selection.

Initially, both the Virginia Plan and the New Jersey Plan placed presidential selection with the national legislature. However, adopting a bicameral legislature coupled with the Connecticut Compromise reinvigorated debate over the mode of presidential selection. Differences in the distribution of state power to the two houses caused concern about a legislative election, especially as these differences related to other questions dealing with the separation of powers, length of term, and reelection.[10] If presidential selection remained with the legislature, any changes to the institutional design of Congress also altered preferences for the mode of electing the executive. The development of the electoral college was a continuation of the Connecticut Compromise, resulting in a federal institution aimed at reconciling differences between the large and small states.[11] The federal component of the electoral college was hardly the only concern at the convention; other considerations such as slavery and executive independence from the legislature also influenced debates on the presidential selection system. While Article II, Section 1, may have incorporated federalism into the mode of presidential selection, how the states would exercise their constitutional power of selecting presidential electors and why they would choose a particular method remained to be seen.

Based on debates at the constitutional convention of 1787, there was no clear indication of a consensus. For example, during the debates over presidential selection, James Wilson proposed using the district system, Elbridge Gerry proposed having state governors choose presidential electors, and Oliver Ellsworth insisted that state legislatures should appoint electors.[12] After September 4 and the Committee of Eleven delegated the choice of electors to the states, there was no genuine discussion about a preferred method. Rather, debates fundamentally centered on other details of the proposed presidential selection system, specifically, the procedures and the relative state voting power during a contingency election in the event no candidate secured an electoral majority.

The lack of consensus on how states would select electors persisted during the ratification debates. For example, in *The Federalist*, Madison wrote, "Without the intervention of the State Legislatures, the President of the United States cannot be elected at all. They must in all cases have a great share in his appointment, and will, perhaps, in most cases, of themselves determine it."[13] However, Hamilton also wrote in *The Federalist* that the president would be elected by "electors chosen for that purpose by the people,"[14] and "the election of the President once in four years by persons immediately chosen by the people for that purpose" allowed for a "due dependence on the people" and a "due responsibility."[15] Furthermore, during the ratification debates, there was no real opposition to the provision delegating authority to the state legislatures to select presidential electors. It is for this reason that Hamilton was able to proclaim that the electoral college was "almost the only part of the system, of any consequence, which has escaped without severe censure or which has received the slightest mark of approbation from its opponents."[16] The textual indeterminacies of Article II, Section 1, gave rise to the important questions of how states would choose presidential electors and why they would prefer a particular method. The answers to these questions structured how the presidential selection system would work in the federal system and the political and constitutional principles it was intended to embody.

State Methods of Selecting Electors in the Early Republic: Practices and Debates

During the constitutional convention, there was no discussion of a uniform mode of selecting electors because the Constitution empowered states to employ any mode its legislature deemed appropriate. Until the

1830s, consistency in method was rare. States constantly alternated between three common modes of selection: by state legislature, by popular elections in districts, and by popular elections using an at-large, general ticket. Occasionally, states employed a hybrid system or experimented with other methods such as the state legislature selecting electors in a type of runoff election based on popular voting in districts. From 1787 to 1836, there was a substantial increase in the number of states selecting electors by general ticket. After John Quincy Adams's contested election in 1824, most states adopted the general ticket method, thereby moving toward a uniform method of selecting electors without the need for a constitutional or congressional mandate. The emergence and acceptance of political parties had a significant impact on the development of appointing presidential electors because it provided party incentives to aggregate a state's electoral college votes in favor of one candidate and maximize a political party's influence on the election.

Once the Constitution was ratified in 1788, states were required to quickly adopt a method of selecting electors for the first presidential election. However, for the most part, states had little concern over their method of selection given the certainty that George Washington would be elected. This allowed states to widely experiment with different methods. For the first presidential election, ten states participated, as North Carolina and Rhode Island had yet to ratify the Constitution and New York's legislature failed to agree on a method of selecting electors, making the state ineligible to cast its votes. Of the ten voting states, four, Connecticut, New Jersey, South Carolina, and Georgia had their legislatures select their electors. Two states, Pennsylvania and Maryland, adopted the general ticket method, allowing the people to vote for as many electors as the state was allotted. Two states, Virginia and Delaware, selected electors using the district method. Delaware allowed individuals to vote for electors based on counties, with the top three statewide vote recipients chosen as electors. And two states, New Hampshire and Massachusetts, used a hybrid system, with the former allowing for legislative selection in the event of electors failing to receive a majority of the popular vote and the latter allowing each of its districts to select two electors and the legislature selecting one elector from the two in addition to two electors chosen at large. Despite the various methods used by the states, George Washington was unanimously selected as the first president. Yet the selection of John Adams as vice president, which was not unanimous, foreshadowed the need to adopt a method of selecting electors that would ensure electoral victory when the candidate did not receive unanimous support.

By 1792, the method used by state legislatures to choose electors became the subject of political debate in response to the emerging Republican opposition. Now having both experience and time, states had an opportunity to reassess their mode of selecting electors and make desired changes. New Hampshire adopted the general ticket method by removing the legislative contingency in the event an elector did not receive the majority of votes and replaced it with a runoff election. The largest change occurred in states using legislative selection: Delaware replaced its general ticket method with the legislative method; and Rhode Island, Connecticut, New York, North Carolina, and Vermont all opted for legislative selection. Changing methods for selecting electors coupled with the emergence of partisan politics introduced the need to coordinate electoral efforts. While President Washington's reelection was all but assured, Hamilton feared Adams's vice presidential victory would be less than unanimous because of the mode of selecting presidential electors. In a letter to John Steele, Hamilton lamented that "Mr. Adams [would] have a nearly unanimous vote . . . in New York if the Electors were to be chosen by the people, but as they will be chosen by the Legislature, and as a majority of the existing Assembly are Clintonians, the electors will, I fear, be of the same complexion."[17] Ensuring Adams received all of New York's electoral votes was crucial for his election, as Hamilton attempted to predict election outcomes. The electoral rules in each state affected the outcome of the election, and, given the absence of a uniform form of selecting electors, partisans would have to account for these variations. For Hamilton, because "the electors *nominated* by the same interest will all, or nearly all, favor Mr. Adams," the Federalists would prefer a winner-take-all system in states controlled by the Federalists.[18] In states where Republicans carried a majority, the Federalists were best served by a system that awarded electoral votes based on district outcomes.

During the 1792 election, ten of the fifteen states used legislative selection, constituting half of the total number of electoral college votes. The 1796 election brought modest changes to the overall methods previously used as New Hampshire returned to a hybrid system, Maryland switched from the general ticket to the district method, North Carolina changed from legislative selection to the district method, Georgia replaced legislative appointment with the general ticket method, and newcomer Tennessee adopted a hybrid system in which the legislature chose three electors for each county and these electors in the three counties each elected one elector. In the previous two presidential elections, the Federalist Party had benefited from the widespread popularity of George Washington in that they only had to ensure John Adams received the second highest number of votes. Unfortunately for the Federalists, John Adams did not share Washington's notoriety, bringing the method of selecting electors to the political forefront.

In order to successfully challenge the Federalists, the Republicans had to coordinate electoral efforts and navigate the various state methods for selecting electors.[19] As partisan conflicts intensified, elector selection dramatically affected the outcomes of the presidential elections and the partisan nature of government. Political actors' preferences for elector selection were heavily influenced by their partisanship and the majority or minority status of their party in the separate states. Party development meant that electors never fulfilled the initial constitutional design of the electoral college acting as an independent body in presidential selection. Electors were not immune to public opinion or national partisan alignments. "Instead," explains Jeffrey L. Pasley, "the activities of the notables in 1796 generally served to *stimulate* popular political opinion and *promote* national political alignments in their local communities."[20] Early state experimentation with various methods of elector selection, along with the increasing role of partisanship, led to much discussion about the propriety of these methods, especially from 1800 onward. This debate played out in part in Congress, which considered whether to require a uniform system. A number of prominent founders also joined the debate. Hamilton, Jefferson, and Madison all maintained at various points that the district system was the most principled method.

In November 1800, in response to the partisan influences on the various methods for selecting electors, an amendment was proposed in Congress to permanently establish the district system by "dividing each State into a number of districts, equal to the number of electors to be chosen in such State."[21] The amendment was then referred to a select committee to provide more details on the proposition. In January 1801, Senator

Wilson Cary Nicholas (DR-VA) reported on the committee's inconclusive findings. Nicholas first addressed the constitutionality of the various modes in use, because the amendment was necessary if a particular method in practice was considered unconstitutional. The ambiguity of the "existing provisions of the Constitution," he reasoned, granted states great latitude in selecting a particular method for choosing electors, and the committee was "persuaded that the varieties which have practically taken place . . . [were] not beyond the contemplation of those who framed the Constitution."[22] The Constitution allowed for the diversity in methods for elector selection and provided no clear indication as to which methods states should adopt. Adopting the amendment, then, would not be driven by a determination about the unconstitutionality of existing state practices but by a judgment about the propriety of a given method.

Because the committee found no constitutional restrictions, settling on a particular method for selecting electors became a question of "experience and comparison with other modes" to find the method possessing "superior advantages" while also being "liable to fewer or less considerable inconveniencies."[23] The select committee members, however, believed the issue was still in its infancy and that further experience was necessary before they were willing to make any sort of recommendation on the propriety of a particular method. The committee hoped "the good sense of the American people, when aided by further experience," would discover the best method to "combine the expression of the public sentiments of the people of the respective States, with a perfect assurance of the due appointment of the electors for that important purpose."[24] As a result, the committee concluded that the amendment was an inexpedient change to the Constitution, and further debate and practice was required.

The emerging party battles in New York during the 1800 presidential election forced Hamilton to switch his previous preference for selecting New York's electors by general ticket to the district method. As Jefferson's popular support grew, Hamilton turned to New York's mode of elector selection to circumscribe Jefferson's influence in the coming presidential election. Preceding the 1800 presidential election, New York opted for elector selection by the then Federalist-controlled state legislature. However, state legislative elections would transpire before the presidential election, which allowed the Republicans to potentially take over the legislature and selection of presidential electors. As mentioned in chapter 4,

Burr oversaw a well-organized electioneering operation to create a Republican legislative ticket with prominent partisan names in the hope that these distinguished and influential political names would contribute to capturing a legislative majority and aid the party's electoral success.[25] Much to Hamilton's dismay, Burr and the Republicans successfully captured the New York legislature, and, with the "moral certainty . . . that there [would] be an anti-federal majority in the . . . Legislature," Hamilton asked Governor John Jay to call together the existing legislature with the object of "choosing . . . electors by the people in Districts." Being aware of "weighty objections to the measure," Hamilton believed this political strategy was "justified by unequivocal reasons of PUBLIC SAFETY." However, he needed Jay to "appreciate the extreme danger of the crisis" and convey this sense of urgency and necessity to the legislature because the "measure will not fail to be approved by all the federal party; while it will, no doubt, be condemned by the opposite."[26] He was ultimately unsuccessful in securing Jay's support for the measure, and he received no response from Jay. As for Jay, Hamilton's letter was put away among other personal correspondence with the label, "Proposing a measure for party purposes which it wont become me to adopt."[27] Importantly, political actors recognized that their party's success was contingent on the rules regulating the allocation of electoral votes. Those who were in the majority preferred a winner-take-all system so as to maximize their advantage; the minority preferred a district system to fragment the majority's vote total. As Hamilton's party began to dwindle, so did his preference for the general ticket system.

Like Hamilton, Jefferson recognized the importance of using the various modes of elector selection to his advantage in securing Republican electoral outcomes. In a letter to James Monroe, he acknowledged, "All agree that an election by districts would be best, if it could be general; but while 10 states chuse either by their legislatures or by a general ticket, it is folly & worse than folly for the other 6 not to do it."[28] Jefferson understood that the winner-take-all system provided the greatest advantage for his party, and the states carried more weight in the election if their electoral votes were unified rather than fragmented by the district system. Politically, without ensuring that all votes went to their party, the Republicans could suffer from the same misfortune as their rivals in the 1796 election, when Jefferson captured the vice presidency. If, for example, Virginia fragmented its electoral vote while Federalist states did not, the Democratic-Republicans were susceptible to losing votes without the prospect of gaining others in Federalist states. The best election strategy was to ensure that a state's entire electoral vote was allocated to the political party's preferred candidate. Although his principled preference was the district system, Jefferson recognized the need to unify a state's electoral vote, especially in the states with a Republican majority; otherwise his party could be vulnerable to electoral defeat.[29]

In addition to the electoral disadvantage, the problem with the general ticket system, according to Jefferson, was the status of his minority party. In the states not using the district system, "the minority is entirely unrepresented; & their majorities not only have the weight of their whole state in their scale, but have the benefit of so much of our minorities as can succeed at a district election."[30] Adopting the general ticket in states where the Republicans were minorities meant that the districts supporting Jefferson were lost to the Federalists. This electoral effect would likewise have an impact on the development of electoral representation and the construction of public sentiment.

For Jefferson, there were essentially three types of public sentiment: the one (a national sentiment), the few (a state sentiment), and the many (a district sentiment). The question became which provided the best representation of the public, for "a representation of a part by great, & a part by small sections, would give a result very different from what would be the sentiment of the whole people of the U.S., were they assembled together." In other words, "it is . . . a question whether we will divide the U.S. into 16 [states] or 137 districts."[31] The result of the presidential election should reflect public sentiment, and the district method, "being more chequered, & representing the people in smaller sections, would be more likely to be an exact representation of their diversified sentiments."[32] The one neglects to capture the diversity of sentiments in the few, and, in like manner, the few fails to reflect the diversity of the many. For Jefferson, selection of presidential electors by districts best constructed and represented public sentiment, and if the president's job was to "bring public opinion to a set of declared principles," the district system, which accounted for more diversity, would provide a more precise estimation of public opinion.[33]

Like Jefferson, Madison endorsed selecting presidential electors by the district system, going so far as to outline a corrective "for the faulty part of the Constitution" regarding presidential selection. In an 1823 letter to George Hays, he described the "final arrangement" for presidential selection during the constitutional convention as "not exempt from a degree of the hurrying influence produced by fatigue and impatience in all such Bodies, tho' the degree was much less than usually prevails in them."[34] Madison opposed the provision granting states plenary power in selecting electors, and he believed the "district mode was mostly, if not exclusively in view when the Constitution was framed and adopted." More to the point, he thought the states began using the general ticket or legislative method as the "only expedient for baffling the policy of the particular States which had set the example."[35] Since the Articles of Confederation, he had recognized the "injustice of the laws of States" and the "multiplicity" and "mutability" of their laws apt to bring "more into question the fundamental principle of republican Government."[36] The continual alteration of election law to serve political purposes and the refusal to implement the selection of electors by districts were further evidence of the states' "vicious legislation" that needed to be remedied. The states, by adopting the general ticket or legislative selection method, created a concentration of state power in presidential elections that needed to be contained and dissipated. And this concentration of power had adverse effects on the status of minorities.

Like Jefferson, Madison centered his critique of the general ticket method on the status of minority votes. He believed that it was necessary to account for the diversity of opinion within a state and that the general ticket method was a "great departure from the Republican principle of numerical equality."[37] Moreover, the district system had the added benefits of breaking geographic or political factions: when the states "make their elections by districts, some of these differing in sentiment from others, and sympathizing with that of districts in other States, they are so knit together as to break the force of those geographic and other noxious parties which might render the repulsive too strong for the cohesive tendencies with the Political System."[38] The district system aggregated the minority votes in the separate states, thereby providing a measure of opposition to the majority. Under the general ticket method, the minority votes were silenced, keeping the majority, both political and geographic, insulated from any oppositional forces. Subsequently, Madison outlined an amendment that would have substantially altered the mode of presidential selection in order to remedy the deficiencies in Article II, Section 1.

Madison shared his personal view on the necessary changes to the mode of presidential selection with George Hays in 1823, George McDuffie in 1824, and Robert Taylor in 1826. McDuffie was one of the primary advocates for the district system and a constitutional amendment following the contested election of President John Quincy Adams. He even asked for Madison's opinion on the districting proposition that was proposed in 1826. Madison, however, was hesitant to share his view because he perceived McDuffie was "disposed to overvalue" his opinion on the matter.[39] In fact, Madison explicitly stated in all the letters that he wished to keep his view on presidential selection confined to these private correspondences.

Madison's proposition would have restored the electoral college to what he believed was the founders' original intent for the institution in two important ways: by establishing elector selection by districts and changing the actual voting procedures by both the electors and Congress should no majority winner emerge from the vote of the electors. According to Madison's proposition, "Each Elector to give two votes, one naming his first choice, the other his next choice. If there be a majority of all the votes on the first list for the same person, he of course to be President; if not, and there be a majority, (which may well happen) on the other list for the same person, he then to be the final choice."[40] If there were no majorities on either list, he proposed having Congress, by joint ballot, choose from the two recipients receiving the most votes. The process would be the same for vice president, allowing electors to cast a total of four votes: two for president and two for vice president. He held to the belief expressed during the constitutional convention that electors should exercise independent judgment in their voting rather than simply pledge their votes to a particular party, as had become the accepted practice. Because the electors were given two votes for both president and vice president, he believed they "may be intentionally left sometimes to their own judgment, guided by further information that may be acquired by them: and finally, what is of material importance, they will be able, when ascertaining . . . that the first choice of their Constituents is utterly hopeless, to substitute, in their electoral vote the name known to be their second choice."[41] That is, Madison still saw value in maintaining the system of electors as long as they were selected by districts and given the opportunity to filter prospective presidential and vice presidential candidates through a double ballot system for each office.

Partisanship and principle were central to early political developments in the mode of selecting presidential electors. As political parties formed, politicians pursued election rules that secured all their states electoral votes for their preferred candidate. As the Republicans demonstrated in New York during the 1800 election, state legislative selection of electors was one of the most effective means of ensuring total allocation of electoral college votes to a party's preferred candidate. The election of 1800 saw the highest number of states (ten of the sixteen) selecting electors by the state legislature. Pragmatic partisanship trumped a more principled preference for selecting electors using the district method, as Hamilton, Jefferson, and Madison all believed the district system was more favorable to minorities. Until 1820, legislative selection remained the preferred method of selecting electors by the majority of states because it eliminated most of the uncertainty about who would be selected as an elector and how he would vote, a point closely related to the lack of partisan competition during the time after the Federalist Party was no longer competitive in elections.[42] The election of 1824, however, marked the rise of the general ticket method and the demise of all other methods for selecting electors. In this way, the election of 1824 and its aftermath was a key moment in the development of the electoral college because of the ensuing widespread adoption of the general ticket method as the best method for selecting electors. Those advocating for the general ticket method also provided a principled rationale for it based on a particular understanding of partyism and majority rule.

PARTYISM AND ELECTOR SELECTION
AFTER THE 1824 ELECTION

As in 1800, the presidential election of 1824 was ultimately decided in the House of Representatives and led to a renewed determination to amend the system. Because 131 electoral college votes were required to secure the presidency and Jackson's 99 votes fell well short of the required majority, the election went to a contingency election in the House. Following the Twelfth Amendment's rules, the House chose from the top three candidates, Andrew Jackson, John Quincy Adams, and William H. Crawford. Presidential candidate Henry Clay was eliminated because he received four electoral votes fewer than Crawford despite receiving more popular votes. Clay, however, played a significant role in the election because, as the influential Speaker of the House, he was able to use his authority to help secure Adams's election. Once the House elected Adams president, he made Clay his secretary of state. Jackson and his supporters cast doubt on the legitimacy of the presidential selection system by claiming his defeat was due to this "corrupt bargain." The 1824 election served as poignant evidence of everything that was to be feared from presidential selection by Congress. Although the immediate problem in 1824 was the House voting method, political actors considered that reexamining the entire mode of presidential election, including elector selection, was a necessity.[43] In 1826, an amendment was once again proposed to uniformly establish elector selection by districts. While this was not the first time an amendment had been pursued along these lines, it is worth focusing on this one because it was the first time political actors appealed to both federalism and a defense of the general ticket based on majority rule as reasons to oppose amending the electoral college.

John Quincy Adams's seemingly antidemocratic election victory created a new question of electoral legitimacy. In the previous nine presidential elections, the system had produced a president who won the electoral vote and who was arguably the popular choice. Now the public and the electoral system was forced to address the legitimacy of a House election that deviated from the "sense of the people." The public had not been required to determine if it would support the House if its choice in the contingency election deviated from popular sentiment.[44] After all, nothing in the Constitution requires members of Congress to vote for the candidate with the most popular votes in the contingency election. The question of Jackson's popularity further complicated matters. His lead in the electoral college vote totals did not necessarily mean he was more popular than the other candidates. The Three-Fifths Compromise inflated Jackson's lead. Without it, Adams would have been leading Jackson 83 votes to 77.[45] Participation in the popular vote did not dramatically increase during the 1824 election, and partisan voters for both candidates were equally ardent in their support.[46] More to the point, some states that supported Adams, such as New York, did not register popular votes, which cast doubts on claims that Jackson was more "popular" than Adams.[47] The legislatures in six states chose electors, providing no direct measure of popular preference. The method of selecting electors became a key variable in constructing an appropriate understanding of the "sense of the people" in presidential elections.

After the election of 1824, there was a significant increase in the number of states that selected electors by general ticket. In 1824, twelve states used a general ticket, five states used the district method, six states opted for legislative selection, and one state used a hybrid method. In 1828, eighteen states selected electors by general ticket, and the district method, legislative selection, and a hybrid system were each used in only two states. Consequently, a proposed constitutional amendment that would have required all states to adopt the district method for selecting presidential electors coincided with this substantial increase in the number of states using the general ticket system. The proposed amendment would have drastically changed the nature of Article II, Section 1, by requiring states to adopt a particular method for selecting electors—a method that had never been the most widely used—thereby reducing the states' constitutional authority over the matter. Although the proposed amendment was ultimately rejected, it served a significant purpose, in that state legislatures' plenary constitutional power to determine the method of selecting electors—not actually selecting the electors—was firmly established, something the Supreme Court later affirmed in 1892 in *McPherson v. Blacker*. While debating the amendment, political actors articulated a new understanding of majority rule that served as a foundational justification for the general ticket system, rejecting previous principled preferences for the district method as the best mode of ascertaining a "sense of the people" in presidential elections.

In response to the crisis of 1824, a constitutional amendment was proposed in the House requiring a uniform method of voting by districts and removing the constitutional provision for a contingency election in the House.[48] In essence, the proposed amendment aimed at constitutionally establishing the preference for the district method that had previously been abandoned due to electoral expediency and partisan posturing. Once again, there were two central issues at stake during the amendment debates: whether states should retain authority over elector selection and which method, the district or general ticket, best achieved majority rule.

On February 15, 1826, Representative McDuffie (SC), addressing the partisan nature of how states selecting electors, argued for a "permanent [and] a uniform system of voting for president," because allowing states to determine elector selection made the election rules "all liable to be changed according to the varying views and fluctuating fortunes of political parties."[49] Without the amendment, political parties would continue to adopt methods of selecting electors that promoted their individual interests and created "gross and palpable injustice[s]" and "political inequalities."[50] Permanently and uniformly adopting the general ticket system, however, was not an appropriate remedy, because, according to McDuffie, it destroyed the minority's vote in the state and transferred the votes given by the minority in favor of their preferred candidate to another.[51] Like Jefferson and Madison, McDuffie argued that the general ticket method distorted the popular vote, resulting in voter misrepresentation and incorrectly ascertaining the will of the people. If the purpose of presidential selection was to reflect public will, then the mode of selection should be conducive to creating the "real will of the People, instead of the artificial will of the State," and, by consequence, the "artificial will" of political parties in the states.[52] McDuffie refused to sacrifice the central tenets of republicanism, as he understood them, for arguments grounded in principles of federalism. Proponents of the amendment emphasized establishing a particular understanding of majority rule over the constitutional propriety of retaining state sovereignty in presidential elector selection.

For proponents of the amendment, republicanism and federalism could not coincide as long as the states used the general ticket system, which inflated popular support and thereby distorted electoral accountability. This point was particularly important given the adoption of the Twelfth Amendment and its purpose of making presidential electoral accountability possible. President Jefferson understood the Twelfth Amendment as a necessary constitutional change to create a "union of opinion," thereby making it possible for him to theoretically claim approval of his actions during his first term in office, including his broad use of executive power.[53] His reelection can be understood as an attempt at elective responsibility in that the public was given the opportunity to reprimand him if he had abused his power. However, for McDuffie, Jefferson's claim to public support through reelection was ultimately suspect because the "union of opinion" meant to justify his actions was constructed using electoral rules that may have inflated his support, particularly his partisan support. Put simply, Jefferson could not know if the public supported him as long as the public was not selecting electors or if his support was inflated by the general ticket method. The debates over the Twelfth Amendment never took up the question of elector selection; the primary focus was ensuring that electors would distinguish their votes for president and vice president and reducing the number of candidates on the ballot in the case of a contingency election. The proposed amendment in the 1820s can be understood as an attempt to complete the Twelfth Amendment by giving a more accurate indication of public sentiment, through the district method, and thereby accounting for opposition voices typically silenced by the general ticket system.

Opponents of the amendment, however, did not view republicanism and federalism as necessarily incompatible and attempted to reconcile the states' constitutional power to select electors with an understanding of the general ticket method that fulfilled a certain conception of majority rule and electoral accountability. On February 17, 1826, Representative Henry R. Storrs (NY) responded to McDuffie's arguments by first articulating a defense of the states' plenary power in selecting presidential electors, with a particular reference to the constitutional convention. The "delicate" system of presidential election, argued Storrs, was eventually grounded on principles consistent "with the separate sovereignty of the States, and the preservation of the just relative influence and interests of each." Moreover, "this part of the plan of the Federal Government was received in the State Conventions with less objection than almost any other."[54] The federal nature of the presidential selection system was well entrenched, as many opponents of the amendment included references to the constitutional convention, the ratification debates, and the *Federalist Papers* to substantiate the claim that the power of selecting electors was intended to be given solely to the states. Any changes to the system had to adhere to the "original principles" and "practical operation" of the constitutionally established electoral distribution of power within the federal system of presidential selection.

Having first established the states' authority over elector selection,

Storrs proceeded to defend the general ticket as the best way to ascertain the will of the people and establish majority rule. As Storrs explained, "In the election of President, the expression of the will of the *People* of the *several States*, as *distinct political communities*, was intended to be preserved inviolably" by the Constitution.[55] In advancing this argument, Storrs shifted the commitment to majoritarian politics from a notion of a "People" constructed from a national majority (as McDuffie had previously articulated) to one based on the original parties of the constitutional compact, a majority consisting of the "People" in a state. The general ticket system was the best way to ascertain the will of the people in a state. Given this shift, Storrs criticized the district system because of its tendency to fragment and weaken the majority of a given state. To illustrate this point, he considered the effect of the district system on New York's presidential vote: "Let us suppose that the aggregate of all the surplus majorities in nineteen of these districts, every one of which are in favor of one person, is fifteen thousand votes—and that the aggregate of these majorities in the remaining seventeen districts, all of whom are for a different person, amount to twenty thousand."[56] The winning candidate would not have received a majority of popular votes despite winning the majority of districts. In the district system, "the minority of a State may effectually defeat the will of a majority" and make states susceptible to intrigue, as it would "enable party leaders to bring into market a large share of [a state's] electoral votes, who would otherwise despair of success, on a general ticket throughout the State."[57] Substantiating this point, Representative Andrew Stevenson (VA) explained that the larger states exacerbated this exaggeration of minority support:

> Let me suppose that nineteen twentieths of a state are in favor of A for President, and one district, on the borders of the State, wishes to go with an adjoining State, for B, do you not, by this amendment, enable that district to defeat the wishes and interests of its own state, and to take one from the number of its electoral votes? Do you not break the force of State interest and will, and especially the large States, and enable local and partial interests to defeat the general interest of the State? Sir, . . . , by this amendment, Virginia, voting by districts, would not be Virginia still.[58]

In other words, the district system provided minority parties with an electoral advantage at the expense of constructing a majority that accurately reflected the partisan interests of the state.

The general ticket system, then, would allow political parties to maximize their influence in the presidential election by unifying all of a state's electoral college votes in favor of the state majority's preferred presidential candidate. In this sense, the "general will of the People of all the States" was created by the individual majorities in each state, and only through the general ticket would "the will of the People of the several States . . . strictly regarded, [take] its full effect on the election of the President."[59] Representative William S. Archer (VA) substantiated this point by maintaining that, "in relation to the Executive officer, the mode of election by general ticket was better calculated than that by districts, to afford a just and sound expression of the public sentiment—the object of the elective function."[60] In contrast to previous preferences for the district system, the popular will was now understood as a federal will constructed from the popular will of the separate states, and the district system was seen as tending to break, if not undermine, these majorities.

While much of the discussion on the proposed amendment centered on federalism and majority rule, political parties and partyism underscored many of the opinions on the preferred method for selecting electors. A minority party within a state preferred the district plan so as to have a voice in the presidential election; a majority party within a state preferred the general ticket so as to capture the entire slate of electoral votes. For those opposed to the amendment, partyism provided a salutary check on the party in government that could not be achieved if the district system was uniformly adopted. Put simply, the district method "depreciate[d] party."[61] Bringing political parties to the forefront, Representative Churchill C. Cambreleng (NY) argued partyism was a necessary component of republican government by providing electoral accountability: "And does that gentleman [McDuffie] expect to defeat the unwise measures of an Administration, sustained by the patronage of all the Departments and the Executive—backed, too, by an overflowing Treasury—without the agency of party?"[62] Furthermore, he connected the salutary benefits of political parties to the election of 1800: "Party is indispensable to every Administration—it is essential to the existence of our institutions"; "it never yet injured any free country—the power of party was never abused here but once: the evil was instantly corrected, by the People—the political revolution of 1800 was the consequence."[63] Far from viewing partyism as a political feature to be feared, Cambreleng recognized the benefits of party competition and articulated a pro-party position: "The conflict of parties is a noble conflict—of mind to mind, genius to genius. It is to such periods of high excitement—to these wars of intellect, that we are indebted for almost all that is great and valuable in political science."[64] Partyism contributed to republicanism and governmental accountability only if a state's electoral power was undivided.[65] The general ticket better served as a check on (or support for) the party in government because it ensured that the full weight of the majority's partisan preference within a state was exerted in presidential selection.

On April 1, 1826, the proposed amendment was defeated by a vote of 90 to 102.[66] This was not the last challenge to the electoral college, as the institution was subject to numerous other constitutional amendment proposals and litigation. However, subsequent amendment proposals had to overcome the federal and majoritarian arguments supporting the institution. For example, in response to a proposed amendment in 1828, the federal argument was used again to ground opposition to the district plan. Critics argued that the proposed amendment "would be a proposition to take from the State Legislature a power which they now possess." If the "States shall agree to be laid off into districts . . . their relative weight shall be destroyed."[67] In addition, in 1834, justification for a proposal to institute a uniform district system again focused on the status of minority votes as a way of challenging the majority rule established by the general ticket system: "The general-ticket system was unfriendly to the rights of the people, it enabled the majority to impress the votes of the minority, and that ought to condemn it in a country of equal rights."[68] With various methods employed prior to the 1824 election, advocates of the district plan, like Madison and Jefferson, used the status of minority votes to settle the question of elector selection. Once the general ticket method, and its conception of majority rule, became the settled method, advocates of the district plan used this minority vote counterargument to challenge the status quo and its "unequal" majority rule.

Given the unsuccessful attempts to amend the Constitution, opponents of the general ticket method turned to the courts. The 1892 Supreme Court case of *McPherson v. Blacker* further entrenched the federal nature of the electoral college. In that case the Court affirmed, "The appointment and mode of appointment of electors belong exclusively to the states under the constitution of the United States."[69] In 1968, the United States District Court for the Eastern District of Virginia affirmed the majoritarian foundation of the general ticket method. In *Williams v. Virginia State Board of Elections*, plaintiffs brought suit against Virginia's statute requiring that electors be selected by general ticket. The plaintiffs argued three points: (1) the district method was intended by Article II, Section 1; (2) the general ticket selection of electors violated the principle of "one person, one vote" in the equal protection clause of the Fourteenth Amendment; and (3) the general ticket system afforded citizens of larger states an increased opportunity to influence the selection of president than citizens of a smaller state.

The District Court dismissed the first argument because it could not be definitively determined that the drafters of Article II, Section 1, intended states to choose electors by congressional or other districts. Moreover, the method of selecting electors was a political question beyond the scope of judicial review. The District Court then addressed the constitutionality of the general ticket method by assessing the status of minority voters and the claim of voter disenfranchisement. Affirming the majoritarian nature of elections, the District Court reasoned, "Admittedly, once the electoral slate is chosen, it speaks only for the element with the largest number of votes. This in a sense is discrimination against the minority voters, but in a democratic society the majority must rule, unless the discrimination is invidious."[70] The District Court found no evidence of invidious discrimination by the general ticket method. It then favorably assessed Virginia's choice of the general ticket method to ensure majority rule. Virginia could have adopted the district method to "fairly reflect the popular vote but thereby weaken the potential impact of Virginia as a State in the nationwide counting of electoral ballots," or it could have adopted the general ticket method "to allow the majority to rule and thereby maximize the impact of Virginia's 12 electoral votes in the electoral college tally. The latter course was taken, and we cannot say unwisely."[71] Like the conclusion reached during the 1826 congressional debates over a proposed constitutional amendment, the District Court affirmed that the general ticket method coincided with majority rule without necessarily endangering minority rights. The general ticket method all but ensured that the full weight of the majority's preference within a state was exerted in the presidential election.

Following the election of 1800, Jefferson and his party's claim to political legitimacy could only be achieved if the results of the presidential election reflected the popular will. The Twelfth Amendment was adopted to ensure that the results of the House contingency election reflected popular will by attempting to reduce the probability the House could select a minority candidate. It, however, only addressed presidential balloting procedures and the House contingency election. It did not touch the electoral college and the electoral process by which public sentiment would be constructed. While parties were able to unify their presidential tickets, without accounting for how states selected presidential electors, the issue of popular will, and whether a party could claim popular support in a presidential election, remained in question. To address this issue, political actors continued to develop institutional rules supporting partyism and party politics, as they dealt with the constitutional indeterminacies of Article II, Section 1.

At the constitutional convention, the electoral college was intended to provide the new system of government with a federal component, as Article II, Section 1, empowered state legislatures to determine the method of selecting presidential electors. With no other constitutional direction, states were left to construct constitutional norms for how and why electors would be selected. In early presidential elections, states experimented with various methods, and as partisanship and political parties emerged, states began to select electors pragmatically in the hope of securing the election of their preferred presidential candidate. Early preferences, particularly of Madison and Jefferson, for a district method, which was believed the best way to achieve majority rule in presidential elections, were sacrificed for state legislative selection or the general ticket system, because these methods ensured that a state and party could exert all their influence in the presidential contest.

Elector selection by state legislature was the most widely used method from 1789 to 1820. After the contentious election of 1824, however, the general ticket method became the primary method for selecting electors. As a result of the 1824 election, an amendment was proposed in the

House of Representatives requiring states to adopt the district method. The amendment was ultimately rejected; yet the debates became an important moment in the development of the electoral college because members of the House reaffirmed the federal nature of the presidential selection system in that states had plenary power over selecting electors. Furthermore, representatives articulated a new understanding of majority rule based on the general ticket system, thereby replacing previous understandings of majority rule and the preference for the district system. This majority rule based on the general ticket method became an important factor in the further development and institutionalization of American political parties and the two-party system. Adopting the general ticket system was an essential precursor to an institutionalized two-party system.[72] As Epstein writes, "An electoral college majority is a nearly certain product of the two-candidate competition that our major parties ordinarily, if not quite uniformly provided."[73] Any subsequent attempts to transform the electoral college would have to overcome this principled defense of a partisan conception of majority rule that empowered states and political parties to maximize their influence within a federal system of presidential selection. This development, combined with the Twelfth Amendment, further entrenched the constitutional construction of partyism in presidential elections.

CHAPTER 7

Partyism, the Elections Clause, and the House of Representatives

According to Article I, Section 4, of the Constitution, the "times, places, and manner of holding elections for senators and representatives shall be prescribed in each state by the legislature thereof; but the Congress may at any time by law make or alter such regulations, except as to the places of choosing senators." For congressional elections, states are not constitutionally granted plenary power like they are with the selection of presidential electors and allocation of Electoral College votes. Historically, Congress has "made" and "altered" election law, particularly regarding how members of the House are elected once representatives are apportioned to a state. The first attempt to establish national standards for House elections came in 1842 when Congress required representatives to be elected by single-member districts. While Congress followed the Constitution by apportioning representatives after the decennial census, adding the single-member district requirement initiated debate over the constitutionality of the districting mandate and the extent of Congress's power granted by Article I, Section 4.

This chapter examines the constitutional constructions pertaining to Congress's power to "make or alter" regulations in reference to the times, places, and manner clause. Prior to the 1842 law requiring single-member districts, the states experimented with various methods for electing members to the House of Representatives, including at-large elections and multimember districts to provide urban areas with more representatives. The debates over mandating single-member districts raised questions regarding Congress's power in relation to the clause, as well as substantive constitutional questions about representation and constructing competitive elections, particularly in House elections.

The effect of the 1842 law further institutionalized the two-party system in American politics. American election law has created conditions conducive to the entrenchment of a two-party system. The most prominent of these conditions is the rule that divides each state into single-member districts, with each district electing one representative.[1] While scholarship on the 1842 Apportionment Act focuses on partisan explanations for why it passed, there were also rhetorical justifications the Whig Party used to legitimize its electoral changes. In particular, it constructed an understanding of representation based on political parties. The 1842 requirement for single-member districts is part of the larger developmental trajectory of the two-party Constitution in the United States. The 1842 mandate institutionalized party competition for and within Congress just as the First Amendment was interpreted for party competition in the electorate and the Twelfth Amendment and Electoral College for presidential party competition.

By most historical accounts, 1828 marks the emergence of political parties and party politics. This institutionalized party development is often connected to Martin Van Buren, who is credited with providing a rationale for partyism and its importance to American politics.[2] While Van Buren did much to organize the Democratic Party around Andrew Jackson, the North/South sectional coalition constructed to elect President Jackson could not hold for Van Buren, as growing opposition from southerners and antislavery northerners fragmented the party. The historian Sean Wilentz writes, "The burdens of these cross-pressures would be borne most heavily by Martin Van Buren, first in his presidential campaign in 1836 and then for the rest of his political career. Their full weight would only be felt, however, once the southern and northern anti-Jacksonian forces coalesced."[3] Van Buren, the New York politician, could not command the loyalty of Southerners like Jackson, and this lack of unity allowed the Whig Party to form and seriously challenge the Democrats. Utilizing the Democratic Party's electoral strategy, the Whigs united around the war hero William Henry Harrison for the 1840 presidential election, easily defeating the incumbent Van Buren. This two-party competition between the Whigs and the Democrats was not simply the product of the party developments in the 1820s. Rather, it is connected to constitutional developments that transpired long before Van Buren and party politics during the Jacksonian era.

Electoral Laws and the Two-Party System

Laws regulating elections have significant political consequences for establishing the characteristics of democracy in the United States. Scholars look to these laws to explain institutional and democratic characteristics, such as the durability of the two-party system.[4] Perhaps one of the most famous is Maurice Duverger's explanation for the existence and dominance of the two-party system. According to Duverger's law, a single-member district system with a simple plurality rule, sometimes referred to as "first past the post," tends toward a system with only two competitive parties. As a corollary, "the simple-majority system with second-ballot and proportional representation favors multipartyism."[5] Building on Duverger's theory, Gary W. Cox argued that the single-member district with a plurality rule does not necessarily mean there will be only two candidates but a maximum of two viable candidates, particularly at the district level.[6] Two-party competition is more likely in this situation because rational voters and rational parties tend to support candidates who have a real prospect of winning.[7] Because there is no consolation prize for being runner-up when only one seat is available, parties and voters tend to choose between only two leading candidates. This means that in a single-member district system where there is only one seat ($x = 1$), voters and parties will support as many as two ($x + 1$) parties.[8] The requirement for single-member districts has created conditions conducive to institutionalizing partyism and party duopoly in the United States.

There are, however, no constitutional requirements that representation in the House be allocated using single-member districts. The adoption of single-member districts was the result of federal law, as congressional delegates debated the extent to which the Constitution empowered Congress to mandate that states adopt a particular method of electing representatives. With passage of the Apportionment Act of 1842, representatives constructed a new constitutional understanding of the powers granted to Congress by Article I, Section 4. At the constitutional convention and during ratification debates, the times, places, and manner clause was a necessary, albeit extremely limited, means of ensuring that the states did not disrupt or subvert the national government by failing to hold congressional elections. Critics of the Constitution feared the clause was too ambiguous and gave too much power to Congress at the expense of state governments. The original limited, self-preservation argument was superseded by a more expansive understanding of the clause that allowed Congress to require single-member districts, thereby establishing one of the key electoral configurations and politically entrenching a two-party system in the constitutional regime. To understand further why the United States has a two-party system, one must return to the constitutional debates that established this feature of the constitutional order.

The Founders and the Times, Places, and Manner Clause

During the constitutional convention, the times, places, and manner clause did not elicit extensive debate because it was introduced in the later stages by the Committee of Detail. Throughout the convention, delegates disagreed on how to properly define congressional power, with some delegates, like Edmund Randolph, supporting broad grants of power and other delegates, like Charles Pinckney and John Rutledge, arguing for an exact enumeration of congressional powers.[9] On August 6, the Committee of Detail introduced its version of Article I, which included a list of enumerated powers. Among the powers was the times, places, and manner clause. Discussion of the clause proceeded by separating it into its two parts: first, the power granted to state legislatures to "prescribe" the times, places, and manner of holding elections; and second, the power granted to the national government to alter the election provisions made by the states. Like many aspects of the Constitution, discussion of the clause became a debate about the nature of federalism in the new republic.

The debate centered on whether the second portion granting congressional power to supersede state prescriptions was necessary. Pinckney and Rutledge proposed to completely eliminate this part of the clause, believing state legislatures could and should be relied on in all cases of choosing representatives.[10] Because one of the purposes for calling a constitutional convention was the creation of a national government capable of defending itself from state encroachments, eliminating the second part was imprudent. Madison reminded delegates that a stronger national government was necessary because states often failed or refused to pursue the common good because of their local prejudices. States would abuse such a discretionary power to influence public policy by manipulating electoral rules to favor particular candidates and transfer inequalities within the state legislature to the national legislature.[11] With no check on the states' power to determine the times, places, and manner of elections, the House of Representatives could become a creature of the state legislatures rather than a representative body of the people. Rufus King and Gouverneur Morris likewise defended congressional power over elections because they feared states could completely undermine and frustrate Congress by refusing to hold elections.[12]

Proponents of maintaining congressional power over elections were successful, and both parts of the clause were retained. The clause went through one more minor change before the final version was accepted on September 14, a few days before the constitutional convention concluded. As delegates voted on the final version of the proposed Constitution, a qualification to congressional power was added and unanimously adopted relating to the Senate. While Congress had power over state election law, this addition to the clause prohibited the national legislature from determining the place for electing senators. This addition was meant to complete the federal character of the clause by ensuring that House elections did not disrupt the "national" character of the House. It also ensured that Senate elections adhered to the constitutional requirements that state legislatures select senators, maintaining the "federal" character of the Senate.

The times, places, and manner clause, while not heavily debated in the constitutional convention, became a source of contention during the ratification process. The Anti-Federalists were committed to a strict reading of the Constitution; the national government should only exercise powers that were explicitly enumerated. Implied powers were dangerous and could lead to tyranny. To avoid the dangers of the national government exercising implied powers, they took issue with any phrases in the Constitution that were too broad or overly ambiguous. Article I, Section 4, exemplified constitutional clauses that could be broadly interpreted to subvert state sovereignty and eliminate federalism from the proposed system. Their specific critique of the times, places, and manner clause reversed Madison's defense of it at the convention. While he argued for its necessity based on his fear that state legislatures would manipulate electoral laws to their advantage, the Anti-Federalists argued that the national legislature may use its power to regulate elections to "secure the choice of a particular description of men."[13] This concern coincided with state partyism prior to the Constitution and the geographic division between urban coastal cities and rural inland areas. Congress could alter the times, places, and manner of elections to make it more difficult for voters dispersed throughout the inland towns to participate. This would deprive areas of adequate representation, and the Anti-Federalists feared Congress could use Article I, Section 4, to make the House more aristocratic and less democratic.[14]

The Anti-Federalists recognized that electoral laws determined the nature of representation in the House Representatives. The times, places, and manner clause was key to institutionalizing fair and adequate representation. However, it needed to include language that required states to use a district system for House elections to ensure equal and fair representation. The district system, argued the Anti-Federalists, secured representation from all parts of the community and ensured that representatives had an electoral connection to the localized interests of their constituents.[15] While Anti-Federalists typically appealed to state sovereignty as a challenge to the proposed Constitution, the regulation of House elections was different. They advocated for granting Congress additional enumerated powers and clearly delineating power between the national and state governments. In line with the federal spirit of Article I, Section 4, Congress would be granted enumerated powers to create state electoral districts and, from time to time, to regulate the size of the districts to keep the number of representatives proportionate to the number of constituents across all districts.[16] Congress should also be granted power over election laws only if a state neglected to hold elections. Since it was impossible to enumerate all regulations related to elections, those that are incapable of being fixed by the Constitution should be left to the states, thereby reserving much of the power over elections to them. According to the Anti-Federalists' proposals, the federal sphere of constitutional powers was further defined and clarified, minimizing the prospect of abuse by both the national and state governments.

During the state ratifying conventions, discussion centered on concerns similar to those raised during the constitutional convention in that the clause was necessary to preserve the institutional integrity of Congress. The power to regulate elections was accepted as necessary, and debates focused on where the power would be lodged, with the states or with the national government. Proponents of the Constitution favored empowering the national government because state governments could not be trusted; opponents favored empowering the states, fearful of tyranny at the national level. If any alterations to Article I, Section 4, were suggested, they primarily sought to make Congress's power over elections more limited and explicit by adding language that would only allow Congress to exercise their power when states failed to hold elections.[17] This proposed addition, however, was never incorporated because it was thought unnecessary. No other official alterations were made to the clause, and its meaning was initially settled in that Congress could only exercise its limited power over state election laws in terms of self-preservation.[18] This left the language of the clause and the nature and scope of Congress's power to regulate state election law relatively ambiguous.

This early understanding of the times, places, and manner clause was not seriously challenged until 1842, when, for the first time, Congress interpreted its power to regulate elections as a grant of power to require states to adopt a particular method of electing members to the House of Representatives. This new constitutional construction provided Congress with broader powers in determining state election laws, which resulted in a congressional mandate that states elect representatives using single-member districts, just as the Anti-Federalists had argued prior to ratifying the Constitution.

POST-RATIFICATION DEVELOPMENTS

Following ratification of the Constitution and the first census, the question of how to apportion House members among the states became central. The Second Congress faced a difficult task with the first Apportionment Act because it was required to interpret what the Constitution meant by its stipulation that "the Number of Representatives shall not exceed one for every thirty thousand."[19] Initially, the total number of representatives was determined by dividing the total population of a state by a fixed number (the House proposed 30,000, and the Senate proposed 33,000) and rounding down, producing a House of 112 members (based on the House's ratio) or 105 (based on the Senate's ratio).[20] Overall, the first five apportionment acts increased the size of the House but said nothing of how states should elect representatives.

During this time, while Congress determined the number of representatives, states determined their own methods of electing members to the House. Article I, Section 4, of the Constitution delegated many of the procedural aspects of electing congressional representatives to the states, including suffrage qualifications, polling places, and the manner of choosing representatives. As states experimented with various forms of election types, disputes arose over the meaning of the times, places, and manner clause, because different election methods resulted in differences in both forms of representation and who was represented.

During the early decades of the nineteenth century, states primarily used two methods of selecting representatives to the House: a single-member district system and an at-large, general ticket system. When electing by single-member districts, a state was divided into as many electoral districts as there were seats available, with each district having one representative. Under the general ticket system, representatives were elected as an entire multimember delegation, with voters given a block of candidates for which they could vote. Some states, usually larger ones like New York and Pennsylvania, used a single-member district system but allowed for some multimember districts in order to provide adequate representation to highly populated districts. Patterns in states' preferences quickly became discernible as larger states adopted the district method while smaller states preferred election by general ticket. This distinction had political significance as the two-party system became institutionalized.[21] Similar to the choosing of electors for the electoral college, the manner of selecting representatives had ramifications for the partisan composition of Congress. The general ticket system provided for a unified partisan delegation, whereas the district system allowed for diversity in the partisan composition based on the variety of preferences in the districts. The at-large selection of congressional representatives was driven largely by state parties as a way to effectively translate their majority control of the state into control of their House delegation. Smaller states likewise preferred this method because it unified partisan preferences in both the House and the Senate, providing them with a disproportionately influential voting bloc when combined with other small states.[22] Conversely, larger states, electing by districts, gave minorities a voice in the House delegation, but this also resulted in greater political division among the states' congressional delegation.

Given the perceived advantage to the smaller states and political parties, from 1800 to 1826, at least thirty-four proposed constitutional amendments and bills were introduced, as large states attempted to abolish the general ticket selection of representatives to the House.[23] Many of the proposed amendments connected using districts with the electoral college. The amendments required that states select representatives and presidential electors from the same districts, with the final two presidential electors chosen by the state legislature. John Nicholas (DR-VA) introduced the first of these types of amendments in 1800. His proposal was referred to a committee, but since an amendment to the Constitution was unnecessary as Congress already had power to regulate House elections, including how representatives were elected, it was rejected.[24] This assumption about congressional power was not definitive. From 1816 to 1822, attempts to amend the Constitution gained momentum, with amendments in 1819, 1820, and 1821 receiving the requisite two-thirds support in the Senate before dying in the House. In the course of debates over these amendments, members of Congress expressed uncertainty regarding their power over House elections and their ability to require that states adopt a particular method for electing representatives.[25] States' rights were a central feature of the opposition to these amendments because there was no convincing argument as to why the states should be denied the right to determine the best method for electing their own representatives. After 1822 and the controversial election of 1824, amendments related to districting the House were halted in favor of those that would fix the system of presidential election. The movement toward a uniform method for selecting representatives did not gain significant traction until the 1840s, when the Whig Party became a credible challenge to the Democratic Party.

The Whig Party formed during the early 1830s in opposition to President Jackson and the Democratic Party. The rise of modern party and electoral politics is often attributed to this era. Competition between the Whigs and the Democrats, explains Alexander Keyssar, created a "strong and vibrant national party system" where "both party loyalty and party identification became prominent elements of public life."[26] With the exceptions of race and gender, most voting restrictions were eliminated, and this mass enfranchisement resulted in an enormous increase in participants in the political process. From 1820 to 1842, the number of ballots cast in elections for the House of Representatives increased over 500 percent.[27] Political parties both benefited and suffered from this increase in participation. Parties could establish electoral dominance from a substantial increase in electoral support; but voting was unpredictable, meaning parties could not rely on a constant political base for support. Electoral fates could change dramatically from one election cycle to the next, as a party could command a solid majority only to find itself in the minority in the subsequent election.

Economics played a central role in the emergence of the Whig Party. The volatile economic environment allowed parties to appeal to voters by developing cohesive and distinct economic platforms. This also tied party politicians to their party platform and influenced voting behavior in Congress so they could have a stable record to tout during reelection efforts.[28] Following President Jackson's reelection in 1832, division over the Second Bank of the United States and the nullification crisis escalated opposition to the Democratic Party as opponents like Henry Clay, Daniel Webster, and former Jacksonians led by John C. Calhoun denounced what they perceived as Jackson's aggrandizement of executive power. To counter the alleged abuse of executive power, the newly formed Whigs looked to Congress as a means of censuring President Jackson and the Democratic Party.[29]

While starting off as a minority party, the Whigs successfully captured control of both Congress and the White House by 1840. Amid economic decline, the Whigs successfully ran on the prospect of chartering a new national bank. In the 1840 presidential election, President Van Buren faced a Whig Party united behind its candidate, war hero William Henry Harrison. Harrison easily defeated the incumbent president, receiving 234 electoral college votes to Van Buren's 60. President Harrison used his inaugural address to repudiate the Democratic Party and its policies. To address economic decline, Harrison promised to implement Henry Clay's American system, which included establishing a tariff, a national bank, and federal subsidies. He also promised to restore the proper balance of power between Congress and the executive by using his veto more sparingly than President Jackson had and deferring to Congress on legislative matters. His promises and the Whigs' control of the presidency, however, was short-lived; President Harrison died in 1841, a mere thirty days after he took the oath of office. Vice President John Tyler, a former Democrat, took his place and immediately challenged Whig leadership in Congress. Deviating from many of Harrison's promises, Tyler twice vetoed bills to create a national bank, to which the congressional Whigs responded by officially disavowing him for abandoning and betraying their party.[30]

In addition to being challenged by the executive branch, the Whig Party saw its majority status in Congress threatened by changes in how states elected their representatives to the House. Electing representatives through single-member districts benefited the Whigs, most of whom were urban dwellers, whereas electing representatives through the general ticket method allowed the larger rural, predominantly Democratic electorate to overwhelm the urban vote and capture the entire state delegation.[31] In states using the general ticket system, even if the Whigs captured 49 percent of the vote, they would still lose all seats for the state, providing them with no representation in the House of Representatives. The lack of representation became a central issue for the Whigs in 1840, as the Democratic-controlled Alabama state legislature switched from electing members of the House by districts to the general-ticket method in order to get more representatives of the Democratic Party elected to Congress.[32] Prior to the change, the Whigs held two of Alabama's five seats; after the change, the Democrats won all five. Alabama's governor, Arthur B. Bagby, preferred the general ticket method because it countered any increases in support for the Whigs. The majority of Alabama voters were Democrats who lived in the northern part of the state. A general ticket election allowed the Democratic majority to elect all of the state's representatives, whereas the Whigs could capture two or three districts under the districting plan.[33] Party politics and representation were key components for the Whigs because the method of selecting representatives determined the partisan configuration of the House. Whigs looked to the uniform adoption of single-member districts as a way to secure both fair representation and their partisan influence in Congress.

The Whig Party became the majority party in Congress in 1840. Following the 1840 census, they were in position to challenge state electoral law by putting single-member districts on the legislative agenda. Making this change was important because they had suffered electoral losses in state and local races. For example, they won only about 33 percent of House elections in 1842–43, down from 60 percent during the 1840–41 cycle.[34] Perhaps more important, they also lost state legislative and gubernatorial races at the very time that state governments determined the method for selecting House Representatives and drawing district lines following the 1840 census.[35] Enacting this change at the congressional level could prevent them from losing representatives in states where the Democrats controlled the legislatures. Debates over the adoption of single-member districts were driven by party politics, and the electoral reforms included in the 1842 Apportionment Act introduced essential features of the two-party system.[36]

1842 APPORTIONMENT ACT: ELECTORAL RULES AND PARTYISM

Following the 1840 census, Representative Horace Everett (W-VT) chaired the Select Committee on the Apportionment of Representatives to address changes to apportionment as a result of population changes. On January 22, 1842, he reported that the committee had set the ratio at one representative for every 68,000 residents, thereby reducing the total number of representatives in the House for the first time. The ratio was an important starting point for discussion on apportionment, as the Whigs wanted to reduce the size of the House because they believed its continual growth had made it impossible for it to be a deliberative assembly. Representative John Thompson (W-KY) argued that the size of the House was susceptible to confusion and disorder, and Representative William Allen (D-OH) complained that the body had become so numerous that it was often difficult to hear proceedings, causing many representatives to leave or become frustrated.[37] Any additional increases to the House, warned Representative Joseph Underwood (W-KY), would result in mob rule.[38] Representative Richard Thompson (W-IN) feared that due to its large size, the House would fail to produce intelligent legislation.[39]

Those opposed to reducing the chamber's size argued that a larger House was more representative and better reflected the interests of the people. Representative Richard Davis (D-NY) believed a larger House allowed for a more diversified body of representatives and the representation of the "hard-handed mechanics and farmers."[40] This point was particularly relevant because, according to the 1840 census, 69 percent of Americans worked in agriculture, yet lawyers dominated the House. There were very few farmers in Congress, and some occupations, like bakers or butchers, were not represented at all.[41] Opponents of reducing the size of the House were concerned with the quality of representation and how well representatives mirrored their constituents demographically.

Early support for reducing the size of the House, however, did not follow the partisan divide between the Whigs and the Democrats. Some Whigs joined with the Democrats in advocating for an increase in the size of the House. This revealed a growing divide within the Whig Party regarding property and politics. Conservative Whigs, who feared that democratization endangered property, wanted a smaller House to alter the debating style and the decision-making process that a larger House created and the Democrats desired. Younger Whigs disagreed, believing that the masses could become important defenders of property; like many Democrats, they viewed a larger House, even with its increased crowds and noise, as embodying a more democratic ideal of representation.[42] This division among the Whigs led many to vote with the Democrats, and on May 3, the House passed a bill specifying the ratio of 50,179 residents per House member, which would have increased the size of that chamber from 242 to 305.

The bill did not survive the Senate, however. Many senators worried that an increase in House size would give it too much power and disrupt the balance between the two chambers. In addition, some senators were concerned about the distribution of power between northern and southern states. Southern states had an interest in reducing the size of the House, because a larger House benefited the more populous northern states by giving them more seats. A smaller House also reduced the number of representatives needed to construct a majority coalition, and the smaller the numbers needed to build a majority coalition, the fewer concessions the southern members would have to make to northern members in building a winning coalition.[43] In addition to these calculations of sectional advantages, senators expressed concern regarding the legislative efficiency of the House. One senator opined that "the sessions [would be] drawn out to such an intolerable length as to be a reasonable complaint."[44] Too numerous a House would make it democratic only in appearance.

On June 10, the Whig-controlled Senate returned the Apportionment Bill with a ratio (70,680) that reduced the size of the House from 242 to 223 members. Initially, the House rejected the Senate's change, and the Senate refused to make additional alterations. However, on June 17, the Whigs gained enough support in the House to accept the Senate's higher ratio. Why the House ultimately acquiesced is not entirely clear.[45] Much of the debate on the Senate's ratio centered less on the fact that the ratio had been increased and the number of representatives reduced and more on the constitutionality of representing fractions. The Senate's proposed ratio included giving an additional representative if the remaining fraction of the population was greater than half the proposed ratio. Those representatives supporting the Senate's increased ratio (and smaller House) again appealed to legislative efficiency, as they were "unwilling, for the sake of adding respectability, to destroy the efficiency of the democratic principle." A smaller number of representatives was sufficient to accomplish all the business, no matter how minor, that came before Congress.[46] This higher ratio prioritized legislative efficiency over adequate representation, a significant deviation from all previous apportionment acts.

To compensate for the loss in representation that a smaller House size entailed, the Whigs also pursued the uniform system of single-member districts for House elections. They believed that representatives would better reflect and be known by their constituencies if elected by a district rather than the entire state. On April 26, the Apportionment Act was amended to require states to adopt single-member districts for the election of representatives to the House. Representative William Halstead (W-NJ), instructed by the Committee of Elections, reported on the amendment, which became Section 2 of the Apportionment Act. The proposed amendment read:

And be it further enacted, That in every case where a State is entitled to more than one Representative, the number to which each State shall be entitled under this apportionment shall be elected by districts, composed of contiguous territory, equal in number to the number of Representatives to which the State may be entitled; no one district electing more than one Representative.[47]

As in the ratio debate, the Whigs holding a majority did not guarantee that the new districting amendment would pass, as sectional lines again divided the Whig Party. Although voting on the districting amendment largely followed party lines, Whigs representing slave-holding states were the exception: while 93 percent of the Whig members from free states (68 votes) voted for single-member districts, only 65 percent of Whigs from slave states (30 votes) voted for the amendment. By contrast, sectional division did not fracture the Democratic Party's voting: 98 percent (40 votes) opposed the districting amendment in free states, and 95 percent (37 votes) opposed it in slave states.[48] The opposition to Section 2 was centered on the constitutionality of the plan. Democrats and many southern Whigs argued that the Constitution granted Congress no such power. Passing the districting amendment required supporters to provide a convincing constitutional argument that Article I, Section 4, could be understood in broader terms to legitimize the districting amendment.

In general, supporters of Section 2 viewed the provision as both constitutional and good policy; opponents attempted to maintain the status quo by using familiar arguments from the founding era that Congress could interfere with state election law only if states failed to hold elections. Representative William L. Goggin (W-VA) was hesitant to fully support the amendment, making reference to Madison and quoting at length from his notes at the constitutional convention to argue that power over elections was to be used only as a "last resort" to ensure that "the wheels of the General Government might not stop" if states failed to hold elections.[49] His real issue was with the general ticket system, which he abhorred. If they understood Congress to have the power to require districting, it could also require states to adopt the general ticket system. Adopting the districting amendment required supporters to be convincing on the question of its constitutionality and the issue of good policy. On the matter of policy, supporters of Section 2 relied on arguments about the representation produced by the district system against that of the general ticket system to legitimize the districting amendment. The Whigs argued that single-member districts improved the quality of representation, particularly for minority parties within a state.

The debate echoed those during ratification, with the contested constitutionality of Section 2 centering on a broad or narrow reading of Article I, Section 4. Representative Halstead defended the districting amendment by drawing attention to the language of the Constitution, emphasizing that Congress was given power to regulate the times, places, and manner of holding state elections. The districting principle was well within Congress's power given this language. Representative Walter T. Colquitt (D-GA), however, rejected this interpretation and asserted that the districting amendment was unconstitutional because it provided for additional qualifications for members of the House and abridged the right of voters to select representatives. The Constitution clearly establishes the qualifications for those eligible for election to the House. Article I, Section 4, likewise did not contain the term "qualification" when enumerating congressional power over elections. If the districting amendment required representatives to live in the district from which he was elected, then it unconstitutionally abridged the residency qualifications already fixed in Article I, Section 2. Moreover, districting a state violated the constitutional provision for electing representatives in Article I, Section 2, which establishes that representatives be elected by the people of a state, not a fraction of the state. Under the district plan, voters would only be voting for a fraction of the state's representatives. According to the Constitution, each voter is entitled to vote for "as many members as the State is entitled to send to Congress."[50] The addition of Section 2 far overreached the power granted to Congress because the word *manner* does not give Congress power to determine who can vote, where they live, and how many candidates they can vote for.[51] Like Colquitt, Representative Andrew Kennedy (D-IN) pointed to the plain construction of Article I, Section 4:

Time did not comprehend the power to district; it meant when the people should come together. *Place* did not mean such power, for it referred to where the people should come together; and *manner* referred to nothing else but as to how the election should be held; the mode in which the sovereign people, for time being, shall transfer their power. These terms could not therefore embrace in them the power to district.[52]

Preliminary debates on the districting amendment once again introduced the continual debate between broad and strict readings of the Constitution, and debate on Section 2 was further complicated as representatives became embroiled in a dispute over federalism.

The addition of Section 2 to the Apportionment Act signaled that there was more at stake than deciding the size of the House. Section 2 disrupted the currently accepted balance between national power and states' rights. At the time, the pendulum of federalism had moved toward state sovereignty. Elvin T. Lim writes that the Jacksonian era was "the golden age of states' rights," as it produced "a durable retrenchment in federal authority from the height it had enjoyed during the Era of Good Feelings."[53] The districting amendment struck at the very heart of the federal question, and representatives were keenly aware of how its acceptance would change the dynamics of federalism. Representative John Gelston Floyd (D-NY) was strongly opposed to Section 2 because it was not simply a matter between districting and the general ticket. Rather, he said, this was the "embodiment of the Federal doctrine of centralization," which aimed at strengthening the government at the expense of the people.[54] He went so far as to state that Congress had yet to pursue an act "so odious as this," with abolitionist movements in the North and nullification in the South being less of a danger to states' rights than the districting amendment.[55] To that point, power over elections had been considered a state prerogative. The states' rights defenders emphasized the lack of delegated powers in the Constitution that allowed Congress to impose electoral regulations on the states, firmly entrenching the matter on the side of state sovereignty.

In response to their opponents, defenders of the districting amendment held that Section 2 was not a constitutional overreach and that it was firmly grounded in the power delegated to Congress in Article I, Section 4, to regulate the states' electoral systems. Representatives Garrett Davis (W-KY) and Joseph L. Tillinghast (W-RI) viewed Article I, Section 4, as a type of dormant clause in that states had power over elections if Congress had not acted. If Congress did exercise its power over elections, it became the exclusive right of Congress.[56] Furthermore, the language of Section 2, reasoned Tillinghast, was sufficiently narrow in that the amendment did not necessarily grant Congress power to district the states; it only called on the states to district, which was completely different.[57] Supporters attempted to temper the accusations made regarding a complete assumption of state sovereignty because Section 2 required states to adopt the district method while still allowing the states to perform the actual districting.

The Whigs were also well aware that the manner of electing representatives, by districts or general ticket, determined the nature of representation. With Section 2 being added to the Apportionment Act, the discussion of representation was framed in majority/minority terms. Supporters of the district plan understood it as providing better representation to minorities, whereas the general ticket system failed to represent them at all. The institutional design of the House made minority representation possible, more than any other branch of government. Even though the Whigs were positioned to benefit from single-member districts, some Democrats recognized the principled justification of the districting amendment and the legitimate purpose it served of improving representation. Representative John Campbell (D-SC), one of the only Democrats to support the amendment, believed the "true principle of the Constitution" was representation of both majorities and minorities. The general ticket method went against this principle because it suppressed minority voices. The "principles of Democratic Government," he argued, required the voice of the minority; without it, the majority could not govern.[58] More recently, Stephen Calabrese has substantiated this position empirically. He found that diversity in ideological representation increased when states shifted from general ticket elections, which a single party typically won, to single-member districts. Likewise, ideological diversity decreased when states changed from a single-member to a general ticket system.[59] In other words, the nature of congressional representation was contingent on the method of electing representatives, since, compared to the general ticket method, single-member districts allowed for more ideological diversity in representation.

The disparity in election law across states had important political ramifications for the recurring division between large and small states and the issue of slavery. Representative Horace Everett (W-VT) pointed out that the smaller states adopted the general ticket because it gave them "political power" over the larger states.[60] This strategy violated the Connecticut Compromise in the original constitutional compact, under which the larger states were supposed to benefit from proportionate representation in the House while smaller states had an advantage through equal representation in the Senate.[61] With the larger states using the district method and the smaller ones using the general ticket, the latter gained a political advantage in both houses of Congress: the district method fragmented a state's delegation in the House, while the general ticket system allowed for a more politically unified delegation that could exert influence disproportionate to its number of representatives. States like Georgia, New Jersey, and Alabama, which elected by general ticket, maintained a smaller number of representatives. Yet, "on all party questions, they had a stronger voice than the largest States, who went on the district plan."[62]

However, for several reasons, the larger states did not simply adopt the general ticket system to eliminate the smaller states' advantage. Everett argued that the large states should refrain from doing so, since this would sharply reduce the influence of the small states in the House. The large states did not adopt the general ticket system "partly from the influence of moral principle and a regard to the general good, and partly on considerations of convenience." The Union would not endure, he argued, if the large states used the general ticket.[63] The larger states used the district system for decades because it provided fairer and more equitable representation to the various interests and parties in those states than the general ticket system could.[64] The decision for the large states was framed around a central dilemma: inadequate representation (via the general ticket method) versus a reduction in the state's influence and power in the House (by retaining the district method). Large states were unwilling to adopt the general ticket method to increase their power at the expense of adequate representation. From the standpoint of the large states, the solution to their dilemma was to require states to uniformly adopt the district method, in order to restore Congress to its proper equilibrium between large and small states and to provide fair and equitable representation to all parties and interests in each state.

In addition, representatives believed that the cross-state variation in election law had political ramifications for the debate on slavery. The northern states primarily used the district method, while southern states adopted the general ticket system. As with the small states protecting their interests, the southern states' delegates could unite to create a durable voting bloc more easily than the northern states.[65] However, this advantage only existed if there continued to be a disparity in election law, with the northern states continuing to use the districting method and the southern states continuing to use the general ticket. Representative Garrett Davis (W-KY) recognized that the "peculiar principles" of the South and "every interest it cherished" would actually be protected by the uniform adoption of the district system, because the more populous northern states adopting the general ticket system would overwhelm the southern states' united power. Many representatives believed that without the districting amendment, all the states would eventually adopt the general ticket system to maximize their influence in Congress, even at the expense of reducing the representation of diverse interests in the states.[66]

The size of the House and sectional issues were all concerns during the debates that help explain support and opposition for Section 2. The districting requirement also produced a sustained debate over the role of political parties, which was closely related to a normative understanding of how representation should function in a two-party system. Rather than emphasize demographic characteristics, such as occupation, representatives framed the discussion of representation in terms of party, with the district system allowing for greater minority or opposition party representation. Hence representatives infused a constitutional construction of Article I, Section 4, with debates over the relationship between partyism and representation in the House.

Emboldened by the issue of representation, Whigs advocated for the district system as a constitutional method for securing fair representation not just for their own party, but for all political parties, which they believed existed since ratification of the Constitution. "This government," Representative Daniel D. Barnard (W-NY) declared, "was now, ever had been, and ever would be, because it ever must be, carried on and administered by party." He "scouted the idea of conducting the Government without party; and when he heard gentlemen profess such a purpose, he thought they meant very little of what they said: it was an idle dream. And if the Government must proceed on party principles, how unfairly did the present unregulated system work."[67] Far from interpreting constitutional history as working against parties, he recognized the reality of partyism and the role it played in politics. Electoral laws needed to reflect and enhance party government, not work against it. Joining Barnard, Representative Everett praised the districting amendment because it recognized party government and ensured that the party system functioned fairly.[68] In contrast to the district system, Representative Davis argued, the general ticket system provided representation only for one political party: "If all the States adopted the general ticket system, five of the large States would have a majority on the [House] floor. They would be elected by the same political party; and the consequence would be, that a little more than one quarter of the people of the United States would constitute a majority and governing power in this House." If the general ticket system persisted, he continued, "they would have no popular representation here."[69] A fairly functioning party system needed to provide representation for both the minority and the majority party, and the district system was the only way this was possible.

Despite the Whigs' understanding of representation and partyism, some Democrats accused them of pursing this change for partisan purposes. Representative William W. Payne (D-AL), believed the Whigs were using their concern over representation to obscure the fact that this was a partisan maneuver to perpetuate their political power. If the Whigs were given the constitutional power to adjust election laws, they, or any future party, could simply alter the rules again to their advantage. They wanted districting today, he argued, because "it suited the interests of the dominant party: and perhaps, the next Congress would undertake to establish the general ticket system."[70] By accusing the Whigs of party positioning, Payne meant to decry party constitutionalism in that "if this principle was adopted by this Congress, instead of coming here to legislate for the whole republic, their successors would have in their eye their own security, and the party in power would seek to perpetuate its own existence, and to sink those that were opposed to them in party politics."[71] For Payne, following the Constitution-against-parties thesis, if the Whigs prevailed, parties would subvert the Constitution's long-established regime by corrupting the House with partyism and sacrificing deliberation on public business for private, partisan interests.

As debate on the districting amendment progressed, some Democrats began supporting Section 2 on grounds of fair representation. Representative Sampson H. Butler (D-SC) defended Section 2 as both constitutional and good policy because the principles of fair representation offered by the district system took precedence over any partisan considerations.

Republicanism, according to Butler, required the district method, and "if he could fill up this hall with his own party, by adopting the general ticket system, he would not do it; because he believed it would result in the ultimate ruin of this country and the prostration of liberty."[72] In the Senate, Albert White (W-IN) endorsed districting the House on grounds of fair representation as well. "Was [Section 2]," he asked, "not a question of whether representation in the popular branch of the National Legislature shall be a popular representation or a party representation?" For Senator White, districting allowed for fair party representation while also enhancing representation. Constructing representation based on districts provided a closer electoral connection because constituents could keep their representative personally accountable to them, something the general ticket system failed to provide.[73] In other words, the districting amendment was not simply a partisan maneuver by the Whig Party. Rather, they believed districting improved representation, particularly for the developing two-party system and the minority party in a state. The general ticket method failed to represent minority parties; single-member districts provided representation for a minority capable of capturing the majority vote within a district.

On May 3, 1842, the Whigs' districting amendment passed by a bare majority (101 to 99), and on June 10, the Senate approved the apportionment bill by a 25 to 19 vote. For the first time, Congress passed an apportionment bill that reduced the size of the House and required representatives to be selected using single-member districts. Although President Tyler eventually signed the bill into law, he did so with great hesitation, going so far as to attach a presidential signing statement questioning its constitutionality. Following its enactment, controversy over the districting requirement ensued during the Twenty-Eighth Congress after four states—Georgia, Missouri, Mississippi, and New Hampshire—elected members in 1842 using the general ticket system. The Whigs, who suffered enormous electoral defeats and lost their slim majority in the House, adamantly protested and moved that the representatives elected by the general ticket method, all of whom were Democrats, not be seated and granted full participation in House proceedings.[74] The Democrats, now the majority, did not acquiesce to their requests. Although a few states did not initially adhere to the districting requirement, the legal tradition of requiring single-member district elections took hold in

American politics. Although the 1842 Apportionment Act expired at the next census, other congressional laws requiring single-member districts replaced it,[75] and subsequent Supreme Court decisions reaffirmed what the Whigs initially established, the constitutionality of the districting principle.[76]

The concern about Section 2 focused on parties and the two-party system providing fair representation to both the Whigs and Democrats. In so doing, the Apportionment Act of 1842 further entrenched political parties in American politics by creating electoral rules favoring a two-party system. As representatives debated the constitutionality and propriety of the measure, it was clear that the meaning of Section 2 and the associated concept of representation were framed in terms of parties, particularly the two major parties. At the time, the Whigs and the Democrats were the only parties running candidates in the majority of states and in the majority of districts. The Apportionment Act was understood to provide fair representation for the two major parties and not necessarily for third parties. During this time, support for third party candidates and challenges to the two major parties were extremely low. It was the longest absence of third party challenges during that century.[77] Theoretically, third party candidates, particularly for the House, would fare better electorally under a district rather than a general ticket system, and the district system would allow for third party and independent candidate representation in the House. However, the act primarily addressed and corrected representation for the two major parties within the two-party system. It was passed primarily, if not solely, with the two major parties in mind. Consequently, "the 1842 Act," explains Andrew Hacker, "was a major step towards proportional representation to the distribution of votes" for the two major political parties.[78]

The Apportionment Act of 1842 broadened the scope of Article I, Section 4, and enhanced congressional power over elections. The Whigs and some Democrats desiring to replace general ticket elections with the district system constructed authority over congressional elections in relatively broad terms. Their broad construction established a power that allowed Congress to override state election laws for more than narrowly defined instances of state inaction or emergency. During the constitutional convention and ratification debates, the ambiguous language of the times, places, and manner clause was interpreted as a necessary yet limited power. This newly constructed power, however, was not entirely new, because the Anti-Federalists had advocated for electing members to the House of Representatives by districts during the ratification debate. The construction of Article 1, Section 4, centered on two central tenets of American politics, federalism and representation.

Until 1842, congressional redistricting had been solely a state function, and the broad construction of congressional power over elections was the first of many subsequent federal statutory laws prescribing electoral methods. In 1872, Congress added another requirement to the districting mandate in that districts should be drawn with approximately an equal number of inhabitants per district.[79] In 1901, the Apportionment Act included prescriptions for districts made of contiguous and compact territories and, as practicable as possible, an equal number of inhabitants. This language was repeated in apportionment acts until 1929, when Congress adopted the Permanent Apportionment Act containing no districting standards, and after 1929, Congress imposed no standards on congressional districting. States would not have regulations imposed on them again until 1967, when Congress once again required elections for the House of Representatives by geographically based districts. In the wake of *Baker v. Carr* and *Wesberry v. Sanders*, the Supreme Court assumed a participatory role in governing congressional redistricting through judicial interpretation and constitutional law.[80] The Apportionment Act of 1842 initiated a substantive shift in governing authority as the national government, whether through Congress or the Supreme Court, became substantially more involved in the "manner" of choosing representatives to the House.

In addition to the ramifications for federalism, the Apportionment Act of 1842 had substantive effects on the concept of representation because elections by single-member districts altered the relationship between representatives and constituents. During the debates at this time, many representatives recognized that the single-member district requirement allowed for a closer relationship between the people and their representatives. Voters could know a candidate from their district more easily than from their state. Likewise, representatives were more accountable to their constituents under a single-member district system than under the general ticket system.[81] Many representatives believed a smaller House limited the chaotic nature of participatory democracy and enhanced deliberative democracy. As Craig T. Borowiak explains, "The zeal of 'jealous republicans' needed to be checked lest it generate onerous obligations of accountability that would hamper good government."[82] The compromise of 1842, then, produced a House that was more distant yet also closer to the people in that there were fewer representatives, but these representatives would better reflect their constituents. These issues of representation and better reflecting constituents were closely related to the question of political parties.

Throughout the debates on Section 2 of the Apportionment Act, the Democrats accused the Whigs of supporting districting solely for partisan purposes, while the Whigs insisted theirs was a position of principle. It is true that the Whigs would have been the primary beneficiaries of reducing the size of the House and adopting the district system. However, the Whigs and certain Democrats constructed a principled account of representation within a two-party system to justify their insistence on the district method, thereby further incorporating political parties and partyism into the constitutional regime.

Partyism and the Twenty-Fourth Amendment

Entrenching the Two-Party Constitution

In many contemporary democracies, political parties have been identified as essential institutions for the organization of political participation and the execution of democratic politics. For decades, party scholars have idealized partyism and promoted stronger parties as the means of achieving democratic goals.[1] Conversely, contemporary antipartyism is also prevalent, as parties are blamed for low participation in elections, accused of being controlled by special interest groups or wealthy donors, criticized for being either too extreme or not extreme enough, or denounced for being unresponsive to public opinion or public interest.[2] Political parties in the United States are often caught between promotion for their salutary benefits and discredit for their obstinate partisanship. Any attempt to strengthen or promote political parties must come to terms with the arguments against partyism. This includes understanding their role in a constitutional system that was intended to work against them. As this study has shown, political parties emerged as an institutional device by which popular sovereignty, albeit popular sovereignty based on partisanship, could legitimately exercise its authority in politics. That is, political actors constructed constitutional meaning in an effort to legitimize the emerging partisan practices during a time when the Constitution, as many scholars argue, was intended to work against parties and partyism.

THE CONSTITUTION AND POPULAR SOVEREIGNTY

Despite no explicit mention of political parties, the Constitution is a partisan document. In Charles R. Kesler's words, the Constitution is "partisan above all because it stands for a particular kind of government, for republican government, which it undertakes to guarantee to the states."[3] The governing document became partisan because of contestation over defining foundational concepts like popular sovereignty and republicanism and how these concepts would function in political practice. The first political parties formed around competing conceptions of republicanism and the governmental practices that would make the newly founded republic successful.[4] Although the Constitution was theoretically based on the concept of majority rule, how the commitment to popular sovereignty would function in political practice remained to be seen.

In many regards, the Constitution was an experiment in self-government, and even though the new government was founded on popular sovereignty, the meaning of republicanism, and its distinction from a democracy, was highly disputed.[5] "Even before the revolution," argues Christian G. Fritz, "colonial Americans had wondered how to discover the people's will, express that will, render government responsive to it, and balance popular opinion against the public interest."[6] The Declaration of Independence asserted that "Governments are instituted among Men, deriving their just powers from the consent of the governed," raising a question regarding the precise understanding of who constituted "the governed." The Declaration was legitimized by the unanimous support of the "thirteen united States of America," a conception of the consent of the governed that carried over to the "league of friendship," based on state sovereignty, in the Articles of Confederation. The Constitution, however, created a "more perfect union" by including notions of popular sovereignty as an addition to the claims of state sovereignty.[7] The Preamble, by invoking "We the People," expressed the notion of popular government, but it also constituted the first action by "the People" in that the people exercised their right to ordain and establish the Constitution.

Not only was ratification an expression and exercise of popular self-rule, but proponents of the Constitution emphasized that the document itself contained principles of popular sovereignty and republicanism. During the ratification process, the Anti-Federalists argued that the Constitution created an aristocratic government, perpetuating the very principles repudiated by the American Revolution. Toward the end of the constitutional convention, John Dickenson proclaimed, "When this plan goes forth it will be attacked by the popular leaders. Aristocracy will be the watchword; the Shibboleth among its adversaries." He recognized that constitutional shortcomings would be the product of inexperience.[8] Many opponents of the Constitution feared that, despite all the democratic rhetoric, the government was still fundamentally aristocratic.[9] In response to these claims, supporters described the Constitution as "wholly popular" or "strictly republican," not aristocratic.[10] That is, the democratic nature of the Constitution became a fundamental question.

Throughout the *Federalist Papers*, Madison and Hamilton connected popular sovereignty and republican government with the Constitution. In Federalist No. 22, Hamilton established the central pillar of the republican experiment, the "fundamental maxim of republican government, which requires that the sense of the majority should prevail."[11] In Federalist No. 39, Madison specifically addressed the Anti-Federalists' aristocratic concerns: "The first question that offers itself is, whether the general form and aspect of the government be strictly republican." And, setting the stakes, Madison argued that "if the plan of the convention . . . be found to depart from the republican character, its advocates must abandon it as no longer defensible."[12] However, he further argued, history had shown that monarchies and aristocracies were classified as republics.[13] The United States would constitute a republic only if it was a "government which derives all its powers directly or indirectly from the great body of the people," because "the genius of republican liberty seems to demand on one side, not only that all power should be derived from the people, but that those intrusted with it should be kept in dependence on the people."[14] Theoretically, the Constitution was understood to link republican government with popular sovereignty and majority rule.

Nevertheless, it was uncertain how the Constitution would establish a truly republican government in practice. It was not long before parties emerged to help settle this uncertainty.

REPUBLICANISM AND THE FIRST PARTY SYSTEM

The ideological and policy division between Alexander Hamilton and Thomas Jefferson and James Madison led to the development of party competition between the Federalists and the Democratic-Republicans.[15] Bridging the ideological and policy gap, explains John Aldrich, required more than "vote trades among opposing leaders or by other forms of piecemeal, issue-by-issue compromise, [so] these leaders—first Hamilton, then Jefferson and Madison—turned to organizing their supports."[16] Early in his congressional career, Madison lost on key constitutional and policy issues, such as President Washington's use of executive power to declare neutrality in relation to France and England, Congress's power to charter a national bank, and the assumption of war debts. As Jeremy Bailey stated, "Rather than accepting these losses as the necessary consequence of deliberation, or as settled by the compromise and consensus required to survive the separation of powers, Madison instead chose the extra-constitutional path of organized opposition."[17] Importantly, Madison's decision to turn to party organization and political opposition brought the centrality of public opinion to the fore and provided the means by which popular sovereignty conferred legitimacy on the government. Governmental actions were not settled until they were subject to the public's judgment through competitive partisan elections.

In the *Federalist Papers*, Madison argued that the Constitution was indeed republican in that popular sovereignty was the central feature. As he pursued party organization, Madison later argued that by turning to public opinion, his opposition party was the embodiment of these true republican principles.[18] In his essays published in the *National Gazette*, he claimed public opinion was sovereign in every free government because it sets bounds to governmental action.[19] His party was grounded on the authority of the people, being "friends to" popular sovereignty, while the Federalists were opposed to republican principles and "the republican spirit of the people."[20] With his emphasis on popular sovereignty, Madison recognized the difficulty of ascertaining public opinion, especially in the extended republic.

> The larger a country, the less easy for its real opinion to be ascertained, and the less difficult to be counterfeited; when ascertained or presumed, the more respectable it is in the eyes of the individuals. This is favorable to the authority of government. For the same reason, the more extensive a country, the more insignificant is each individual in his own eyes. This may be unfavorable to liberty.[21]

His solution to this problem was the printing press and the circulation of newspapers.[22] The Federalists' Alien and Sedition Acts aimed at silencing the partisan press, which the Republicans believed constituted an attack on public opinion and republicanism. If the newly formed Republican Party was going to rely on an appeal to the public, it would need to ensure that constitutional and electoral rules allowed them to effectually "interpose a common manifestation of their sentiments" in opposition to the Federalists.[23] The Republicans relied on party competition as a means of challenging the Federalists through the authority of majority rule. Partyism was the means by which the constitutional commitment to majority rule and popular sovereignty was realized in the early republic.

The Constitution was supposed to work against the Republicans' party efforts, or at least make them temporary. But what if the dominant narrative is mistaken? What if, during these early partisan battles, the Constitution empowered parties rather than constrained them? This study provides a new narrative of political parties that emphasizes how political actors used the Constitution to fulfill the constitutional promise of popular sovereignty through partisan competition. The first party battle between the Republicans and the Federalists made the Constitution subject to politics, as political actors combined constitutional text with dominant, yet competing principles and interests.[24] During these partisan battles, indeterminacies in the Constitution's text were interpreted through the lenses of partyism and party competition. Moreover, constitutional text and meaning were created to establish rules by which partisan competition would transpire. Political actors constitutionally entrenched partyism and party practices at the very time many scholars believe the Constitution was supposed to be working against political parties.

POLITICAL PARTIES AND CONSTRUCTING MAJORITY RULE

This book has shown how political actors used the Constitution to institutionalize early party practices. The nature and scope of participation in the political and policy-making process were defined by these early constitutional constructions and creations centered on partyism. I have argued that although the Constitution does not explicitly mention political parties, various constitutional provisions were interpreted or created to have the Constitution work for rather than against parties and party competition. In so doing, political parties and party competition established the political rules and norms by which majority rule would be constructed. The First Amendment, the Twelfth Amendment, the electoral college, and single-member congressional districts all created a particular dimension of majority rule and allowed for various types of majorities, unified by partisan principles and interests, to legitimately exert their will in the political process. The early partisan competition between the Federalists and the Democratic-Republicans made majority rule workable and established the grounds on which democracy in the United States was executed.

In 1964, political parties eventually became recognized in the constitutional text with the ratification of the Twenty-Fourth Amendment. The amendment prohibits the use of poll taxes in federal elections. Specifically, the language of the amendment establishes "the right of citizens of the United States to vote in any primary or other election." Unlike the Fifteenth, Nineteenth, and Twenty-Sixth Amendments, which also deal with voting rights, the Twenty-Fourth Amendment is the only one that specifically identifies primary elections.[25] Primary elections are fundamentally party elections because they constitute the nominating procedure by which partisan voters are given the opportunity to select which candidates will run for office under the party name. The vast majority of states utilize primary elections for nominating candidates and electing governmental officials. The primary system also dominates the presidential nominating process. Political parties, however, predate primary elections, as leaders and activists in the early party organizations chose the party's nominees, not the voting public. The adoption of primary elections was part of reforms aimed at making the nomination and election process more democratic. "The plan [for adopting presidential primaries]," writes James Ceaser, "was to transform the delegate selection process into what in effect would be a national party plebiscite in which the people would choose the nominee."[26] Primary elections aimed at producing majority rule from partisan voters during the nomination process, thereby ensuring that candidates were supported by popular will in general elections. Through primary elections, partyism has become a constitutionally recognized feature of the electoral landscape in the United States.

Originally, methods for nominating candidates were fundamentally private matters managed by political parties outside the realm of state intervention.[27] Because political parties were initially considered private associations, they were only minimally limited by the constitutional constraints applicable to governmental actors. In the early 1900s, as states attempted to regulate primary elections, the Supreme Court determined that political party primaries were outside the scope of federal law and the elections clause in Article I, Section 4.[28] Based on this, states and parties, especially in the South, engaged in practices that disenfranchised voters and suppressed minority participation in primaries, thereby distorting majority rule even within the partisan nomination process. As a result, the Supreme Court once again addressed whether political parties were private associations or state actors.

In four cases, known as the *White Primary Cases*, the Supreme Court concluded that primaries were subject to constitutional limitations.[29] These cases all arose in Texas, as the state legislature and the Democratic Party attempted to prohibit African Americans from participating in primaries. "White primaries" were used throughout the southern states, which were predominantly Democratic, with elections being solidly one-party competitions. Exclusion from the primary election was ultimately a form of disenfranchisement. As Nathaniel Persily explained, "The incumbent officeholders, the party functionaries in the cloak of state law, and the individuals with power equal that of official state actors to determine the content of the ballot used the primaries to disenfranchise the class of voters that the Fourteenth and Fifteenth Amendments were enacted to protect."[30] Although primaries were initially viewed as private affairs, in the *White Primary Cases*, the Supreme Court understood them as state actions, making parties and primaries subject to and constrained by the Constitution. The ruling in these cases, however, applied only to exclusion in the nominating process based on race.

The mention of primary elections in the Twenty-Fourth Amendment is all the more poignant given the previous attempts at voter disenfranchisement in primary elections. The language of the Twenty-Fourth Amendment extended beyond exclusion based on race and addressed attempts to exclude participation in primaries based on class. After Reconstruction, the southern states adopted poll taxes to prevent poor African Americans and whites from voting without violating the Fifteenth Amendment. In *Breedlove v. Suttles* (1937), the use of poll taxes survived legal scrutiny because the Supreme Court deemed that the privilege of voting was granted by the state, and the state may determine suffrage qualifications as long as it does not violate the provisions of the Fifteenth and Nineteenth Amendments. The use of poll taxes, like white primaries, had negative consequences for party competition and the legitimacy of elections because popular will could not be accurately ascertained if a large portion of voters was excluded from participating in contested elections. The Twenty-Fourth Amendment was important in the continued development of the constitutional project of popular sovereignty because it recognized the importance of assessing public will through participation in party-based primary elections as part of the electoral process.

Because the Twenty-Fourth Amendment applied only to federal elections, subsequent federal and state statutes were required to reach state and local elections. Congress responded with the 1965 Voting Rights Act, which broadly attacked electoral devices used to disenfranchise African Americans, encompassing the use of the poll tax at the state and local levels. Moreover, in *Harper v. Virginia Board of Elections* (1966), the Supreme Court determined that Virginia's poll tax violated the equal protection clause of the Fourteenth Amendment, which overturned its previous decision in *Breedlove v. Suttles*. As a result of these electoral reforms, the number of voters participating in elections swelled, particularly in the South. For example, Akhil Reed Amar explains, "in Mississippi—which had a long history of discriminatory poll-tax laws and policies—black voter registration zoomed from less than 10 percent in 1964 to nearly 60 percent within a few years."[31] As early party leaders believed, if election results were intended to reflect popular will, then the primary process by which candidates are nominated for office should be no different. The institutionalization of primaries, argues Gerald M. Pomper, "is that rare reform that accomplished its intended aim, the substitution of individualist political action for that of cohesive party majorities."[32] Just as the first parties used constitutional constructions to establish majority rule based on partisanship, through the Twenty-Fourth Amendment, the Constitution was amended to recognize the long-standing role of partyism and political parties in the execution and outcomes of the electoral process.

THE CONSTITUTION-FOR-PARTIES AND MAJORITY RULE

The way in which early parties were incorporated into American constitutionalism reveals a constitutional commitment to majority rule, even if the majority emerges as an opposition party in open, partisan competition. The constitutional constructions and creations that grounded early party practices were all made with the intent of ensuring majoritarian results during the electoral process. The early interpretation of the First Amendment established the press as a central tool of political parties in creating a majority by disseminating information and printing party-based ballots. The Twelfth Amendment ensured that the result of the presidential election reflected majority will and that the executive office would be unified around a single political party. Building on the Twelfth Amendment, the construction of Article II, Section 1, clarified the nature and purpose of the electoral college and how best to construct majorities that reflected the partisan preferences of the separate states. Similar to constructing representative majorities in presidential elections, Article I, Section 4, was constructed to ensure that partisan majorities were appropriately represented through single-member districts in the House of Representatives, creating institutional rules conducive to a two-party system. Like these early constitutional developments, the Twenty-Fourth Amendment recognized political parties in the electoral process by ensuring that primary elections were inclusive, albeit still partisan.[33] These constitutional developments ensured that majority rule was based on popular will through the design of various institutions and asking if various electoral rules create representative majorities within the federal system.

In general, these early constitutional developments require us to reconsider the paradox of political parties during the early republic. Factionalism and partisan competition had been endemic to democratic regimes, a historical observation of which the founders were well aware. Regarding partyism and the Constitution, scholarship on party development in the early republic has articulated two paradoxical claims: the Constitution-against-parties thesis and that the founders who had no use for parties relied on political parties. To overcome this paradox, scholars have articulated an argument that the founders of the first political parties did not turn to partyism as a permanent feature of American constitutionalism. Parties were temporarily useful, and a party system was to be avoided.[34] For many scholars, the institutionalization of the party system and political parties did not occur until Martin Van Buren provided the theoretical defense of party competition and President Andrew Jackson put it into practice. Importantly, for this argument, the party system connected the presidency to popular will by making it accountable to a popular party. As this book has shown, the actual foundation of popular party support and the institutionalized party system was forged during the very time these scholars posit that the Constitution was intended to work against partyism.

The evidence in this book challenges our understanding of the Constitution-against-parties thesis by detailing how political actors constructed and created constitutional meaning to ground early party practices. This book presents a broader understanding of party development by considering how these early party practices were supported by the Constitution. This broader perspective reveals how the theory of popular sovereignty and majority rule were put into political practice by means of partyism. By using the Constitution to ground these party practices, these political actors created the authoritative norms and governing institutions for party-based governmental practices that extended well beyond the era in which they were established.

Even today, the relationship between political parties and the Constitution remains complex, as the terms by which majority rule is constituted and fulfilled have changed with the expansion of suffrage and further entrenchment of partyism. For decades, legal scholars have been focused on the legal parameters within which the political process transpires. These scholars emphasize germane topics such as voting rights, campaign finance, and redistricting. More recently, political parties have received special attention as scholars recognize, with much hostility, just how influential parties, party organizations, and the two-party system are in the political process.[35]

Central to this special attention is the balance between party autonomy and associational rights with constitutional constraints applicable to state actors. Indeed, both aspects are central to party functions as party activities are often actions of both private organizations and state actors, as in primary elections. Political parties, argues Nathaniel Persily, occupy a complex "space in the American political system at the interstices of government, civil society, and individual identity."[36] Given the early constitutional commitment to majoritarian politics, and its further application in party primaries, questions involving partyism can be framed by assessing the impact that legal rules and policy, such as campaign finance, ballot access, and redistricting, will have on how majorities are constructed at the various institutional levels and in what ways these constructed majorities are representative. In this, we can determine the manner in which the constitutional promise of popular sovereignty and majority rule is achieved, even if done so through a commitment to partyism.

NOTES

INTRODUCTION. Antipartyism and the Constitution

1. For the clearest discussion of this point, see Richard Hofstadter, *The Idea of a Party System: The Rise of Legitimate Opposition in the United States, 1780–1840* (Berkeley: University of California Press, 1969), in which he influentially described the Constitution as a Constitution-against-parties. See also Gerald Leonard, *The Invention of Party Politics: Federalism, Popular Sovereignty, and Constitutional Development in Jacksonian Illinois* (Chapel Hill: University of North Carolina Press, 2002), ch. 1.

2. Sidney M. Milkis, *Political Parties and Constitutional Government: Remaking American Democracy* (Baltimore, MD: Johns Hopkins University Press, 1999), 1.

3. John H. Aldrich, *Why Parties? A Second Look* (Chicago: University of Chicago Press, 2011), 295.

4. Alexander Hamilton, John Jay, and James Madison, *The Federalist: A Commentary on the Constitution of the United States*, ed. Robert Scigliano (New York: Modern Library, 2000), 54; hereafter *The Federalist*.

5. Hofstadter, *The Idea of a Party System*.

6. "From Thomas Jefferson to Francis Hopkinson, 13 March 1789," *Founders Online*, National Archives, last modified June 29, 2017, http://founders .archives.gov/documents/Jefferson/01-14-02-0402. Original source: *The Papers of Thomas Jefferson*, vol. 14, *8 October 1788–26 March 1789*, ed. Julian P. Boyd (Princeton: Princeton University Press, 1958), 649–51.

7. George Washington "Farewell Address, 19 September 1796," in *The Papers of George Washington*, http://gwpapers.virginia.edu/documents_gw/farewell /transcript.html.

217

8. James Madison, *Selected Writings of James Madison*, ed. with introd. by Ralph Ketcham (Indianapolis, IN: Hackett, 2006), 40.

9. Ibid., 41.

10. Hofstadter, *The Idea of a Party System*, 53.

11. Federalist No. 10 contains Madison's oft-cited definition of *faction*: "By faction I understand a number of citizens, whether amounting to a majority or minority of the whole, who are united and actuated by some common impulse of passion, or of interest, adverse to the rights of other citizens, or to the permanent and aggregate interests of the community." *The Federalist*, 54.

12. Madison, *Selected Writings*, 41.

13. Aldrich, *Why Parties?*, 98.

14. For example, E. E. Schattschneider considered his work on parties his most important academic accomplishment. In *Party Government in the United States* (New York: Rinehart & Company, 1942), Schattschneider went so far as to say, "The political parties created democracy and modern democracy is unthinkable save in terms of parties" (1). Echoing Schattschneider, Clinton Rossiter, in *Parties and Politics in America* (Ithaca, NY: Cornell University Press, 1964), claimed there is "no America without democracy, no democracy without politics, and no politics without parties" (1).

15. Milkis, *Political Parties and Constitutional Government*, 2. See also Larry J. Sabato and Bruce Larson, *The Party's Just Begun: Shaping Political Parties for America's Future* (New York: Longman, 2002). In particular, chapter 1 discusses many of the ways in which parties uniquely contribute to the political process.

16. Hofstadter, *The Idea of a Party System*, 53.

17. See William Nisbet Chambers, *Political Parties in a New Nation: The American Experience, 1776–1809* (Oxford: Oxford University Press, 1963); Joseph Charles, *The Origins of the American Party System: Three Essays* (Williamsburg, VA: Institute of Early American History and Culture, 1956); Hofstadter, *The Idea of a Party System*; Scott C. James, "Patronage Regimes and American Party Development from 'The Age of Jackson' to the Progressive Era," *British Journal of Political Science* 38, no. 1 (January 2006): 39–60; Joel H. Silbey, *The Partisan Imperative: The Dynamics of American Politics before the Civil War* (Oxford: Oxford University Press, 1985); Michael F. Holt, *Political Parties and American Political Development from the Age of Jackson to the Age of Lincoln* (Baton Rouge: Louisiana State University Press, 1992) and *The Rise and Fall of the American Whig Party: Jacksonian Politics and the Onset of the Civil War* (Oxford: Oxford University Press, 1999); Scott C. James, *Presidents, Parties, and the State: A Party System Perspective on Democratic Regulatory Choice, 1884–1936* (Cambridge: Cambridge University Press, 2000); John Coleman, *Party Decline in America: Policy, Politics, and the Fiscal State* (Princeton, NJ: Princeton University

Press, 1996); John C. Green and Paul S. Herrnson, eds., *Responsible Partisanship? The Evolution of American Political Parties since 1950* (Lawrence: University Press of Kansas, 2003); Everett Carl Ladd Jr. and Charles D. Hadley, *Transformations of the American Party System* (New York: Norton, 1978); A. James Reichley, *The Life of the Parties: A History of American Political Parties* (New York: Free Press, 1992). In addition, see Karen Orren and Stephen Skowronek, *The Search for American Political Development* (New York: Cambridge University Press, 2004), for a useful definition of American political development as "a durable shift in governing authority" (123).

18. Sabato and Larson, *The Party's Just Begun.*

19. Aldrich, *Why Parties?*, 130–59.

20. Reichley, in *The Life of the Parties*, organizes the history of parties using the following eras: The Founding to the Civil War Era, the Republican Era, the New Deal Era, and the Contemporary Era.

21. V. O. Key Jr., "A Theory of Critical Elections," *Journal of Politics* 17 (1955): 3–18; and "Secular Realignment and the Party System," *Journal of Politics* 21 (May 1959): 198–210; James L. Sundquist, *Dynamics of the Party System: Alignment and Realignment of Political Parties in the United States*, 2nd ed. (Washington, DC: Brookings Institution Press, 1983); Walter Dean Burnham, *Critical Elections and the Mainsprings of American Politics* (New York: Norton, 1970); Jerome M. Clubb, William H. Flanigan, and Nancy H. Zingale, *Partisan Realignment: Voters, Parties, and Government in American History* (Thousand Oaks, CA: Sage, 1980); John Petrocik, *Party Coalitions: Realignment and the Decline of the New Deal Party System* (Chicago: University of Chicago Press, 1981). On the other hand, scholars have questioned the validity of realignment claims, pointing to such variables as divisions over policy positions or short-term variables like recessions to explain changes in partisan voting behavior. See David R. Mayhew, *Electoral Realignments: A Critique of an American Genre* (New Haven, CT: Yale University Press, 2002); Edward G. Carmines, John P. McIver, and James A. Stimson, "Unrealized Partisanship: A Theory of Delalignment," *Journal of Politics* 49 (May): 376–400; Russell J. Dalton, Scott C. Flanagan, and Paul Allen Beck, eds., *Electoral Change in Advanced Industrial Democracies: Realignment or Dealignment?* (Princeton, NJ: Princeton University Press, 1984).

22. Orren and Skowronek, *The Search for American Political Development*, 61.

23. Sidney M. Milkis, *The President and the Parties: The Transformation of the American Party System since the New Deal* (New York: Oxford University Press, 1993).

24. As Milkis explained it, "The vitality of the American Constitution has come from its alliance with democratic debate about its meaning. Critical elec-

tions have been, so to speak, surrogate constitutional conventions, in which the American people have been drawn into partisan disputes about the proper understanding of their fundamental principles and institutional arrangements." As a result, the Right "has been lost amid the petty, virulent partisanship that has racked the nation's capital during the past thirty years. In its rediscovery might come the recognition that liberty requires the art of political association no less than the demand for rights. With this recognition, we would have reason to expect a true renewal of party" (*The President and the Parties*, 186).

25. Aldrich, *Why Parties?*, 56.

26. Ralph Nader, for example, may have made an impact on the 2000 presidential election as a third party candidate. However, his influence in the 2008 election was limited. So third parties can at times be important agents in a system of "strategic interactions," but their impact is not continuous over time like that of the two major parties.

27. This macrolevel approach signals that there was no real substantive change in the competitive two-party system between the 1830s and 1960s. For example, according to the "party eras" approach, significant changes in the parties transpired between the Jacksonian era and the Civil War era as the Whig Party lost national prominence and gave way to the rise of the Republican Party. Moreover, as indicated by Aldrich, the Democratic Party was unable to maintain its sectional alliance as slavery became a national issue, and the Republican Party benefited from creating an electoral coalition between the Northeast and the Northwest. See Aldrich, *Why Parties?*, chs. 4, 5. However, while the parties changed, the system did not; it was still based on the mass political party system already established. This system did not undergo any durable changes until the 1960s with the decline of the mass party system and the development of the candidate-centered system and the rise of conditional party government.

28. Marty Cohen, David Karol, Hans Noel, and John Zaller, *The Party Decides: Presidential Nominations before and after Reform* (Chicago: University of Chicago Press, 2008). Cohen et al. expand the typical definition of a political party by including what they deem a major political actor in the development of political parties, "intense policy demanders." They define intense policy demanders by using three criteria: "They are (1) animated by a demand or a set of demands, (2) politically active on behalf of their demands, and (3) numerous enough to be influential. Formal organization is often present but not essential" (30). As such, party organization and party development are not merely a product of ambitious politicians working within a politician-centered party, as politicians now must respond to these intense activists and their demands for policy.

29. Leon D. Epstein, *Political Parties in the American Mold* (Madison: University of Wisconsin Press, 1986), 11–12.

30. Leonard, *The Invention of Party Politics*, 34.

31. Robert C. Wigton, *The Parties in Court: American Political Parties under the Constitution* (Lanham, MD: Lexington Books, 2014), 2.

32. Keith Whittington, *Constitutional Construction: Divided Powers and Constitutional Meaning* (Cambridge, MA: Harvard University Press, 1999), 5. See also Stephen M. Griffen, *American Constitutionalism* (Princeton, NJ: Princeton University Press, 1996); Bruce Ackerman, *We the People*, vol. 1 (Cambridge, MA: Harvard University Press, 1991); Barry Friedman, "Dialogue and Judicial Review," *Michigan Law Review* 91 (1993): 577; Wayne D. Moore, *Constitutional Rights and Powers of the People* (Princeton, NJ: Princeton University Press, 1988).

33. Whittington, *Constitutional Construction*, 5.

34. Akhil Reed Amar, *America's Unwritten Constitution: The Precedents and Principles We Live By* (New York: Basic Books, 2012). Amar's account primarily focuses on the Twelfth, Thirteenth, Fourteenth, Fifteenth, and Twenty-Fourth Amendments to the Constitution, which puts his developmental account mostly beyond the key development stage before the institutionalization of the two-party system.

CHAPTER ONE. Antiparty Constitutionalism
and the Tradition of Political Parties

1. Gerald M. Pomper, *Passions and Interests: Political Party Concepts of American Democracy* (Lawrence: University Press of Kansas, 1992), 132.

2. *The Federalist*, 55.

3. Giocanni Sartori, *Parties and Party Systems: A Framework for Analysis* (New York: Cambridge University Press, 1976), 26; emphasis in the original.

4. Richard Hofstadter, *The Idea of a Party System: The Rise of Legitimate Opposition in the United States, 1780–1840* (Berkeley: University of California Press, 1969).

5. Harvey C. Mansfield, *Statesmanship and Party Government: A Study of Burke and Bolingbroke* (Chicago: University of Chicago Press 1965), 1.

6. "Thomas Jefferson to John Adams, 27 June 1813," *Founders Online*, National Archives, last modified June 29, 2017, http://founders.archives.gov/documents/Jefferson/03-06-02-0206. Original source: *The Papers of Thomas Jefferson*, Retirement Series, vol. 6, *11 March to 27 November 1813*, ed. J. Jefferson Looney (Princeton, NJ: Princeton University Press, 2009), 231–35.

7. Nancy Rosenblum, *On the Side of Angels: An Appreciation of Parties and Partisanship* (Princeton, NJ: Princeton University Press, 2008), 25. Rosenblum

usefully categorizes the antiparty tradition as "holism" and "divisiveness." According to Rosenblum, "The terrain of historical antipartyism has two high points, two 'glorious traditions.'" And she uses "holism" to classify the tradition that sees "parties as unwholesome parts." Further, "all social and political groups threaten the unity and integrity of the political order" (25). Conversely, "divisiveness" refers to the tradition that "accepts social and political parts and partiality but sees parties as dangerously divisive. It is one thing to accept divisions and to institutionalize pluralism in a system of political representation. It is another thing to organize political conflict within or among acceptable parts by means of accusatory 'party'" (25).

8. Plato, *The Republic*, trans. Allen Bloom (New York: Basic Books, 1991), 30.

9. Ibid., 141.

10. Ibid., 111.

11. Ibid., 113–14.

12. Aristotle, in *Politics*, challenged Plato on this point: "Further with respect to the end which he asserts the city should have, it is, as has just been said, impossible; but how one should distinguish [a sense in which it is possible] is not discussed. I mean, that it is best for the city to be as far as possible entirely one; for this is the presupposition Socrates adopts. And yet it is evident that as it becomes increasingly one it will no longer be a city. For the city is in its nature a sort of multitude, and as it becomes more a unity it will be a household instead of a city, and a human being instead of a household; for we would surely say that the household is more a unity than the city, and the individual than the household. So even if one were able to do this, one ought not do it, as it would destroy the city. Now the city is made up not only of a number of human beings, but also of human beings differing in kind: a city does not arise from persons who are similar"; Aristotle, *Politics*, trans. Carnes Lord (Chicago: University of Chicago Press, 1984), 55–56.

13. Thomas Hobbes, *The Leviathan*, ed. with introd. and notes Edwin Curley (Indianapolis, IN: Hackett, 1994), 76.

14. Ibid., 75.

15. Ibid., 212.

16. Ibid., 78.

17. Ibid., 23.

18. Ibid., 217.

19. Ibid., 76.

20. Jean-Jacques Rousseau, *On the Social Contract*, trans. Donald A. Cress, introd. Peter Gay (Indianapolis, IN: Hackett, 1987), 17.

21. Bryan Garsten, *Saving Persuasion: A Defense of Rhetoric and Judgment* (Cambridge, MA: Harvard University Press, 2006), 58.

22. Rousseau, *On the Social Contract*, 80.

23. Ibid., 30.

24. Ibid.

25. Rosenblum, *On the Side of Angels*, 34.

26. Ibid., 110.

27. David Hume, "Of the Parties of Great Britain," in *Political Essays* (New York: Cambridge University Press, 1994), 40.

28. David Hume, *Essays, Moral, Political, and Literary* (ed. 1882), I, 110–11.

29. Craig Smith, "The Scottish Enlightenment's Reflection on Mixed Government," *Giornale di Storia Constituzionale*, no. 20/II (Semester 2010): 125.

30. Hofstadter, *The Idea of a Party System*, 27.

31. Hume, *Essays, Moral, Political, and Literary*, 110–11, 119, 127–28.

32. Quoted in Duncan Forbes, *Hume's Philosophic Politics* (New York: Cambridge University Press, 1975), 128.

33. See John Allphin Morre Jr., "James Madison, David Hume, and Modern Political Parties," in *James Madison: Philosopher, Founder, and Statesman*, ed. John R. Vile, William D. Pederson, and Frank J. Williams (Athens: Ohio University Press, 2008), 209–26; Douglas Adair, "'That Politics May Be Reduced to a Science': David Hume, James Madison and the Tenth Federalist," and "'Experience Must Be Our Only Guide': History, Democratic Theory, and the United States Constitution," in *Fame and the Founding Fathers*, ed. Trevor Colbourn (New York: Norton, 1974), 75–123; Drew McCoy, *The Last of the Fathers: James Madison and the Republican Legacy* (Cambridge: Cambridge University Press, 1989).

34. *The Federalist*, 55.

35. John H. Aldrich, *Why Parties? A Second Look* (Chicago: University of Chicago Press, 2011), 27.

36. See, e.g., Milkis, *Political Parties*, ch. 2.

37. Hofstadter, *The Idea of a Party System*, 9–16.

38. Ellen Goodman, *The Origins of the Western Legal Tradition: From Thales to the Tudors* (Annandale, NWS: Federation Press, 1995), 260.

39. John F. Hoadley, *Origins of American Political Parties, 1789–1803* (Lexington: University Press of Kentucky, 1986), 21.

40. Ibid., 21.

41. John M. Murrin, "The Great Inversion, or Court versus Country: A Comparison of the Revolution Settlements in England (1688–1721) and America (1776–1816)," in *Three British Revolutions: 1641, 1688, 1776*, ed. J. G. A. Pocock (Princeton, NJ: Princeton University Press, 1980), 368–453, 379.

42. Karl Loewenstein, *British Cabinet Government* (New York: Oxford University Press, 1967), 78–79.

43. Hoadley, *Origins of American Political Parties*, 22.

44. Loewenstein, *British Cabinet Government*, 84.

45. Peter Jupp, *The Governing of Britain, 1688–1848: The Executive, Parliament, and the People* (New York: Routledge, 2006), 64.

46. Hofstadter, *The Idea of a Party System*, 19.

47. See Mansfield, *Statesmanship and Party Government*.

48. Bernard Bailyn, *The Origins of American Politics* (New York: Vintage Books, 2011), 35.

49. Gerald Leonard, *The Invention of Party Politics: Federalism, Popular Sovereignty, and Constitutional Development in Jacksonian Illinois* (Chapel Hill: University of North Carolina Press, 2002), 22.

50. Loewenstein, *British Cabinet Government*, 90–91.

51. Ibid., 92.

52. Hoadley, *Origins of American Political Parties*, 24.

53. Hofstadter, *The Idea of a Party System*, 16–39.

54. Quoted in Hoadley, *Origins of American Political Parties*, 8–9.

55. Hofstadter, *The Idea of a Party System*, 2–3.

56. Ibid., 218.

57. See James W. Ceaser, *Presidential Selection: Theory and Development* (Princeton, NJ: Princeton University Press, 1979); Marc Landy and Sidney M. Milkis, *Presidential Greatness* (Lawrence: University Press of Kansas, 2000). Ceaser provides a useful account of Van Buren's efforts to develop a competitive party system as a precursor to Jacksonian politics, and Landy and Milkis argue that President Jackson oversaw a democratic revolution based on embracing parties and partyism.

58. Hofstadter, *The Idea of a Party System*, 219.

59. Leonard, *Invention of Party Politics*. See also Michael Wallace, "Changing Concepts of Party," *American Historical Review* 74 (1968): 453–91, 469–71; John Niven, *Martin Van Buren: The Romantic Age of American Politics* (New York: Oxford University Press, 1983), chs. 1–6; Donald Cole, *Van Buren and the American Political System* (Princeton, NJ: Princeton University Press, 1984), chs. 1–3.

60. Quoted in Hofstadter, *The Idea of a Party System*, 222.

61. George Clinton, *The Martling Man* (New York: Columbian, 1819), 5–6, 8.

62. Quoted in Ceaser, *Presidential Selection*, 124.

63. Robert Vincent Remini, *Van Buren and the Making of the Democratic Party* (New York: Columbia University Press, 1959), 24.

64. Hofstadter, *The Idea of a Party System*, 227.

65. Martin Van Buren, *Inquiry into the Origin and Course of Political Parties in the United States* (New York: Hurd and Houghton, 1867), 3–4.

66. See Harry V. Jaffa, "The Nature and Origin of the American Party System," in *Political Parties U.S.A.*, ed. Robert A. Goldwin (Chicago: Rand McNally, 1964).

67. Martin Van Buren, *The Autobiography of Martin Van Buren*, ed. John Clement Fitzpatrick (n.p.: Nabu Press, 2010), 192–93.

68. Ceaser, *Presidential Selection*, 125.

69. Van Buren, *Inquiry into the Origin*, 4–5.

70. In *Why Parties?*, Aldrich rightfully describes this shift from antiparty constitutionalism to institutionalized partisan competition in the following way: "By 1828 Van Buren saw the opportunity for a mass political party centered on principle, a revival of principles of the 'true' Jeffersonian and Madisonian sort. It was to be a new party form designed to align with the success of the experiment in increasingly mass-based democracy, and based on the idea that no person would be more important than the party. It was not to be, that is, the personality-dominated party Van Buren had observed in New York or the nation" (301).

71. Aldrich finds that competitive elections and mobilization efforts increased participation as "the Democratic Party organizational measure increased turnout . . . in those states organized in 1828" (*Why Parties?*, 125–26). Moreover, similar results were found for 1832 and 1836; turnout was higher in states with organizational measures than in those not yet organized.

72. See Ceaser, *Presidential Selection*, ch. 3, esp. 123–27.

73. According to Robert V. Remini, organizers "earnestly sought a reaffirmation of the Jeffersonian principles of states' rights as the fundamental philosophy of the Democratic Party" (*The Election of Andrew Jackson* [Philadelphia: Lippincott, 1963], 53).

Moreover, Van Buren recognized the importance of committing to Jeffersonian principle of states' rights as "it is the best and probably the only practicable mode of concentrating the entire vote of the opposition [to Adams] and of effecting what is of still greater importance, the substantial reorganization of the old Republican party." And he believed that the Democrats could "only get rid of the present, and restore a better state of things, by combining Genl. Jackson's personal popularity with the portion of old party feeling yet remaining" (Martin Van Buren's Letter to Thomas Ritchie, January 13, 1827, in *The Evolution of Political Parties, Campaigns, and Elections*, ed. Randall E. Adkins [Washington DC: CQ Press, 2008], 67).

74. Martin Van Buren's Letter to Thomas Ritchie, 68.

75. Gerald Leonard, in *The Invention of Party Politics*, likewise recognizes the way in which Van Buren broke with the antiparty tradition: "The permanent and thorough organization of a political party comprehending every democratic citizen was a great step beyond what Jefferson had contemplated" (43). Leonard provides a useful account of Van Buren's thought and how he connected democracy and popular constitutionalism with political parties.

76. Van Buren, *Inquiry into the Origin*, 5.

77. For example, Aldrich argued that the Democratic-Republicans and Federalists were "not fully" political parties; "such parties did not emerge until later, when Martin Van Buren and others invented this new form" (*Why Parties?*, 99). Likewise Milkis argued, "The emergence of open party conflict altered the Constitution, which was now joined to a doctrine of local self-government. But Jefferson and Madison were dedicated to transforming government, not necessarily to establishing a permanent, formal two-party system. Although it was party that cultivated popular support for republican principles and reforms, Jefferson and Madison appeared to hope that this task would be short term, that the flaws of the original constitutional design might prove to be temporary. Once the Federalists and their program of executive aggrandizement were defeated, they hoped, the Republican party could safely wither away, restoring the nonpartisan character of the Constitution" (*Political Parties*, 22).

78. This statement, from Tennessee congressman John Bell, a Whig, was typical of the Whigs' animosity toward political parties. Cited in Joel H. Silbey, "Election of 1836," in *History of American Presidential Elections*, 4 vols., ed. Arthur Schlesinger Jr. (New York: Chelsea House, 1971), 1:630. Silbey's account provides a relatively comprehensive account of the Whigs' opposition to political parties (585–86). See also Ceaser, *Presidential Selection*, 139.

79. The three candidates were William Henry Harrison, from the Midwest; Daniel Webster, from the East; and Hugh White, from the South.

80. Andrew Stevenson, Silas Wright, et al., "Statement by Democratic Republicans of the United States" in Schlesinger, *History of American Presidential Elections*, 1:623, 625.

81. Aldrich, *Why Parties?*, 128.

CHAPTER TWO.   Partyism prior to the Constitution

1. James Madison, *Selected Writings of James Madison*, ed. with introd. Ralph Ketcham (Indianapolis, IN: Hackett, 2006), 225.

2. Ibid., 225–26. In the essay, Madison identifies three "interesting" periods of parties in the United States: (1) the division between those who supported the cause of independence and those who did not; (2) the division between those who supported ratification of the Constitution and those who did not; and (3) the division between those who supported the concept of republican, self-government and those who do not. Madison believed the third party period was the most natural and durable among political societies.

3. Gordon S. Wood, *The Creation of the American Republic, 1776–1787* (Chapel Hill: University of North Carolina Press, 1998), 129.

4. Ibid., 130.

5. Ibid., 132.

6. "The Resolutions and Recommendations of Congress, May 10–15, 1776," Digital History, www.digitalhistory.uh.edu/disp_textbook.cfm?smtID=3&psid=3940.

7. Jackson Turner Main, *Political Parties before the Constitution* (Chapel Hill, NC: University of North Carolina Press, 1973).

8. William Nisbit Chambers, *Political Parties in a New Nation: The American Experience, 1776–1809* (New York: Oxford University Press, 1963), 21.

9. Bernard Bailyn, *The Origins of American Politics* (New York: Vintage Books, 2011), 60–61.

10. Ibid., 64.

11. Ibid., 66; Keith I. Polakoff, *Political Parties in American History* (New York: John Wiley & Sons, 1981).

12. Bailyn, *Origins of American Politics*, 67–69.

13. Main, *Political Parties before the Constitution*, 3.

14. Polakoff, *Political Parties in American History*, 5.

15. Edgar E. Robinson, *The Evolution of American Political Parties: A Sketch of Party Development* (New York: Harcourt, Brace and Company, 1924), 21.

16. Quoted in Wood, *The Creation of the American Republic*, 146.

17. Robinson, *The Evolution of American Political Parties*, 29.

18. Madison, *Selected Writings of James Madison*, 225.

19. John F. Hoadley, *Origins of American Political Parties, 1789–1803* (Lexington: University of Kentucky Press, 1986), 26; see also Roy F. Nichols, *The Invention of the American Political Parties* (New York: Macmillan, 1967).

20. Main, *Political Parties before the Constitution*, 15.

21. Polakoff, *Political Parties in American History*, 9.

22. This account relies on Main's *Political Parties before the Constitution*, which provides a comprehensive account of party development within the states prior to the Constitution by analyzing role call votes in the state legislatures.

23. Main, *Political Parties before the Constitution*, 174.

24. Robert L. Brunhouse, *The Counter-Revolution in Pennsylvania, 1776–1790* (Harrisburg: Pennsylvania Historical and Museum Commission, 1971), 15.

25. Ibid., 142.

26. Ibid., 16.

27. Ibid., 13.

28. Main, *Political Parties before the Constitution*, 183.

29. Brunhouse, *The Counter-Revolution in Pennsylvania*, 41.

30. Ibid., 18.

31. Main, *Political Parties before the Constitution*, 185.

32. Quoted in Main, *Political Parties before the Constitution*, 186.

33. Brunhouse, *Counter-Revolution in Pennsylvania*, 77–79.

34. Main, *Political Parties before the Constitution*, 189.

35. Ibid., 203.

36. Carl Lotus Becker, *The History of Political Parties in the Province of New York 1760–1776* (Madison: University of Wisconsin Press, 1960).

37. Polakoff, *Political Parties in America History*, 18.

38. Main, *Political Parties before the Constitution*, 123.

39. Ibid., 126.

40. Ibid., 127.

41. John P. Kaminski, *George Clinton: Yeoman Politician of the New Republic* (Madison, WI: Madison House Publishers, 1993), 77–79.

42. Main, *Political Parties before the Constitution*, 128–42. During the five legislative sessions following 1784, "the legislators recorded nearly two hundred votes or vote groups, 70 percent of which proved significant as indicators of party" (128).

43. Alfred F. Young, "Party Rivalry in New York," in *The First Party System: Federalists and Republicans*, ed. William N. Chambers (New York: John Wiley & Sons, 1972), 93–98.

44. See Ronald P. Formisano, *The Transformation of Political Culture: Massachusetts Parties, 1790s–1840s* (New York: Oxford University Press, 1983), 24–33.

45. Main, *Political Parties before the Constitution*, 249.

46. Norman K. Risjord and Gordon DenBoer, "The Evolution of Political Parties in Virginia, 1782–1800," *Journal of American History* 60, no. 4 (1974): 961–84, 963–64.

47. "To James Madison from Richard Henry Lee, 20 November 1784," Founders Online, National Archives, last modified June 29, 2017, http://founders .archives.gov/documents/Madison/01-08-02-0076. Original source: *The Papers of James Madison*, vol. 8, *10 March 1784–28 March 1786,* ed. Robert A. Rutland and William M. E. Rachal (Chicago: University of Chicago Press, 1973), 144–47.

48. Risjord and DenBoer, "The Evolution of Political Parties in Virginia," 965.

49. Main, *Political Parties before the Constitution*, 257.

50. Risjord and DenBoer, "The Evolution of Political Parties in Virginia," 966.

51. See "George Washington to David Stuart, Nov. 30, 1785," National Museum of American History, http://americanhistory.si.edu/documentsgallery/exhibitions /gwletter_6.html.

52. "To Thomas Jefferson from Archibald Stuart, 17 October 1785," *Founders Online,* National Archives, last modified June 29, 2017, http://founders.archives .gov/documents/Jefferson/01-08-02-0504. Original source: *The Papers of Thomas Jefferson*, vol. 8, *25 February–31 October 1785,* ed. Julian P. Boyd (Princeton, NJ: Princeton University Press, 1953), 644–47.

53. Risjord and DenBoer, "The Evolution of Political Parties in Virginia," 967.

54. Ibid., 970.

55. "To Thomas Jefferson from James Madison, 9 December 1787," *Founders Online,* National Archives, last modified June 29, 2017, http://founders.archives.gov/documents/Jefferson/01-12-02-0418. Original source: *The Papers of Thomas Jefferson,* vol. 12, *7 August 1787–31 March 1788,* ed. Julian P. Boyd (Princeton, NJ: Princeton University Press, 1955), 408–13.

56. Risjord and DenBoer, "The Evolution of Political Parties in Virginia," 971.

57. Ibid., 973.

58. Main, *Political Parties before the Constitution,* 84.

59. Ibid., 86.

60. Claire Priest, "Colonial Courts and Secured Credit: Early American Commercial Litigation and Shays' Rebellion," *Yale Law Journal* 108, no. 8 (1999): 2413–50, 2440.

61. Main, *Political Parties before the Constitution,* 88.

62. Ibid., 88.

63. Priest, "Colonial Courts and Secured Credit," 2442.

64. Main, *Political Parties before the Constitution,* 109.

65. Ibid., 118.

66. Ibid., 119.

67. Ibid., 296–97.

68. Ibid., 297.

69. Ibid., 297–98.

70. Ibid., 301.

71. Ibid., 302.

72. Keith L. Dougherty, *Collective Action under the Articles of Confederation* (New York: Cambridge University Press, 2001), 5.

73. Ibid., 30.

74. Hoadley, *Origins of American Political Parties,* 27.

75. "From Alexander Hamilton to James Duane, [3 September 1780]," *Founders Online,* National Archives, last modified June 29, 2017, http://founders.archives.gov/documents/Hamilton/01-02-02-0838. Original source: *The Papers of Alexander Hamilton,* vol. 2, *1779–1781,* ed. Harold C. Syrett (New York: Columbia University Press, 1961), 400–418.

76. "Proposed Amendment of Articles of Confederation, [12 March] 1781," *Founders Online,* National Archives, last modified June 29, 2017, http://founders.archives.gov/documents/Madison/01-03-02-0007. Original source: *The Papers of James Madison,* vol. 3, *3 March 1781–31 December 1781,* ed. William T. Hutchinson and William M. E. Rachal (Chicago: University of Chicago Press, 1963), 17–20.

77. Ibid.

78. Madison, *Selected Writings of James Madison*, 35–42.

79. See, e.g., David O. Stewart, *The Men Who Invented the Constitution* (New York: Simon & Schuster Paperbacks, 2007).

80. Hoadley, *Origins of American Political Parties*, 29.

81. Michael Allen Gillespie, "Political Parties and the American Founding," in *American Political Parties and Constitutional Politics*, ed. Peter W. Schramm and Bradford P. Wilson (Lanham, MD: Rowman & Littlefield, 1993), 17–43, 37.

82. William Nisbit Chambers, *Political Parties in a New Nation*, 29.

83. Herbert James Henderson, *Party Politics in the Continental Congress* (New York: McGraw-Hill, 1974), 420.

84. Hofstadter, *The Idea of a Party System*, 40, 8.

CHAPTER THREE. Partyism and the First Amendment

1. Richard Hofstadter, *The Idea of a Party System: The Rise of Legitimate Opposition in the United States, 1780–1840* (Berkeley: University of California Press, 1969), 107.

2. For example, as Justice Holmes argued, we would not think twice about prohibiting citizens from yelling "Fire" falsely in a crowded theater. The types of speech that approximate falsely yelling fire "has plagued first amendment theory," and the vast ways in which speech can be expressed contributes to the difficult task of formulating "principles that separate the protected from the unprotected." William B. Lockhart et al., *Constitutional Law: Cases, Comments, Questions*, 8th ed. (St. Paul, MN: West Publishing Co., 1996), 614.

3. For more on the difficulty of developing a general theory of free speech, see Larry Alexander and Paul Horton, "The Impossibility of a Free Speech Principle," 78 *Northwestern University Law Review* 1319 (1983); Daniel Farber and Phillip Frickey, "Practical Reason and the First Amendment," 34 *UCLA Law Review* 1615 (1987); Steven Shiffrin, "The First Amendment and Economic Regulation: Away from a General Theory of the First Amendment," 78 *Northwestern University Law Review* 1212 (1983); Lawrence Tribe, "Toward a Metatheory of Free Speech," *Southwestern University Law Review* 237 (1978).

4. In *Schenck v. United States* (1919) Justice Holmes develops the case-by-case principle of "clear and present danger." According to Holmes, "The question in every case is whether the words used are used in such circumstances and are of such nature as to create a clear and present danger that they will bring about the substantive evils that the United States Congress has a right to prevent. It is a question of proximity and degree. When a nation is at war, many things that might be said in times of peace are such a hindrance to its effort that their utter-

ance will not be endured so long as men fight, and that no Court could regard them as protected by any constitutional right." *Schenck v. United States* 437 (1919), quoted in Howard Gillman, Mark A. Graber, and Keith E. Whittington, *American Constitutionalism: Powers, Rights, and Liberties* (New York: Oxford University Press, 2015), 446.

5. The defendants were convicted of violating the Espionage Act of 1917 by printing and distributing fliers that questioned the constitutionality of the military draft during World War I. The defendants claimed their actions were protected by the First Amendment.

6. See Michael Gibson, "The Supreme Court and Freedom of Expression from 1791 to 1917," *Fordham Law Review* 55 (1986): 263. According to Gibson, before 1917 "the Court issued opinions in over sixty cases that today we would consider as concerning the first amendment" (255). Moreover, due to the limited number of cases, the Court was "unable to address many important areas, [and] it also never developed a first amendment specialist . . . who would ponder the intricacies of the amendment and the long-range effects of the Court's decisions" (270). Overall, the case law on freedom of expression does not pay much attention to cases prior to 1917 because the "Court's early decisions present no threat to the modern interpretation of the first amendment. Instead, the early decisions are examples of how the Constitution's guarantees of free speech and a free press should not be interpreted. They deservedly have been left dormant" (267).

7. Akhil Reed Amar, *The Bill of Rights: Creation and Reconstruction* (Harrisonburg, VA: R. R. Donnelley & Sons, 1998), 21.

8. Keith Whittington, *Constitutional Construction: Divided Powers and Constitutional Meaning* (Cambridge, MA: Harvard University Press, 1999), 13.

9. For example, James Madison argued that certain constitutional questions required that the states "themselves must be the rightful judges," as states "in their sovereign capacity can be called for by occasions only, deeply and essentially affecting the vital principles of their political system." See James Madison, *Selected Writings of James Madison*, ed. with introd. Ralph Ketcham (Indianapolis, IN: Hackett, 2006), 250–51.

10. Leonard W. Levy, *Emergence of a Free Press* (New York: Oxford University Press, 1985).

11. Jeffrey L. Pasley, *"The Tyranny of Printers": Newspaper Politics in the Early American Republic* (Charlottesville: University of Virginia Press, 2001), 350.

12. On this point, see Amar, *The Bill of Rights*. In particular, Amar argues that "although the First amendment's text is broad enough to protect the rights of unpopular minorities (like Jehovah's Witnesses and Communists), the Amendment's historical and structural core was to safeguard the rights of popular majorities (like the Republicans of the late 1790s) against a possibly unrepresentative

and self-interested Congress." Furthermore, "our First amendment's focus on Congress suggests that its primary target was attenuated representation, not overweening majoritarianism. Congress was singled out precisely because it was *less* likely to reflect majority will" (21–22).

13. John H. Aldrich, *Why Parties? A Second Look* (Chicago: University of Chicago Press, 2011). The relevance of this freedom of the press development has been understated. For example, according to Aldrich, the first parties (Federalists and Republicans) "fell far short of the true modern political party"; "these national parties were not much in the way of electoral parties . . . seeking to mobilize the public, provide voice for the new democracy, and aggregate the public interest" (94).

14. Jeffrey L. Pasley, "'The Two National Gazettes': Newspapers and the Embodiment of American Political Parties," *Early American Literature* 35, no. 1 (2000): 51–86, 52.

15. Gordon Wood, *Empire of Liberty: A History of the Early Republic, 1789–1815* (New York: Oxford University Press, 2009), 252. See also Pasley, *"The Tyranny of Printers"*; Donald H. Stewart, *The Opposition Press of the Federalist Period* (Albany: State University of New York Press, 1969); Richard D. Brown, *Knowledge Is Power: The Diffusion of Information in Early America, 1700–1865* (New York: Oxford University Press, 1989); Richard Buel Jr., *Securing the Revolution: Ideology in American Politics, 1789–1815* (Ithaca, NY: Iuniverse, 1972); Marcus Daniel, *Scandal and Civility: Journalism and the Birth of American Democracy* (New York: Oxford University Press, 2009).

16. Pasley, "'The Two National Gazettes,'" 52.

17. Pasley, *"The Tyranny of Printers."*

18. Tocqueville, *Democracy in America*, 493.

19. For example, Todd Estes found that, contrary to standard accounts of the Federalist Party, the Federalists were much more attuned to public opinion and the press during debates over the Jay Treaty. Todd Estes, "Shaping the Politics of Public Opinion: Federalists and the Jay Treaty Debate," *Journal of the Early Republic* 20, no. 3 (Autumn 2000): 393–422, 403. See also Todd Estes, *The Jay Treaty Debate, Public Opinion, and the Evolution of Early American Political Culture* (Amherst: University of Massachusetts Press, 2008). Estes argues that the Federalists have long been mischaracterized as being opposed to courting public opinion and using the press to mobilize public support. See, e.g., David Hackett Fischer, *The Revolution of American Conservatism: The Federalist Party in the Era of Jeffersonian Democracy* (New York: Harper and Row, 1965); Linda K. Kerber, *Federalists in Dissent: Imagery and Ideology in Jeffersonian America* (Ithaca, NY: Cornell University Press, 1970); James M. Banner, *To the Hartford Convention: The Federalists and the Origins of Party Politics in Massachusetts, 1789–1815* (New York: Knopf, 1970); Shaw Livermore, *The Twilight of Federalism: The Disintegration of the Federalist*

Party, 1815–1830 (Princeton, NJ: Gordian Press, 1962); and James H. Broussard, *The Southern Federalists, 1800–1816* (Baton Rouge: Louisiana State University Press, 1978). As a result, Estes argues that during the debate over the Jay Treaty, the Federalists actually established the foundation for popular politics. See also Stanley Elkins and Eric McKitrick, *The Age of Federalism: The Early American Republic* (New York: Oxford University Press, 1993); Lisle A. Rose, *Prologue to Democracy: The Federalists in the South, 1789–1800* (Lanham, MD: Lexington Books, 1968); Alfred F. Young, *The Democratic Republicans of New York: The Origins, 1763–1797* (Chapel Hill: University of North Carolina Press, 1967).

20. Hofstadter, *The Idea of a Party System*, 8–9.

21. Thomas Jefferson, *The Essential Jefferson*, ed. Jean M. Yarbrough (Indianapolis, IN: Hackett, 2006), 57.

22. See, e.g., Elkins and McKitrick, *The Age of Federalism*.

23. Geoffrey R. Stone, *Perilous Times: Free Speech in Wartime from the Sedition Act of 1798 to the War on Terrorism* (New York: W. W. Norton, 2004), 23.

24. Quoted in Stone, *Perilous Times*, 35.

25. Quoted in James D. Tagg, "Benjamin Franklin Bache's Attack on George Washington," *Pennsylvania Magazine of History and Biography* (1976): 191–230, 219.

26. "From George Washington to Benjamin Walker, 12 January 1797," *Founders Online,* National Archives, last modified June 29, 2017, http://founders.archives.gov/documents/Washington/99-01-02-00176.

27. *Porcupine's Gazette*, March 17, 1798, quoted in Stone, *Perilous Times*, 35–36.

28. "Printed Version of the 'Reynolds Pamphlet,' 1797," *Founders Online*, National Archives, last modified June 29, 2017, http://founders.archives.gov/documents/Hamilton/01-21-02-0138-0002. Original source: *The Papers of Alexander Hamilton*, vol. 21, *April 1797–July 1798*, ed. Harold C. Syrett (New York: Columbia University Press, 1974), 238–67.

29. Alexander Addison, *Liberty of speech, and the press. A charge to the grand juries of the County Courts of the fifth circuit of the State of Pennsylvania By Alexander Addison. President of those courts. Boston Office of the Columbian Centinel 1799* (Boston, 1799), PDF, Library of Congress, www.loc.gov/item/rbpe.04601100/.

30. *The Papers of George Washington*, Presidential Series, vol. 10, *1 March 1792–15 August 1792,* ed. Robert F. Haggard and Mark A. Manstromarino (Charlottesville: University of Virginia Press, 2002), 349–54.

31. Elkins and McKitrick, *The Age of Federalism*, 375–88; see also Estes, *The Jay Treaty Debate*.

32. "James Madison to James Monroe, Dec. 20, 1795," quoted in *The Republic of Letters: The Correspondence between Thomas Jefferson and James Madison 1776–1826*, vol. 2, *1790–1804*, ed. James Morton Smith (New York: Norton, 1995), 882.

33. Estes, "Shaping the Politics of Public Opinion," 398.

34. Pasley, *"The Tyranny of Printers,"* 105–7. By Pasley's account, in 1795, three quarters of all the newspapers in the country favored the Federalists or did not get involved with politics.

35. Elkins and McKitrick, *The Age of Federalism*, 549–79.

36. Ibid., 118.

37. "From Thomas Jefferson to James Madison, 26 April 1798," *Founders Online*, National Archives, last modified June 29, 2017, http://founders.archives .gov/documents/Jefferson/01-30-02-0209. Original source: *The Papers of Thomas Jefferson*, vol. 30, *1 January 1798–31 January 1799*, ed. Barbara B. Oberg (Princeton, NJ: Princeton University Press, 2003), 299–302.

38. *Abrams v. United States,* 250 U.S. 616, 630 (1919) (Holmes, O. W., dissenting).

39. *New York Times Co. v. United States*, 403 U.S. 713 (1971).

40. See Zechariah Chafee Jr., *Free Speech in the United States* (Cambridge, MA: Harvard University Press, 1941), 16, 29; Henry Schofield, "Freedom of the Press in the United States," *American Sociological Review: Papers and Proceedings* 67 (1914), reprinted in Henry Schofield, *Essays on Constitutional Law and Equity*, ed. Northwestern University Faculty of Law (Boston: Chipman Law Publishing Co., 1921); Wendell Bird, "Liberties of Press and Speech: 'Evidence Does Not Exist to Contradict the . . . Blackstonian Sense' in Late Eighteenth-Century England?," *Oxford Journal of Legal Studies* 36, no. 1 (2016): 1–25.

41. See Levy, *Emergence of a Free Press*; David Jenkins, "The Sedition Act of 1798 and the Incorporation of Seditious Libel into First Amendment Jurisprudence," *American Journal of Legal History* 45, no. 2 (2001): 154–213.

42. Levy, *Emergence of a Free Press*, 252.

43. *A Century of Lawmaking for a New Nation: U.S. Congressional Documents and Debates, 1774-1875*, Statues at Large, 5th Cong., 2nd sess., 596–97.

44. Amar, *The Bill of Rights,* 23.

45. Stephen M. Feldman, *Free Expression and Democracy in America: A History* (Chicago: University of Chicago Press, 2008), 87.

46. James Morton Smith, *Freedom's Fetters: The Alien and Sedition Laws and American Civil Liberties* (Ithaca, NY: Cornell University Press, 1956), 148.

47. Jenkins, "The Sedition Act of 1798," 160.

48. William Blackstone, "Commentaries" (1769), reprinted in Philip B. Kurland and Ralph Lerner, eds., *The Founders' Constitution* (Chicago: University of Chicago Press, 1987), 119. Emphasis in the original.

49. Levy, *Emergence of a Free Press*, 15. Levy demonstrates that this common law understanding was the dominant understanding in early American political development, more than a libertarian understanding, which sought to decriminalize opinions that undermined governmental legitimacy.

50. Jenkins, "The Sedition Act of 1798," 165.

51. Levy, *Emergence of a Free Press*, 37–40.

52. Levy interprets the Sedition Act as a "truly libertarian achievement because it represented the final triumph of the principles of the Zenger case" (*Emergence of a Free Press*, xi).

53. *Annals of Congress*, 5th Cong., 2nd sess., House of Representatives, 2094.

54. Ibid., 2096.

55. Ibid., 2098.

56. James P. Martin, "When Repression Is Democratic and Constitutional: The Federalist Theory of Representation and the Sedition Act of 1798," *University of Chicago Law Review* 66, no. 1 (1999): 117–82, 119. See also Jeremy D. Bailey, *James Madison and Constitutional Imperfection* (New York: Cambridge University Press, 2015), 56–58. Bailey demonstrated that for the Democratic-Republicans the right to instruct representatives, thereby making deliberation a more direct process, was a fundamental principle of republican government. The Federalists, conversely, ascribed to a Burkean model of representation. According to Bailey, Madison took a "middle path," between making public deliberation either a representative or a direct process.

57. *The Federalist*, 458.

58. Ibid.

59. *Annals of Congress*, 4th Cong., 1st sess., House of Representatives, 923.

60. Ibid., 2097.

61. Ibid., 2147–51.

62. Ibid., 2101–3.

63. U.S. Constitution, Article I, Section 8.

64. *Annals of Congress*, 2101.

65. "Commonwealth of Massachusetts. In Senate, February 9, 1799," in *The Virginia Report of 1799–1800, Touching the Alien and Sedition Laws; Together with the Virginia Resolutions of December 21, 1798, the Debate and Proceedings Thereon in the House of Delegates of Virginia and Several Other Documents Illustrative of the Report and Resolutions* (Richmond, 1850), 172.

66. Ibid., 175, 176.

67. Kurt T. Lash and Alicia Harrison, "Minority Report: John Marshall and the Defense of the Alien and Sedition Acts," *Ohio State Law Journal* 68, no. 2 (2007): 451.

68. Lash and Harrison, "Minority Report." Lash and Harrison argue that John Marshall is the primary author of the *Address*. According to these authors, the broad reading of national power that Marshall used in *McCulloch v. Maryland* is too similar to the broad reading of power in the *Address of the Minority* to be merely coincidental.

69. Ibid., 7.

70. *Address of the Minority*, 11.

71. Ibid.

72. Ibid., 12.

73. Ibid., 7.

74. Scholars who attribute the authorship of the *Address of the Minority* to John Marshall point to the similarity in this type of constitutional interpretation to the Supreme Court's decision in *McCulloch v. Maryland*. Chief Justice Marshall argued in *McCulloch v. Maryland*, "Even the 10th amendment, which was framed for the purpose of quieting the excessive jealousies which had been excited, omits the word 'expressly,' and declares only that the powers 'not delegated to the United States, nor prohibited to the States, are reserved to the States or to the people," and "there is no phrase in the [Constitution] which, like the articles of confederation, excludes incidental or implied powers; and which requires that every thing granted shall be expressly and minutely described." Consequently, Congress's constitutionally delegated powers should be "fairly, but liberally" interpreted and understood. *McCulloch v. Maryland*, 17 U.S. 316 (1819).

75. *Address of the Minority*, 12.

76. Ibid., 12–13.

77. Ibid., 13.

78. For a comprehensive account of this understanding of the freedom of the press clause, see Levy, *Emergence of a Free Press,* chs. 7, 8. Levy shows the prominence of this interpretation from the American Revolution to the controversy over the Sedition Act.

79. Pasley, *"The Tyranny of Printers,"* 8.

80. See Elkins and McKitrick, *The Age of Federalism*, 701. For Elkins and McKitrick, the Sedition Act was less about civil liberty and more about the "state of political practice in America," particularly party practices. They write, "Parties, in any modern sense cannot function at all under such a principle [as seditious libel]," and "the Federalists . . . in all their distracted moments, were doing something more against 'sedition'—more, even, than striking at their political opposition in the hope of suppressing it. Whether they knew it or not—perhaps nobody entirely knew it— they were striking out furiously at parties in general, in a desperate effort to turn back the clock," to what can be understood as the Constitution-against-parties.

81. Whittington, *Constitutional Construction*, 42–43. Whittington further details how Chase initiated and aided prosecutions rather than waiting for prosecuted defendants to be brought to him. See also Smith, *Freedom's Fetters*, 342–43, 355.

82. Levy, *Emergence of a Free Press*, 297.

83. Jenkins, "The Sedition Act of 1798," 180; Levy, *Emergence of a Free Press*, 297.

84. Pasley, *"The Tyranny of Printers,"* 153. According to Pasley, the Republicans' response to the Sedition Act intensified newspaper politics in many larger towns and cities. The new newspapers were intended to be partisan, as newspapers

took on a highly charged political stance by incorporating words like *Republican* and *Liberty* in their titles.

85. Ibid., 125.

86. Ibid., 131.

87. Ibid., 51–62.

88. "From Thomas Jefferson to Thomas Mann Randolph, Jr., 15 May 1791," *Founders Online,* National Archives, last modified June 29, 2017, http://founders .archives.gov/documents/Jefferson/01-20-02-0159. Original source: *The Papers of Thomas Jefferson,* vol. 20, *1 April–4 August 1791,* ed. Julian P. Boyd (Princeton, NJ: Princeton University Press, 1982), 414–16.

89. Bailey, *James Madison and Constitutional Imperfection,* 89–90.

90. Lance Banning, *The Sacred Fire of Liberty: James Madison and the Found-ing of the Federal Republic* (Ithaca, NY: Cornell University Press, 1998), 57.

91. See Levy, *Emergence of a Free Press,* 321–25.

92. See Gary Rosen, *American Compact: James Madison and the Problem of Founding* (Lawrence: University Press of Kansas, 1999). Certain scholars have in-terpreted Madison to be completely opposed to democracy: see Charles A. Beard, *An Economic Interpretation of the Constitution* (New York: Free Press, 1913); Rob-ert Dahl, *Preface to Democratic Theory* (Chicago: University of Chicago Press, 1956); and Richard Matthews, "James Madison's Political Theory: Hostage to Democratic Fortune," *Review of Politics* 67 (2005): 49–56. Other scholars have interpreted Madison to be more cautious of democracy: Garry Wills, *Explaining America: The Federalist* (Garden City, NY: Doubleday, 1981); and Garry Wills, *Inventing America: Jefferson's Declaration of Independence* (New York: Mariner Books, 2002); Drew R. McCoy, *The Last of the Fathers: James Madison and the Re-publican Legacy* (New York: Cambridge University Press, 1989).

93. See Martin Diamond, "Democracy and the Federalist: A Reconsid-eration of the Framers' Intent," *American Political Science Review* 53 (1957) 52–68; Banning, *The Sacred Fire of Liberty;* Alan Gibson, "The Madisonian Madison and the Question of Consistency: The Significance and Challenge of Recent Research," *Review of Politics* 64, no. 2 (2002): 311–38; Alan Gibson, "Veneration and Vigi-lance: James Madison and Public Opinion, 1785–1800," *Review of Politics* 67, no. 1 (2005): 5–36; Colleen A. Sheehan, "Public Opinion and the Formation of Civic Character in James Madison's Republican Theory," *Review of Politics* 67 (2005): 37–48; Colleen A. Sheehan, *James Madison and the Spirit of Republican Self Government* (New York: Cambridge University Press, 2009).

94. Both Gibson, "Veneration and Vigilance," and Sheehan, *James Madison,* acknowledge the difficulty Federalist No. 49 presents to their argument for a more democratically consistent Madison. See also Jeremy D. Bailey, "Should We Venerate That Which We Cannot Love? James Madison on Constitutional Im-perfection," *Political Research Quarterly* 65, no. 4 (2012): 732–44.

95. *The Federalist*, 290.

96. For Sheehan, Madison "applied the theory of the importance of the states in marshaling public opinion to practice in his battle to overturn the Alien and Sedition Acts." See Sheehan, *James Madison*, 133.

97. Sheehan, however, does not take the argument to its full conclusion because the Virginia Resolutions were only part of the Republicans' plan to truly fulfill Madison's call to place constitutional limits on elected officials through elections.

98. Pasley, *"The Tyranny of Printers,"* 283.

99. Madison, *Selected Writings*, 50.

100. Ibid., 209.

101. Colleen Sheehan, "Madison's Party Press Essays," *Interpretation: A Journal of Political Philosophy*, 3rd ser., 17 (1990): 355–77, 357.

102. Madison, *Selected Writings*, 208.

103. Ibid., 209.

104. Ibid., 210.

105. Ibid.

106. Ibid.

107. "From Thomas Jefferson to Edward Carrington, 16 January 1787," *Founders Online*, National Archives, last modified June 29, 2017, http://founders.archives.gov/documents/Jefferson/01-11-02-0047. Original source: *The Papers of Thomas Jefferson*, vol. 11, *1 January–6 August 1787*, ed. Julian P. Boyd (Princeton, NJ: Princeton University Press, 1955), 48–50.

108. Madison, *Selected Writings*, 227.

109. Ibid., 226.

110. Ibid., 227.

111. See Aldrich, *Why Parties?*

112. Madison, *Selected Writings*, 213.

113. Ibid., 247.

114. Ibid., 263.

115. Ibid., 249.

116. Amar, *The Bill of Rights*, xii.

117. Pasley, "'The Two National Gazettes,'" 62–63.

118. Quoted in Douglas Bradburn, *The Citizenship Revolution: Politics and the Creation of the American Union, 1774–1804* (Charlottesville: University of Virginia Press, 2009), 170.

119. Ibid., 171.

120. Banning, *The Sacred Fire of Liberty*, 348. Banning however, does not fully connect the newspapers with the emergence of partyism because, he asserts, the opposition leaders, especially Madison and Freneau (the *Gazette*'s editor), did not believe they were creating an opposition party.

121. See Bradburn, *The Citizenship Revolution*, 172.

122. Ibid., 179.

123. "To James Madison from Thomas Jefferson, 5 February 1799," *Founders Online*, National Archives, last modified June 29, 2017, http://founders.archives .gov/documents/Madison/01-17-02-0145. Original source: *The Papers of James Madison*, vol. 17, *31 March 1797–3 March 1801 and supplement 22 January 1778–9 August 1795*, ed. David B. Mattern, J. C. A. Stagg, Jeanne K. Cross, and Susan Holbrook Perdue (Charlottesville: University Press of Virginia, 1991), 225–27.

124. Andrew W. Robertson, "'Look on This Picture . . . And on This!' Nationalism, Localism, and Partisan Images of Otherness in the United States, 1787–1820," *American Historical Review* 106 4 (2001): 1263–80.

125. Tocqueville, *Democracy in America*, 494.

126. "From Thomas Jefferson to James Madison, 23 August 1799," *Founders Online*, National Archives, last modified June 29, 2017, http://founders.archives .gov/documents/Jefferson/01-31-02-0145. Original source: *The Papers of Thomas Jefferson*, vol. 31, *1 February 1799–31 May 1800*, ed. Oberg, 172–74.

127. "To James Madison from Thomas Jefferson, 30 January 1799," *Founders Online*, National Archives, last modified June 29, 2017, http://founders.archives .gov/documents/Madison/01-17-02-0143. Original source: *The Papers of James Madison*, vol. 17, *31 March 1797–3 March 1801 and supplement 22 January 1778–9 August 1795*, ed. Mattern, Stagg, Cross, and Perdue, 223–24.

128. "From Thomas Jefferson to Edmund Pendleton, 14 February 1799," *Founders Online*, National Archives, last modified June 29, 2017, http://founders .archives.gov/documents/Jefferson/01-31-02-0024. Original source: *The Papers of Thomas Jefferson*, vol. 31, *1 February 1799–31 May 1800*, ed. Oberg, 36–39.

129. See Levy, *Emergence of a Free Press*, 282–349.

130. "Thomas Jefferson to Destutt de Tracy, 26 January 1811," *Founders Online*, National Archives, last modified June 29, 2017, http://founders.archives.gov/ documents/Jefferson/03-03-02-0258. Original source: *The Papers of Thomas Jefferson*, Retirement Series, vol. 3, *12 August 1810 to 17 June 1811*, ed. J. Jefferson Looney (Princeton, NJ: Princeton University Press, 2006), 334–39.

131. *The Federalist*, 333.

132. Ibid., 172.

133. K. R. Constantine Gutzman, "The Virginia and Kentucky Resolutions Reconsidered: 'An Appeal to the Real Laws of our Country,'" *Journal of Southern History* 66, no. 3 (August 2000): 473–98, 474.

134. *Debates of the State Conventions on the Federal Constitution as Recommended by the General Convention at Philadelphia in 1787*, ed. Jonathan Elliot (Philadelphia: J. B. Lippincott, 1891), 2:247.

135. Ibid., 3:95.

136. Ibid., 107.

137. Jefferson, *The Essential Jefferson*, 48.
138. Madison, *Selected Writings*, 240.
139. Jefferson, *The Essential Jefferson*, 48, 52.
140. Madison, *Selected Writings*, 241.
141. Ibid., 248.
142. Ibid., 254.
143. Ibid.
144. Ibid., 257.
145. Ibid.
146. Levy, *Emergence of a Free Press*; Jack N. Rakove, *Original Meanings: Politics and Ideas in the Making of the Constitution* (New York: Random House, 2010).
147. See, e.g., Ethelbert D. Warfield, *The Kentucky Resolutions of 1789*, 2nd ed. (New York, 1895); Elkins and McKitrick, *The Age of Federalism*; Wood, *Empire of Liberty*; Buel, *Securing the Revolution*; John C. Miller, *Crisis in Freedom: The Alien and Sedition Acts* (Boston, MA: Atlantic–Little, Brown, 1952); Noble E. Cunningham Jr., *The Jeffersonian Republicans: The Formation of Party Organization, 1789–1801* (Chapel Hill: University of North Carolina Press, 1957); Stewart, *The Opposition Press of the Federalist Period*; Richard Labunski, *James Madison and the Struggle for the Bill of Rights* (New York: Oxford University Press, 2006).
148. Wendell Bird, "Reassessing Responses to the Virginia and Kentucky Resolutions: New Evidence from the Tennessee and Georgia Resolutions and from Other States," *Journal of the Early Republic* 35 (Winter 2015): 519–51, 548.
149. Ibid., 550.
150. Jefferson, *The Essential Jefferson*, 55–56.
151. Levy, *Emergence of a Free Press*, 309–49.
152. Pasley, *"The Tyranny of Printers,"* 350.
153. Tocqueville, *Democracy in America*, 493–95.
154. Pasley, *"The Tyranny of Printers,"* 348–99.

CHAPTER FOUR. Partyism and the Presidential Selection System

1. Jeffrey L. Pasley, *The First Presidential Contest: 1796 and the Founding of American Democracy* (Lawrence: University Press of Kansas, 2013), 309.
2. *The Federalist*, 435.
3. Richard Hofstadter, *The Idea of a Party System: The Rise of Legitimate Opposition in the United States, 1780–1840* (Berkeley: University of California Press, 1969); Bruce Ackerman, *The Failure of the Founding Fathers: Jefferson, Marshall, and the Rise of Presidential Democracy* (Cambridge, MA: Belknap Press of Harvard University Press, 2005); Susan Dunn, *Jefferson's Second Revolution: The Elec-*

tion Crisis of 1800 and the Triumph of Republicanism (Boston, MA: Houghton Mifflin, 2004); Akhil Reed Amar, *America's Constitution: A Biography* (New York: Random House, 2005); Garry Wills, *Negro President: Thomas Jefferson and the Slave Power* (Boston, MA: Houghton Mifflin, 2003); David P. Currie, *The Constitution in Congress: The Jeffersonians 1801–1829* (Chicago: University of Chicago Press, 2001).

4. For example, Susan Dunn, using Jefferson's first inaugural, argued that he viewed his electoral victory as creating "an invincible coalition" that would "ultimately absorb all Americans" by "equating his Republican majority with the entire nation," defining "for all . . . the 'common good'" (Dunn, *Jefferson's Second Revolution*, 223); see also Hofstadter, *The Idea of a Party System*. After his election, Jefferson becomes the centerpiece of Hofstadter's argument that, despite an opposition party successfully winning the presidential election, the idea of a legitimate opposition did not replace the conviction of a "constitution-against-parties." According to Hofstadter, "Such . . . was Jefferson's view of the Federalists: a small faction creeping into the heart of the government under the mantle of Washington and the perverse guidance of Hamilton, addicted to false principles in politics, animated by a foreign loyalty, and given to conspiratorial schemes aiming at the consolidation of government and the return of monarchy." And Jefferson was "sustained" by his optimism that "before long the people through their faithful representatives would take over. And at that point it would be the duty of the Republican party to annihilate the opposition—not by harsh and repressive measures like the Sedition Act, but by the more gentle means of conciliation and absorption that were available to a principled majority party" (*The Idea of a Party*, 127). Leonard Levy pushed this argument to the extreme by emphasizing that President Jefferson's commitment to civil rights, particularly the broad understanding of the First Amendment that protected presses from seditious libel, was not absolute. In other words, Jefferson was not completely opposed to using seditious libel to ensure conciliation and, as Hofstadter phrased it, "annihilation" of an opposition. See Leonard Levy, *Legacy of Suppression: Freedom of Speech and Press in Early American History* (Cambridge, MA: Belknap Press of Harvard University, 1960). On Levy's point, Jefferson's suspect attachment to the First Amendment led him to accept state prosecutions of seditious libel by state officials because the scope of the Bill of Rights had yet to be extended to the states through incorporation. However, Jefferson did not believe, under the First Amendment, that the national government had power to punish seditious libel.

5. James W. Ceaser, *Presidential Selection: Theory and Development* (Princeton, NJ: Princeton University Press, 1979), 88.

6. Ibid., 105–6.

7. *The Federalist*, No. 68, 435.

8. Wadsworth to Hamilton, February, 1789, in *The Works of Alexander Hamilton*, ed. John C. Hamilton (New York, 1850–51).

9. Amar, *America's Constitution*, 337.

10. *The Federalist*, No. 68, 436.

11. Pasley, *The First Presidential Contest*, 308.

12. For example, in *The Idea of a Party System*, Hofstadter argues, "The modern idea of the political party, and with it a fully matured conception of the function of legitimate opposition, flowered first among the second generation of American political leaders—that is, among men who were in the main still children when the Federalists and Republican parties were founded" (212). Subsequently, to explain the acceptance of partyism and a party system, Hofstadter looks to the "Albany Regency as archetypes of the new advocates of party" and focuses on "their leader Martin Van Buren, an intelligent and seasoned exponent of the merging partisan creed, and the first representative of the new generation and mentality to become president" (213). See also Ceaser, *Presidential Selection*.

13. For example, in 1800 Senator James Ross proposed a bill to allow congressional regulation of the electoral count. The bill organized a grand committee composed of six senators and six representatives along with the Chief Justice of the Supreme Court. The committee would have authority to examine "disputed elections of President and Vice President of the United States, and for determining the legality or illegality of the votes given for those officers in the different states." Given the Federalist advantage in both the House and the Senate and a Federalist Chief Justice, the party would maintain a significant advantage in reviewing the electoral college vote and could easily discredit votes for rival Republicans.

14. "Madison's Conversations with Washington, 5–25 May 1792," *Founders Online*, National Archives, last modified June 13, 2018, http://founders.archives.gov/documents/Washington/05-10-02-0222. Original source: *The Papers of George Washington*, Presidential Series, vol. 10, *1 March 1792–15 August 1792*, ed. Robert F. Haggard and Mark A. Mastromarino (Charlottesville: University of Virginia Press, 2002), 349–54.

15. Pasley, *The First Presidential Contest*, 348–406.

16. Jefferson to Edward Rutledge, December 27, 1796, in *The Papers of Thomas Jefferson*, ed. Julian P. Boyd, Charles T. Cullen, John Catanzariti, and Barbara B. Oberg et al., vol. 29 (Princeton, NJ: Princeton University Press, 2002), 232.

17. Ibid.

18. Alexander Hamilton to Rufus King, February 15, 1797, in *The Life and Correspondence of Rufus King: Comprising His Letters, Private and Official, His Public Documents, and His Speeches*, vol. 5 (New York: G. P. Putnam's Sons, 1898).

19. *The Federalist*, No. 70, 447–48.

20. Ibid., 448.

21. Ibid.

22. Ibid., 449.

23. Tadahisa Kuroda, *The Origins of the Twelfth Amendment: The Electoral College in the Early Republic, 1787–1804* (Westport, CT: Greenwood Press, 1994), 99.

24. Kuroda pointed to the difficulty of delegations voting together, especially split delegations: "Whether Republican congressional delegates would vote consistently with their electors remained uncertain, for states generally chose representatives and electors in very different ways and for different purposes. How Federalist delegations, whose state electors had voted for Adams and Pinckney, would act became the central question" (*The Origins of the Twelfth Amendment*, 100).

25. Jeremy D. Bailey, *Thomas Jefferson and Executive Power* (New York: Cambridge University Press, 2007), 199.

26. "From Alexander Hamilton to Gouverneur Morris, 4 March 1802," *Founders Online*, National Archives, last modified June 29, 2017, http://founders .archives.gov/documents/Hamilton/01-25-02-0300. Original source: *The Papers of Alexander Hamilton*, vol. 25, *July 1800–April 1802*, ed. Harold C. Syrett (New York: Columbia University Press, 1977), 558–60.

27. Kuroda, *The Origins of the Twelfth Amendment*, 119.

28. "To Thomas Jefferson from Albert Gallatin, 14 September 1801," *Founders Online*, National Archives, last modified June 29, 2017, http://founders.archives .gov/documents/Jefferson/01-35-02-0222. Original source: *The Papers of Thomas Jefferson*, vol. 35, *1 August–30 November 1801*, ed. Barbara B. Oberg (Princeton, NJ: Princeton University Press, 2008), 284–89.

29. "From Thomas Jefferson to Albert Gallatin, 18 September 1801," *Founders Online*, National Archives, last modified June 29, 2017, http://founders.archives .gov/documents/Jefferson/01-35-02-0245. Original source: *The Papers of Thomas Jefferson*, vol. 35, *1 August–30 November 1801*, 314–15.

30. *Annals of Congress*, 8th Cong., 1st sess., Senate, 19–20.

31. Ibid., 129.

32. *The Federalist*, No. 68, 518.

33. See Wills, *Negro President*.

34. Bailey, *Thomas Jefferson and Executive Power*, 197.

35. See, specifically, Bailey, *Thomas Jefferson and Executive Power*, in which he argues that the original constitutional mode of presidential selection undermined a president's ability to be an expression of the public will and unify public sentiment.

36. See, e.g., Ceaser, *Presidential Selection*; Ackerman, *The Failure of the Founding Fathers*; Amar, *America's Constitution*; Wills, *Negro President*; Currie, *The Constitution in Congress*.

37. See Bailey, *Thomas Jefferson and Executive Power*; Kuroda, *The Origins of the Twelfth Amendment*.

38. Dawson's original proposition reads: "That in all future elections of President and Vice President, the person voted for shall be particularly designated, by declaring which is voted for as President, and which as Vice President." *Annals of Congress*, 8th Cong., 1st sess., House of Representatives, 373.

39. Ibid., 376.

40. Ibid., 377.

41. Bailey explained why the approved House amendment maintained the number of candidates in the contingency election at five: "Either loyalty to House prerogatives or fidelity to their own small states was enough to keep some Republicans from conferring a brighter majority halo on future presidents" (*Thomas Jefferson and Executive Power*, 205). The Senate did not retain the number 5, and the House would later approve the change to the current language, no more than 3.

42. *Annals of Congress*, 8th Cong., 1st sess., House of Representatives, 535–43.

43. Ibid., 536.

44. Ibid., 536–38. Modern scholars have drawn attention to the importance of the three-fifths clause in Jefferson's victory over Adams. See Amar, *America's Constitution*; Wills, *Negro President*.

45. *Annals of Congress*, 8th Cong., 1st sess., Senate, 19–20.

46. Ibid., 17.

47. Ibid., 19.

48. Ibid., 21–22.

49. Ibid., 25. See also Kuroda, *The Origins of the Twelfth Amendment*, 135.

50. *Annals of Congress*, 8th Cong., 1st sess., Senate, 26. On November 4, Clinton formally resigned from the Senate to assume his new position as mayor of New York City.

51. Kuroda, *The Origins of the Twelfth Amendment*, 135; Bailey, *Thomas Jefferson and Executive Power*, 207.

52. *Annals of Congress*, 8th Cong., 1st sess., Senate, 98–100.

53. Ibid., 87–88.

54. Ibid., 87.

55. Ibid., 98.

56. See Ceaser, *Presidential Selection*, 95–96. Here Ceaser recognizes the legal standing of political parties: "In the future, elected officials might attempt to discourage parties by policy or through expressions of disapproval, but they could not suppress them by legal means" (96). However, Ceaser then chooses to underemphasize this point in favor of the unintentional thesis: "If parties began to disintegrate, the Twelfth Amendment had thus inadvertently provided a powerful new justification for recreating them" (106). My argument is that the "justification for recreating them" was not as inadvertent as Ceaser's account assumes.

57. *Annals of Congress*, 8th Cong., 1st sess., Senate, 141.

58. Ibid., 192.

59. Ibid., 89–90.

60. Ibid., 98.

61. Ibid., 99.

62. Ibid., 181.

63. Ibid., 130.

64. See V. O. Key Jr., "A Theory of Critical Elections," *Journal of Politics* 17, no. 1 (1955): 3–18; Philip E. Converse, Angus Campbell, Warren E. Miller, and Donald E. Stokes, "Stability and Change in 1960: A Reinstating Election," *American Political Science Review*, 55 no. 2 (1961): 269–80; Burnham, *Critical Elections*; Sundquist, *Dynamics of the Party System*; Edward G. Carmines and James A. Stimson, *Issue Evolution: Race and the Transformation of American Politics* (Princeton, NJ: Princeton University Press, 1989); Steven Skowronek, *The Politics Presidents Make: Leadership from John Adams to Bill Clinton* (Cambridge, MA: Harvard University Press, 1993); and Alan I. Abramowitz and Kyle L. Saunders, "Ideological Realignment in the US Electorate," *Journal of Politics* 60, no. 3 (1998): 634–52. This literature tends to understand political development as different political eras bounded by critical realignments or punctuated changes in which one party is favored over another, with change coming through the creation of a new ruling majority.

65. See Bailey, *Thomas Jefferson and Executive Power*, 211; Kuroda, *Origins of the Twelfth Amendment*, 146–51.

66. "Thomas Jefferson to Thomas McKean, 17 January, 1804," Manuscript/ Mixed Material, retrieved from Library of Congress, www.loc.gov/item/mtjbib 013099/.

67. Kuroda, *The Origins of the Twelfth Amendment*, 155.

68. Eventually all but Delaware, Connecticut, and Massachusetts, strongholds of the Federalist Party in New England, ratified the proposed Twelfth Amendment. Massachusetts eventually ratified the amendment in 1961.

69. "Thomas Jefferson to Thomas McKean, 17 January, 1804."

70. For a useful account of the ratification process, see Kuroda, *The Origins of the Twelfth Amendment*, ch. 15.

71. Kuroda, *The Origins of the Twelfth Amendment*, 161. See also Joshua D. Hawley, "The Transformative Twelfth Amendment," *William and Mary Law Review* 55 (2013): 1501–86.

72. See Bailey, *Thomas Jefferson and Executive Power*, in which Bailey uses the amendment as evidence against Robert Dahl's contention that the presidential mandate was a myth because there were no empirical tools or measurements by which early presidents were able to know if voters had selected them based on specific policies. Moreover, Dahl argues that the presidential mandate

is "pseudo-democratic" or even imperialistic in that the belief in representing the people undermines other representative bodies, such as Congress, thereby undermining the Constitution's original executive design. Robert A. Dahl, "Myth of the Presidential Mandate," *Political Science Quarterly* 105, no. 3 (Autumn 1990): 355–72.

73. See Skowronek, *The Politics Presidents Make*, for his typology of presidential leadership and leadership categories; two of his four categories (the politics of disjunction and the politics of preemption) are predicated on the existence of an opposition. Moreover, his concept "political time" could not exist without the prospect of an opposition party winning political office. His account, however, does not satisfactorily detail how opposition gained legitimacy in "secular time," especially considering the standard view of opposition in the early republic.

CHAPTER FIVE.   Partyism and Organized Opposition in Elections

1. See Jeremy D. Bailey, *Thomas Jefferson and Executive Power* (New York: Cambridge University Press, 2007). Bailey's account of the election of 1800 and the Twelfth Amendment focuses on the Twelfth Amendment and the politics of presidential character, particularly President Jefferson's. As such, Bailey does not fully connect the ratification of the Twelfth Amendment to the rise of partyism.

2. A. James Reichley, *The Life of the Parties: A History of American Political Parties* (New York: Rowman & Littlefield, 1992), 46.

3. Stanley Elkins and Eric McKitrick, *The Age of Federalism: The Early American Republic, 1788–1800* (New York: Oxford University Press, 1995), 692–93. While recognizing that the Federalists had become a "party," Elkins and McKitrick argue that Federalists believed adaptation to the Democratic-Republicans' party practices was ultimately unthinkable: "The Federalists of 1800 were all but paralyzed in their incapacity to think or act in a truly political way, in any sense that 'political' would come more and more to be understood in the America of the nineteenth century." And "they could not function in a world that accepted, even on sufferance, the existence of parties, nor imagine a time when the idea of 'party' might take on a morality of its own" (693). Subsequently, Elkins and McKitrick miss the efforts, particularly Hamilton's, to create a more unified, competitive party and act in the accepted "political" way of the time.

4. See Elkins and McKitrick, *The Age of Federalism*; Sean Wilentz, *The Rise of American Democracy: Jefferson to Lincoln* (New York: Norton, 2005).

5. Jeffrey L. Pasley, *The First Presidential Contest: 1796 and the Founding of American Democracy* (Lawrence: University Press of Kansas, 2013), 350.

6. Ibid., 351.

7. Wilentz, *The Rise of American Democracy*, 74.

8. Elkins and McKitrick, *The Age of Federalism*, 520.

9. Wilentz, *The Rise of American Democracy*, 74.

10. Wilentz points out that the Democratic-Republicans' efforts were most "staggering" in Philadelphia. According to Wilentz, "More than two in five eligible Philadelphians showed up at the polls and handed the [Democratic-Republican] slate more than 60 percent of the vote—a landslide in what [had] been a solidly Federalist city" (*The Rise of American Democracy*, 74).

11. James Nicholson Statement, December 26, 1803, in Noble E. Cunningham Jr., *The Jeffersonian Republicans: The Formation of Party Organization, 1789–1801* (Chapel Hill: University of North Carolina Press, 1957), quoted on 149.

12. Wilentz, *The Rise of American Democracy*, 85.

13. Ibid., 85.

14. Thomas Jefferson to James Madison, March 4, 1800, in *The Works of Thomas Jefferson*, ed. Paul L. Ford, vol. 9 (New York: Cosimo, Inc., 2009), 123. Emphasis in the original.

15. Wilentz, *The Rise of American Democracy*, 86.

16. Ibid., 87.

17. "James Nicholson to Albert Gallatin, 6 May, 1800," in Henry Adams, *The Life of Albert Gallatin* (Philadelphia, PA: J. B. Lippincott & Co., 1879), 241.

18. "Conversation with Thomas Jefferson, [13 August 1791]," *Founders Online*, National Archives, last modified June 13, 2018, http://founders.archives .gov/documents/Hamilton/01-09-02-0034. Original source: *The Papers of Alexander Hamilton*, vol. 9, *August 1791–December 1791*, ed. Harold C. Syrett (New York: Columbia University Press, 1965), 33–34.

19. See David N. Mayer, *The Constitutional Thought of Thomas Jefferson* (Charlottesville: University of Virginia Press, 1994), 109–10.

20. "Notes of a Conversation with George Washington, 10 July 1792," *Founders Online*, National Archives, last modified June 29, 2017, http://founders .archives.gov/documents/Jefferson/01-24-02-0191. Original source: *The Papers of Thomas Jefferson*, vol. 24, *1 June–31 December 1792*, ed. John Catanzariti (Princeton, NJ: Princeton University Press, 1990), 210–12.

21. Elkins and McKitrick, *The Age of Federalism*.

22. Thomas Jefferson, "First Inaugural Address," in *The Essential Jefferson* ed. Jean M. Yarbrough (Indianapolis, IN: Hackett, 2006), 57. See also Bailey, *Thomas Jefferson and Executive Power*, esp. ch. 5, in which Bailey argues that Jefferson used his first inaugural address as a means linking the presidency with public opinion. Jefferson would declare the guiding principles for his administration so the public would be able to hold him and his party accountable in subsequent elections. By linking Jefferson's view of the inaugural address with his view of the Bill of Rights, Bailey rightly argues that "just as Americans in 1789 needed a text

of liberties by which they could test the powers of the national government, Americans in 1800 needed the president to state principles by which they could test his extraordinary and expansive acts of nation-building" (149).

23. Jefferson, *The Essential Jefferson*, 57–58.

24. Ibid.

25. Ibid.

26. See Stephen G. Kurtz, *The Presidency of John Adams: The Collapse of Federalism, 1795–1800* (Philadelphia: University of Pennsylvania Press, 1957).

27. Quoted in Ron Chernow, *Alexander Hamilton* (New York: Penguin Books, 2005), 557.

28. "From Alexander Hamilton to Rufus King, 5 January 1800," *Founders Online*, National Archives, last modified June 29, 2017, http://founders.archives.gov/documents/Hamilton/01-24-02-0127. Original source: *The Papers of Alexander Hamilton*, vol. 24, 167–71.

29. *Pennsylvania Gazette*, January 8, 1800, in *Legacies of Washington: Being a Collection of the Most Approved Writings of the Late General Washington with an Appendix Containing a Sketch of the Life of this Illustrious Patriot* (Trenton, NJ: Sherman, Mershon & Thomas, 1800), 256.

30. "From Alexander Hamilton to Rufus King, [4 May 1796]," *Founders Online*, National Archives, last modified June 29, 2017, http://founders.archives.gov/documents/Hamilton/01-20-02-0095. Original source: *The Papers of Alexander Hamilton*, vol. 20, *January 1796–March 1797*, ed. Harold C. Syrett (New York: Columbia University Press, 1974), 158–59.

31. "From Alexander Hamilton to Jeremiah Wadsworth, [1 December 1796]," *Founders Online*, National Archives, last modified June 29, 2017, http://founders.archives.gov/documents/Hamilton/01-20-02-0274. Original source: *The Papers of Alexander Hamilton*, vol. 20, 418–19.

32. "John Adams to Abigail Adams, 9 January 1797," *Founders Online*, National Archives, last modified June 29, 2017, http://founders.archives.gov/documents/Adams/04-11-02-0251. Original source: *The Adams Papers*, Adams Family Correspondence, vol. 11, *July 1795–February 1797*, ed. Margaret A. Hogan, C. James Taylor, Sara Martin, Neal E. Millikan, Hobson Woodward, Sara B. Sikes, and Gregg L. Lint (Cambridge, MA: Harvard University Press, 2013), 486–87.

33. E.g., "From Alexander Hamilton to Timothy Pickering, [22 March 1797]," *Founders Online*, National Archives, last modified June 29, 2017, http://founders.archives.gov/documents/Hamilton/01-20-02-0351, original source: *The Papers of Alexander Hamilton*, vol. 20, 545–47; "From Alexander Hamilton to Oliver Wolcott, Junior, [5 June 1798]," *Founders Online*, National Archives, last modified June 29, 2017, http://founders.archives.gov/documents/Hamilton/01-21-02-0270-0001, original source: *The Papers of Alexander Hamilton*, vol. 21, *April*

1797–July 1798, ed. Harold C. Syrett (New York: Columbia University Press, 1974), 485–86.

34. "To Alexander Hamilton from Timothy Pickering, 15 May 1800," *Founders Online,* National Archives, last modified June 29, 2017, http://founders .archives.gov/documents/Hamilton/01-24-02-0402. Original source: *The Papers of Alexander Hamilton*, vol. 24, 490–91.

35. "To Alexander Hamilton from John Rutledge, Junior, 17 July 1800," *Founders Online,* National Archives, last modified June 29, 2017, http://founders .archives.gov/documents/Hamilton/01-25-02-0027-0001. Original source: *The Papers of Alexander Hamilton*, vol. 25, *July 1800–April 1802*, ed. Harold C. Syrett (New York: Columbia University Press, 1977), 30–36.

36. "From Alexander Hamilton to Rufus King, 5 January 1800," *Founders Online,* National Archives, last modified June 29, 2017, http://founders.archives .gov/documents/Hamilton/01-24-02-0127. Original source: *The Papers of Alexander Hamilton*, vol. 24, 167–71.

37. "From Alexander Hamilton to Theodore Sedgwick, 10 May 1800," *Founders Online,* National Archives, last modified June 29, 2017, http://founders .archives.gov/documents/Hamilton/01-24-02-0387; "From Alexander Hamilton to Theodore Sedgwick, [4 May 1800]," *Founders Online,* National Archives, last modified June 29, 2017, http://founders.archives.gov/documents/Hamilton /01-24-02-0365-0002. Original source: *The Papers of Alexander Hamilton*, vol. 24, 474–75 and 444–53, respectively.

38. "From Alexander Hamilton to Oliver Wolcott, Junior, 1 July 1800," *Founders Online,* National Archives, last modified June 29, 2017, http://founders .archives.gov/documents/Hamilton/01-25-02-0004. Original source: *The Papers of Alexander Hamilton*, vol. 25, 4–5.

39. "From Alexander Hamilton to Theodore Sedgwick, 10 May 1800," *Founders Online,* National Archives, last modified June 29, 2017, http://founders .archives.gov/documents/Hamilton/01-24-02-0387. Original source: *The Papers of Alexander Hamilton*, vol. 24, 474–75.

40. Ibid.

41. "From Alexander Hamilton to Oliver Wolcott, Junior, 3 August 1800," *Founders Online,* National Archives, last modified June 29, 2017, http://founders .archives.gov/documents/Hamilton/01-25-02-0039. Original source: *The Papers of Alexander Hamilton*, vol. 25, 54–56.

42. *Letter from Alexander Hamilton, Concerning the Public Conduct and Character of John Adams, Esq. President of the United States, [24 October 1800], Founders Online,* National Archives, last modified June 29, 2017, http://founders.archives .gov/documents/Hamilton/01-25-02-0110-0002. Original source: *The Papers of Alexander Hamilton*, vol. 25, 186–234.

43. Ibid.

44. "To Alexander Hamilton from James A. Bayard, 18 August 1800," *Founders Online*, National Archives, last modified June 29, 2017, http://founders .archives.gov/documents/Hamilton/01-25-02-0051. Original source: *The Papers of Alexander Hamilton*, vol. 25, 68–71.

45. Ibid.

46. "To Alexander Hamilton from Fisher Ames, 26 August 1800," *Founders Online*, National Archives, last modified June 29, 2017, http://founders.archives .gov/documents/Hamilton/01-25-02-0067. Original source: *The Papers of Alexander Hamilton*, vol. 25, 86–88.

47. *Letter from Alexander Hamilton.* See also Susan Dunn, *Jefferson's Second Revolution: The Election Crisis of 1800 and the Triumph of Republicanism* (Boston, MA: Houghton Mifflin, 2004), ch. 8. Dunn connects Hamilton's pamphlet with the Alien and Sedition Acts to demonstrate how the policy was applied only to the Democratic-Republicans. Hamilton was not accused of sedition even though the content of his pamphlet mirrored the Democratic-Republicans' printed opinion of Adams for which they were held accountable.

48. "To Alexander Hamilton from George Cabot, 29 November 1800," *Founders Online*, National Archives, last modified June 29, 2017, http://founders .archives.gov/documents/Hamilton/01-25-02-0122. Original source: *The Papers of Alexander Hamilton*, vol. 25, 247–50.

49. "Introductory Note: *Letter from Alexander Hamilton, Concerning the Public Conduct and Character of John Adams, Esq. President of the United States, [24 October 1800]*," *Founders Online*, National Archives, last modified June 13, 2018, http://founders.archives.gov/documents/Hamilton/01-25-02-0110-0001. Original source: *The Papers of Alexander Hamilton*, vol. 25, 169–85.

50. "To Thomas Jefferson from James Madison, 10 January 1801," *Founders Online*, National Archives, last modified June 29, 2017, http://founders.archives .gov/documents/Jefferson/01-32-02-0311. Original source: *The Papers of Thomas Jefferson*, vol. 32, *1 June 1800–16 February 1801*, ed. Barbara B. Oberg (Princeton, NJ: Princeton University Press, 2005), 436–39.

51. Quoted in "Introductory Note: *Letter from Alexander Hamilton, Concerning the Public Conduct and Character of John Adams, Esq. President of the United States, [24 October 1800]*."

52. Quoted in Dunn, *Jefferson's Second Revolution*, 229.

53. "To Alexander Hamilton from James A. Bayard, 12 April 1802," *Founders Online*, National Archives, last modified June 29, 2017, http://founders .archives.gov/documents/Hamilton/01-25-02-0318. Original source: *The Papers of Alexander Hamilton*, vol. 25, 600–601.

54. "From Alexander Hamilton to James A. Bayard, [16–21] April 1802," *Founders Online*, National Archives, last modified June 29, 2017, http://founders

.archives.gov/documents/Hamilton/01-25-02-0321. Original source: *The Papers of Alexander Hamilton*, vol. 25, 605–10. See also Todd Estes, "Shaping the Politics of Public Opinion: Federalists and the Jay Treaty Debate," *Journal of the Early Republic* 20, no. 3 (Autumn 2000): 393–422; Todd Estes, *The Jay Treaty Debate, Public Opinion, and the Evolution of Early American Political Culture* (Amherst: University of Massachusetts Press, 2008). Estes argues that the Federalists' tactics in winning the political battle over the Jay Treaty would eventually place them at odds with the public, as they would fail to court public opinion during elections.

55. "Fisher Ames to Theodore Dwight, 19 March 1801" in *Works of Fisher Ames with a Selection from His Speeches and Correspondence*, ed. Seth Ames (Boston: Little, Brown, 1854), 1:293–94.

56. Jared Sparks, *The Life of Gouverneur Morris: With Selections from His Correspondence and Miscellaneous Papers* (Boston, MA: Gray & Bowen, 1832), 128.

57. See the American Political Science Association's document on responsible parties: Committee on Political Parties, *Towards a More Responsible Two-Party System* (New York: Rinehart, 1950).

58. "From Alexander Hamilton to James A. Bayard, [16–21] April 1802."

59. Marjorie Randon Hershey, *Party Politics in America* (Indianapolis, IN: Pearson Education, 2011), 6–8. See also V. O. Key Jr., *Politics, Parties, and Pressure Groups* (New York: Crowell, 1958), 180–82.

60. "From Alexander Hamilton to James A. Bayard, [16–21] April 1802." Party scholars have largely overlooked Hamilton's proposed Christian Constitutional Society. Scholarship on the society tends to focus on the "Christian" aspect and whether or not Hamilton was actually promoting Christian politics or merely using religion as propaganda. Two articles asking competing questions best summarize this scholarship: Douglas Adair and Marvin Harvey, "Was Alexander Hamilton a Christian Statesman?," *William and Mary Quarterly*, 3rd ser., 12, no. 2 (April 1955): 308–29; Karl Walling, "Was Alexander Hamilton a Machiavellian Statesman?," *Review of Politics* 57, no. 3 (Summer 1995): 419–47. These accounts largely miss the specific organization of the society at the local, state, and national levels to strengthen the Federalist Party's electoral base.

61. See Richard Hofstadter, *The Idea of a Party System: The Rise of Legitimate Opposition in the United States, 1780–1840* (Berkeley: University of California Press, 1969). Hofstadter argued that for an opposition to be legitimate, it must (1) be constitutional, in that "both government and opposition are bound by the rules of some kind of constitutional consensus"; (2) be responsible, in that the opposition "contains within itself the potential of an actual alternative government[,] . . . a sober attempt to formulate alternative policies which it believes to be capable of execution"; and (3) be effective, in that the opposition is capable of "winning office" and executing its alternative policies (4–5). Hofstadter argues that this conception of a legitimate opposition was outside the realm of possibility for the founders.

62. "To Alexander Hamilton from James A. Bayard, 25 April 1802," *Founders Online*, National Archives, last modified June 29, 2017, http://founders.archives.gov/documents/Hamilton/01-25-02-0323. Original source: *The Papers of Alexander Hamilton*, vol. 25, 613–14.

63. Ibid.

64. Alexis de Tocqueville, *Democracy in America*, trans. Harvey C. Mansfield and Delba Winthrop (Chicago: University of Chicago Press, 2000), 168.

65. Quoted in Linda K. Kerber, *Federalists in Dissent: Imagery and Ideology in Jeffersonian America* (Ithaca, NY: Cornell University Press, 1970), 162.

66. "Timothy Pickering to George Cabot, 29 January 1804," in *The Founders' Constitution,* ed. Philip B. Kurland and Ralph Lerner, vol. 1 (Indianapolis, IN: Liberty Fund, 1987), 235–37.

67. See Kevin M. Gannon, "Escaping 'Mr. Jefferson's Plan of Destruction': New England Federalists and the Idea of a Northern Confederacy, 1803–1804," *Journal of the Early Republic* 21, no. 3 (Autumn 2001): 413-443; Charles Raymond Brown, *The Northern Confederacy According to the Plans of the "Essex Junto," 1796–1814* (Princeton, NJ, 1915).

68. See Bailey, *Thomas Jefferson and Executive Power,* esp. ch. 8, in which Bailey correctly argues that the Twelfth Amendment was intended to ensure that Jefferson could unequivocally claim public support for his use of executive power and his performance as president.

69. Benjamin A. Kleinerman, *The Discretionary President: The Promise and Peril of Executive Power*, (Lawrence: University Press of Kansas, 2009).

70. As Robert A. Dahl argued, the presidential appeal to the public was nothing more than a tool to obscure the reality that the pseudo-democratic president is really an imperial one. See Robert A. Dahl, "The Myth of the Presidential Mandate," *Political Science Quarterly* 105 (1990): 355–72. See also Arthur M. Schlesinger, *The Imperial Presidency* (New York: Hougton Mifflin Company, 1973). Scholarship has responded by addressing ways in which the imperial president can be checked, if a check can be established at all. See, e.g., Kleinerman, *The Discretionary President,* which argues that the judiciary branch cannot successfully check presidential prerogative because the Court, more often than not, will defer to the executive branch. Accordingly, the constitutional solution to the president's extraconstitutional power is legislative elites capable of alerting the public to the executive's abuses. Kleinerman's solution, then, relies on these legislative elites to counter the president's appeal to the public by making one of their own. See also Harvey C. Mansfield Jr., *Taming the Prince: The Ambivalence of Modern Executive Power* (Baltimore, MD: Johns Hopkins University Press, 1993). Counter to Kleinerman, Mansfield is less optimistic about checking presidential prerogative.

71. Samuel Eliot Morison. "Our Most Unpopular War," *Massachusetts Historical Society Proceedings* 80 (1968): 38–54.

72. Despite these modest gains, however, the Federalists still only constituted roughly one-third of the total members of Congress. See Norman K. Risjord, "Election of 1812," in *History of American Presidential Elections, 1789–2008*, ed. Gil Troy, Arthur M. Schlesinger Jr., and Fred L. Israel, vol. 1 (New York: Facts on File, 2011), 249–72.

73. See Donald R. Hinkey, "New England's Defense Problem and the Genesis of the Hartford Convention," *New England Quarterly* 50, no. 4 (December 1977): 587–604.

74. John Quincy Adams to Harrison Gray Otis et al., December 30, 1828; and J. Q. Adams, "To the Citizens of the United States," [1829], in e*Documents Relating to New-England Federalism, 1800–1850*, ed. Henry Adams (Boston, MA, 1877), 56, 221, 238, 245, 265. See also Henry Adams, *History of the United States during the Administrations of Jefferson and Madison* (New York, 1889–91), 8:4–7, 297.

75. Samuel Eliot Morison, *The Life and Letters of Harrison Gray Otis, Federalist, 1765–1848*, vol. 2 (Boston, MA, and New York, 1913), ch. 25; Samuel Eliot Morison, *Harrison Gray Otis, 1765–1848: The Urbane Federalist* (Boston, MA: Houghton Mifflin, 1969), ch. 17.

76. James M. Banner, *To the Hartford Convention: The Federalists and the Origins of Party Politics in Massachusetts, 1789-1815* (New York: Knopf, 1970). Of particular note is the absence of Timothy Pickering from the convention. As the leader of the plan to create the northern confederacy through secession, Pickering was not invited to the convention perhaps as a way of excluding perceived extremists from the Federalist Party. See also J. C. A. Stagg, *Mr. Madison's War: Politics, Diplomacy, and Warfare in the Early American Republic, 1783–1830* (Princeton, NJ: Princeton University Press, 1983). Stagg agrees with Banner that convention participants were not attempting to commit treason, and Stagg emphasizes the Federalists' efforts to avoid secession by excluding extremists like Pickering from the proceedings.

77. See Banner, *To the Hartford Convention*, 343–48; the quotation is from Timothy Pickering, on 346.

78. The Federalists' proposals, however, were moderate only in the sense that they considered them proposals as they would radically restructure the constitutional system. Moreover, while the proposals did not specifically mention plans to secede and create a northern confederacy, nullification and secession were implied if the War of 1812 persisted.

79. Joseph Story to Nathaniel Williams, February 22, 1815, in *Life and Letters of Joseph Story*, ed. William W. Story (Boston, MA, 1851), 1:254.

80. Quoted in Wilentz, *The Rise of American Democracy*, 175.

CHAPTER SIX.   Partyism and the Electoral College

1. See Tadahisa Kuroda, *The Origins of the Twelfth Amendment: The Electoral College in the Early Republic, 1787–1804* (Westport, CT: Greenwood Press, 1994); James W. Ceaser, *Presidential Selection: Theory and Development* (Princeton, NJ: Princeton University Press, 1979).

2. See George C. Edwards III, *Why the Electoral College Is Bad for America* (New Haven, CT: Yale University Press, 2011); Robert A. Dahl, *How Democratic Is the American Constitution?* (New Haven, CT: Yale University Press, 2003); Bruce Ackerman, *The Failure of the Founding Fathers: Jefferson, Marshall, and the Rise of Presidential Democracy* (Cambridge, MA: Belknap Press of Harvard University Press, 2005); Jack N. Rakove, "Presidential Selection: Electoral Fallacies," *Political Science Quarterly* 119, no. 1 (Spring 2004): 21–37; Jack Rakove, *The Unfinished Election of 2000: Leading Scholars Examine America's Strangest Election* (New York: Basic Books, 2002); Sanford Levinson, *Our Undemocratic Constitution: Where the Constitution Goes Wrong (And How We the People Can Correct It)* (New York: Oxford University Press, 2008).

3. See John B. McMaster, *A History of the People of the United States* (New York: D. Appleton and Company, 1883–1913), 4:369–70.

4. See Keith Whittington, *Constitutional Construction: Divided Powers and Constitutional Meaning* (Cambridge, MA: Harvard University Press, 1999).

5. *The Federalist*, 244.

6. Donald Ratcliffe, *The One-Party Presidential Contest: Adams, Jackson, and 1824's Five-Horse Race* (Lawrence: University Press of Kansas, 2015), 4.

7. Ibid., 5.

8. Max Farrand, *The Records of the Federal Convention of 1787* (New Haven, CT: Yale University Press, 1911), 3:13–14.

9. Ibid., 30.

10. John. P. Roche, "The Founding Fathers: A Reform Caucus in Action," *American Political Science Review* 55, no. 4 (1961): 799–816.

11. Shlomo Slonim, "The Electoral College at Philadelphia: The Evolution of an Ad Hoc Congress for Selection of a President," *Journal of American History* 73, no. 1 (1986): 35–58.

12. James Madison, *Notes of Debates in the Federal Convention of 1787 Reported by James Madison*, (Athens: Ohio University Press, 1985), 50, 88, 328.

13. *The Federalist*, 296.

14. Ibid., 385.

15. Ibid., 494.

16. Ibid., 434.

17. "From Alexander Hamilton to John Steele, 15 October 1792," *Founders Online*, National Archives, last modified June 29, 2017, http://founders.archives

.gov/documents/Hamilton/01-12-02-0396. Original source: *The Papers of Alexander Hamilton*, vol. 12, *July 1792–October 1792*, ed. Harold C. Syrett (New York: Columbia University Press, 1967), 567–69.

18. Ibid. Emphasis in the original.

19. See, e.g., Pasley, *The First Presidential Contest*, ch. 8.

20. Ibid., 314. Emphasis in the original.

21. *Annals of Congress,* 6th Cong., 2nd sess., Senate, 785.

22. Ibid., 943.

23. Ibid.

24. Ibid., 945.

25. Stanley Elkins and Eric McKitrick, *The Age of Federalism: The Early American Republic* (New York: Oxford University Press, 1993), 662.

26. "From Alexander Hamilton to John Jay, 7 May 1800," *Founders Online,* National Archives, last modified June 29, 2017, http://founders.archives.gov /documents/Hamilton/01-24-02-0378. Original source: *The Papers of Alexander Hamilton*, vol. 24, *November 1799–June 1800*, ed. Harold C. Syrett (New York: Columbia University Press, 1976), 464–67.

27. Ibid. John Jay's response is given in the footnotes.

28. "From Thomas Jefferson to James Monroe, 12 January 1800," *Founders Online,* National Archives, last modified June 29, 2017, http://founders.archives .gov/documents/Jefferson/01-31-02-0256. Original source: *The Papers of Thomas Jefferson,* vol. 31, *1 February 1799–31 May 1800*, ed. Barbara B. Oberg (Princeton, NJ: Princeton University Press, 2004), 300–301.

29. On this point, in states where there "would be no doubt" of the Democratic-Republican majority, the party would go so far to guarantee all electoral votes went to Jefferson that "the republican party . . . will not consent to elect either by districts or by general ticket. They chuse to do it by their legislature." In other words, in states where one party clearly controls the legislature, legislative appointment of presidential electors was the surest way of ensuring a unified allocation of electors' votes.

30. "From Thomas Jefferson to James Monroe, 12 January 1800."

31. Ibid.

32. Ibid.

33. Jeremy D. Bailey, *Thomas Jefferson and Executive Power* (New York: Cambridge University Press, 2007), 225.

34. "From James Madison to George Hay, 23 August 1823," *Founders Online,* National Archives, last modified June 29, 2017, http://founders.archives.gov/ documents/Madison/04-03-02-0109. Original source: *The Papers of James Madison,* Retirement Series, vol. 3, *1 March 1823–24 February 1826*, ed. David B. Mattern, J. C. A. Stagg, Mary Parke Johnson, and Katherine E. Harbury (Charlottesville: University of Virginia Press, 2016), 108–11.

35. Ibid.

36. James Madison, *Selected Writings of James Madison*, ed. with introd. Ralph Ketcham (Indianapolis, IN: Hackett, 2006), 39.

37. "James Madison to George Hays, 23 August 1823."

38. Ibid.

39. "From James Madison to George McDuffie, 3 January 1824," *Founders Online*, National Archives, last modified June 29, 2017, http://founders.archives .gov/documents/Madison/04-03-02-0212. Original source: *The Papers of James Madison*, Retirement Series, vol. 3, 195–98.

40. "James Madison to George Hays, 23 August 1823."

41. James Madison to Robert Taylor, January 30, 1826, Manuscript/Mixed Material, retrieved from the Library of Congress, www.loc.gov/item/mjm019729.

42. See Ceaser, *Presidential Selection*, 88–122.

43. Ibid., 144.

44. Marc Landy and Sidney M. Milkis, *Presidsential Greatness* (Lawrence: University Press of Kansas, 2000), 84.

45. Ratcliffe, *The One-Party Presidential Contest*, 233.

46. Richard P. McCormick, "New Perspectives on Jacksonian Politics," *The American Historical Review*: 288-301, 298.

47. Ratcliffe, *The One-Party Presidential Contest*, 3.

48. The resolution reads: "That, for the purpose of electing the President and Vice President of the United States, the Constitution ought to be so amended, that a uniform system of voting by districts, shall be established in all the States; and that the Constitution ought to be further amended, in such manner as will prevent the election of the aforesaid officers from devolving upon the respective Houses of Congress." Library of Congress, *Register of Debates: Debates and Proceedings, 1824–1837 Annals*, 19th Cong., 1st sess., 1365; hereafter cited as *Register*.

49. *Register*, 1368, 1367.

50. Ibid., 1368.

51. Ibid., 1370.

52. Ibid., 1372.

53. Bailey, *Thomas Jefferson and Executive Power*, 194.

54. *Register*, 1398.

55. Ibid., 1404. Emphasis in the original.

56. Ibid., 1410.

57. Ibid., 1410, 1401.

58. Ibid., 1526.

59. Ibid., 1410.

60. Ibid., 1450.

61. Ibid., 1545.

62. Ibid.

63. Ibid.

64. Ibid.

65. Ibid., 1549.

66. Of the members identified as Jacksonians, roughly 60 percent (55 of 92) supported the amendment, while around 62 percent (63 of 98) of Adams supporters opposed the amendment. Of the twenty-four states represented, a single vote was cast in four states (Delaware, Illinois, Missouri, and Rhode Island) and no vote was registered for Mississippi. Of the remaining nineteen states, nine (Alabama, Connecticut, Georgia, Indiana, Maryland, New Hampshire, North Carolina, Tennessee, and Vermont) were unified in their vote. Alabama, Maryland, North Carolina, and Tennessee all supported the amendment. Within the voting, state interests often superseded partisan concerns. For example, Connecticut and Georgia both opposed the amendment, with Connecticut's delegates all supporting Adams and Georgia's all supporting Jackson.

67. *Register* 1828, 123.

68. *Register* 1834, 1956.

69. *McPherson v. Blacker*, 146 U.S. 1 (1892).

70. *Williams v. Virginia State Board of Elections*, 288 F. Su622 (E.D. VA. 1968), 627.

71. Ibid., 628.

72. Robert M. Hardaway, *The Electoral College and the Constitution* (Westport, CT: Praeger, 1994), 124.

73. Leon D. Epstein, *Political Parties in the American Mold* (Madison: University of Wisconsin Press, 1986), 81.

CHAPTER SEVEN.   Partyism, the Elections Clause,
and the House of Representatives

1. Ahil Reed Amar, *America's Unwritten Constitution: The Precedents and Principles We Live By* (New York: Basic Books, 2012), 409.

2. See, e.g., John H. Aldrich, *Why Parties? A Second Look* (Chicago: University of Chicago Press, 2011), 102; Richard Hofstadter, *The Idea of a Party System: The Rise of Legitimate Opposition in the United States, 1780–1840* (Berkeley: University of California Press, 1969), ch. 6; Sean Wilentz, *The Rise of American Democracy: Jefferson to Lincoln* (New York: Norton, 2005); Sidney M. Milkis, *Political Parties and Constitutional Government: Remaking American Democracy* (Baltimore, MD: Johns Hopkins University Press, 1999), ch. 2.

3. Wilentz, *The Rise of American Democracy*, 435–36.

4. See Bernard Grofman and Arend Lijphart, eds., *Electoral Laws and Their Political Consequences* (New York: Agathon Press, 1986); Robert G. Moser and Ethan Scheiner, *Electoral System and Political Context: How the Effects of Rules Vary across New and Established Democracies* (New York: Cambridge University Press, 2012); Leon D. Epstein, *Political Parties in the American Mold* (Madison: University of Wisconsin Press, 1986).

5. Maurice Duverger, *Political Parties: Their Organization and Activity in the Modern State,* 1st American ed. (New York: John Wiley & Sons, 1954), 383.

6. Gary W. Cox, *Making Votes Count: Strategic Coordination in the World's Electoral Systems* (New York: Cambridge University Press, 1997).

7. Anthony Downs, *An Economic Theory of Democracy* (Harper and Row, 1957).

8. Scholarship tends to provide two types of explanations for the number of parties, institutional and ideological. The former focuses on the number of seats; the latter, on societal cleavages. Rein Taagepera and Matthew Soberg Shugart, "Predicting the Number of Parties: A Quantitative Model of Duverger's Mechanical Effect," *American Political Science Review* 87, no. 2 (1993): 455–64; Rein Taagepera and Bernard Grofman. "Rethinking Duverger's Law: Predicting the Effective Number of Parties in Plurality and PR Systems—Parties Minus Issues Equals One*," *European Journal of Political Research* 13, no. 4 (1985): 341–52; Octavio Amorim Neto and Gary W. Cox, "Electoral Institutions, Cleavage Structures, and the Number of Parties," *American Journal of Political Science* (1997): 149–74.

9. *Debates,* 31, 43.

10. Ibid., 423.

11. Ibid., 423–24.

12. Ibid.

13. Federal Farmer, No. 3 in *The Founders' Constitution*, vol. 2, ed. Philip B. Kurland and Ralph Lerner (Chicago: University of Chicago Press, 1987), 249.

14. Ibid., 251.

15. Ibid., 249; Brutus, No. 4 in *The Founders' Constitution*, 251.

16. Federal Farmer, No. 12 in *The Founders' Constitution*, 254.

17. According to Pauline Maier's account, Madison, in the Virginia ratifying convention, "defended the provision as it stood and suggested that it already gave Congress the power that Massachusetts and New Hampshire wanted to make explicit. Apparently, he saw no need to change Article I, Section 4, even to remedy the discontent it had caused in many state conventions" (Pauline Maier, *Ratification: The People Debate the Constitution, 1787–1788* [New York: Simon & Schuster, 2010], 448–49).

18. See Maier, *Ratification,* for a more detailed account of the ratification debates over the times, places, and manner clause.

19. U.S. Constitution, Article I, Section 2.

20. Michel L. Balinski and H. Payton Young, *Fair Representation: Meeting the Ideal of One Man, One Vote* (Washington, DC: Brookings Institution Press, 2001), 10–13. Balinksi and Young provide a comprehensive account of the different formulas used to determine representation.

21. Rosemarie Zagarri, *The Politics of Size: Representation in the United States, 1776–1850* (Ithaca, NY: Cornell University Press, 1987), 126.

22. Stephen Calabrese, "Multimember District Congressional Elections," *Legislative Studies Quarterly* 25, no. 4 (2000): 611–43; Stephen Calabrese, "An Explanation of the Continuing Federal Government Mandate of Single-Member Congressional Districts," *Public Choice* 130, no. 1–2 (January 2007): 23–40.

23. Zagarri, *The Politics of Size*, 129.

24. Jay K. Dow, *Electing the House: The Adoption and Performance of the US Single-Member District Electoral System* (Lawrence: University Press of Kansas, 2017), 113.

25. Ibid., 114–15.

26. Alexander Keyssar, *The Right to Vote: The Contested History of Democracy in the United States*, rev. ed. (New York: Basic Books, 2009), 32.

27. Dow, *Electing the House*, 118–19.

28. Ibid., 121; Michael F. Holt, *The Rise and Fall of the American Whig Party: Jacksonian Politics and the Onset of the Civil War* (New York: Oxford University Press, 2003), 153.

29. Holt, *The Rise and Fall of the American Whig Party*, 26–29.

30. Bernard Ivan Tamas, "A Divided Political Elite: Why Congress Banned Multimember Districts in 1842," *New Political Science* 18, no. 1 (March 2006): 23–44.

31. Ibid., 33.

32. Johanna Nicol Shields, "Whigs Reform the 'Bear Garden': Representation and the Apportionment Act of 1842," *Journal of the Early Republic* 5, no. 3 (Autumn, 1985): 355–82, 362.

33. Ibid., 122.

34. Holt, *The Rise and Fall of the American Whig Party*, 122–61.

35. Ibid., 154–55.

36. Michele Rosa-Clot, "The Apportionment Act of 1842: 'An Odious Use of Authority,'" *Parliaments, Estates and Representation* 31, no. 1 (2011): 33–52, 33–34. See also Richard M. McCormick, *The Second American Party System: Party Formation in the Jacksonian Era* (New York: Norton, 1966).

37. *Congressional Globe*, 409, 200.

38. Ibid., 200.

39. Ibid., 436.

40. Ibid., 437.

41. Martin H. Quitt, "Congressional (Partisan) Constitutionalism," *Journal of the Early Republic* 28, no. 4 (Winter 2008): 627–51, 635.

42. Wilentz, *The Rise of American Democracy*, 485. Wilentz provides a useful discussion of the division within the Whig Party by distinguishing between new school Whigs and more conservative, old school Whigs.

43. Charles A. Kromkowski, *Recreating the American Republic: Rules of Apportionment, Constitutional Change, and American Political Development, 1700–1870* (New York: Cambridge University Press, 2002), 336.

44. *Congressional Globe*, 538.

45. Quitt, "Congressional (Partisan) Constitutionalism," 636.

46. *Congressional Globe*, 622.

47. Ibid., 348.

48. For a discussion on the voting blocs that emerged on the districting amendment, see Tamas, "A Divided Political Elite," 39.

49. *Congressional Globe*, 447.

50. Ibid., 446.

51. Ibid., 447.

52. Ibid., 450. Emphasis in the original.

53. Elvin T. Lim, *The Lovers' Quarrel: The Two Foundings and American Political Development* (New York: Oxford University Press, 2014), 78–79. Lim's primary thesis emphasizes the reoccurrence and reconstitution of the Anti-Federalists' (state sovereignty) and Federalists' (national power) political thought in American political development.

54. U.S. Congress, House of Representatives, Appendix to the *Congressional Globe, Speech of Mr. J. G. Floyd of New York, April 27, 1842*, 27th Cong., 2nd sess. (1841–42), 320.

55. Ibid., 322.

56. *Congressional Globe*, 448.

57. *Niles' National Register*, ed. Hezekiah Niles, vol. 62, April 30, 1842, 143. Available at Hathi Trust Digital Library, https://hdl.handle.net/2027/nnc1.cu04634616?urlappend=%3Bseq=155.

58. *Congressional Globe*, 445. Campbell was one of the only Democrats to support the districting amendment as the Whig Party primarily supported the measure. See also Joel Francis Paschal, "The House of Representatives: 'Grand Depository of the Democratic Principle'?," *Law and Contemporary Problems* 17, no. 2 (Spring 1952): 276–89, 281.

59. See Calabrese, "Multimember District," 611–43.

60. *Congressional Globe*, 464.

61. Zagarri, *The Politics of Size*, 127.

62. *Congressional Globe*, 445.

63. Ibid., 464.

64. Zagarri, *The Politics of Size*, 128–30.

65. *Congressional Globe*, 445.

66. Ibid., 463.

67. Ibid., 454.

68. Ibid., 464.

69. Ibid., 448.

70. Ibid., 453.

71. Ibid.

72. Ibid., 471.

73. Ibid., 583.

74. Quitt, "Congressional (Partisan) Constitutionalism," 646.

75. The Apportionment Acts passed in 1862, 1872, 1901, and 1911 all required election by single-member districts. In 1967, Congress passed a law that permanently required single-member district elections by prohibiting general ticket and multimember elections.

76. See Zagarri, *The Politics of Size*, 131.

77. Tamas, "A Divided Political Elite," 31.

78. Andrew Hacker, *Congressional Districting: The Issue of Equal Representation* (Washington, DC: Brookings Institution, 1964), 49.

79. During the 1842 debates, Thomas Benton proposed an amendment to Section 2 that required districts to be drawn with approximately an equal number of inhabitants per district. He observed "that the bill, as it now stands, orders the states to be divided into as many districts as they have members apportioned to them; but, ... a district may contain any number—300,000, for instance, if the city of New York is made one district. Another may only so many hundreds, instead of thousands. If New York has a Democratic population, it might be made a single district; while another portion, with the same amount of population, but all Whigs, might be divided into six districts; giving six party votes on one side against one vote on the other" (*Congressional Globe*, 601). This amendment was initially accepted but was later removed from Section 2 because delegates expressed concern over the meaning of "equal number." Many delegates feared this would mean dividing local counties. At one point in the debates, delegates proposed various numerical ranges within which unequal populations would have to fall, ranging from 5,000 to 20,000. For example, Senator William R. King proposed "that no district should be so far unequal in the number of inhabitants as to exceed 5,000" (*Congressional Globe*, 614). No consensus was reached, and the amendment was eventually dropped.

80. *Baker v. Carr*, 369 U.S. 186 (1962); *Wesberry v. Sanders*, 376 U.S. 1 (1964).

81. Craig T. Borowiak, "Accountability Debates: The Federalists, the Anti-Federalists, and Democratic Deficits," *Journal of Politics* 69, no. 4 (November 2007): 998–1014.

82. Ibid., 1001.

CONCLUSION. Partyism and the Twenty-Fourth Amendment

1. See, e.g., "Toward a More Responsible Two-Party System: A Report of the Committee on Political Parties, American Political Science Association," *American Political Science Review* 44, no. 3, pt. 2 (September 1950); Xandra Kayden and Eddie Mahe Jr., *The Party Goes On* (New York: Basic Books, 1985); Larry J. Sabato and Bruce Larson, *The Party's Just Begun: Shaping Political Parties for America's Future* (New York: Longman, 2002).

2. Nancy Rosenblum, *On the Side of Angels: An Appreciation of Parties and Partisanship* (Princeton, NJ: Princeton University Press, 2008), 456.

3. Charles R. Kesler, "Political Parties, the Constitution, and the Future of American Politics," in *American Political Parties and Constitutional Politics*, ed. Peter W. Schramm and Bradford P. Wilson (Lanham, MD: Rowman & Littlefield, 1993), 229.

4. See John H. Aldrich, *Why Parties? A Second Look* (Chicago: University of Chicago Press, 2011). In chapter 3, Aldrich argues that parties formed around the "fundamental problem [of establishing in practice] just how strong and active the new federal government was to be." He continues, "Basic differences on this, which I call the 'great principle,' rested on differing views of how to make the new republic most likely to succeed. Failure to establish a clear basis of precedent would leave this great principle unresolved and risk revealing the unworkability of an extended republic" (72).

5. In Federalist No. 10, Madison made a distinction between stable republican governments based on popular sovereignty and the instability and danger of strictly democratic governments.

6. Christian G. Fritz, "Alternative Visions of American Constitutionalism: Popular Sovereignty and the Early American Constitutional Debate," *Hastings Constitutional Law Quarterly* 24, no. 2 (Winter 1997): 287–57, 300.

7. See Elvin T. Lim, *The Lovers' Quarrel: The Two Foundings and American Political Development* (New York: Oxford University Press, 2014).

8. *Debates*, 447–48.

9. Federal Farmer No. 9, in *The Anti-Federalist Writings of the Melancton Smith Circle*, ed. Michael Zuckert and Derek Webb (Indianapolis: Liberty Fund, 2009), 83.

10. *The Federalist*, 239; 80. See also Alan Gibson, *Understanding the Founding: The Crucial Questions* (Lawrence: University Press of Kansas, 2007). In particular, Gibson addresses the enduring debate over the democratic nature of the Constitution in chapter 2.

11. *The Federalist*, 132.

12. Ibid., 239.

13. Madison used the examples of Holland, Venice, Poland, and England have all been "frequently placed on the list of republics" despite not adhering to the fundamental maxim of republicanism, popular sovereignty.

14. *The Federalist*, 240, 224.

15. See, e.g., Banning, *The Sacred Fire of Liberty*; Elkins and McKitrick, *The Age of Federalism*.

16. Aldrich, *Why Parties?*, 71.

17. Jeremy D. Bailey, *James Madison and Constitutional Imperfection* (New York: Cambridge University Press, 2015), 89.

18. Colleen A. Sheehan, *The Mind of James Madison: The Legacy of Classical Republicanism* (New York: Cambridge University Press, 2015); Greg Weiner, *Madison's Metronome: The Constitution, Majority Rule, and the Tempo of American Politics* (Lawrence: University Press of Kansas, 2012); Bailey, *James Madison and Constitutional Imperfection*.

19. James Madison, *Selected Writings of James Madison*, ed. with introd. Ralph Ketcham (Indianapolis, IN: Hackett, 2006), 210.

20. "For the *National Gazette*, 31 March 1792," *Founders Online*, National Archives, last modified June 29, 2017, http://founders.archives.gov/documents /Madison/01-14-02-0245. Original source: *The Papers of James Madison*, vol. 14, *6 April 1791–16 March 1793*, ed. Robert A. Rutland and Thomas A. Mason (Charlottesville: University Press of Virginia, 1983), 274–75.

21. Madison, *Selected Writings*, 210.

22. Tocqueville made a similar argument regarding newspapers in *Democracy in America*. In *The Mind of James Madison*, Sheehan points out that Madison's promotion of newspapers as a means of facilitating public opinion was only applicable to large republics. In smaller republics, the proliferation of newspapers may be actually averse to liberty for the same reason he gave in Federalist No. 10 why majority rule was more dangerous in smaller republics.

23. James Madison, "Consolidation," in *Selected Writings*, 209.

24. See Keith Whittington, *Constitutional Construction: Divided Powers and Constitutional Meaning* (Cambridge, MA: Harvard University Press, 1999).

25. Amar argues that there is a connection between all the right-to-vote amendments (Fourteenth, Fifteenth, Nineteenth, Twenty-Fourth, and Twenty-Sixth) and that, as a remarkable fact, "no fewer than five of the fifteen amendments ratified after Jefferson's tenure, explicitly or implicitly address primary elections, and therefore directly address political parties" (Akhil Reed Amar, *America's Unwritten Constitution: The Precedents and Principles We Live* [New York: Basic Books, 2015], 408).

26. James W. Ceaser, *Presidential Selection: Theory and Development* (Princeton, NJ: Princeton University Press, 1979), 220–21.

27. See, e.g., *Grovey v. Townsend*, 295 US 45 (1935).

28. *Newberry v. United States*, 256 US 232 (1921). In the opinion, Justice MacReynolds argued that primary elections "are in no sense elections for an office but merely methods by which party adherents agree upon candidates whom they intend to offer and support for ultimate choice by all qualified electors."

29. The four cases were *Terry v. Adams*, 345 US 461 (1953); *Smith v. Allwright*, 321 US 649 (1944); *Nixon v. Condon*, 286 US 73 (1932); and *Nixon v. Herndon*, 273 US 536 (1927).

30. Nathaniel Persily, "Toward a Functional Defense of Political Party Autonomy," *New York University Law Review* 76 (2001): 750–824, 757–58.

31. Amar, *America's Unwritten Constitution*, 444.

32. Gerald M. Pomper, *Passions and Interests: Political Party Concepts of American Democracy* (Lawrence: University Press of Kansas, 1992), 120.

33. Indeed, the Twenty-Fourth Amendment did not reform the partisan nature of primary elections. Political parties are still granted associational rights based on the First and Fourteenth Amendments. In this way, parties are able to discriminate participation based on ideology, which is much different than discriminating based on age, race, gender, or class.

34. For example, Landy and Milkis explain, "Ironically, the best means for taming factionalism and reconciling rivalry with lawful rotation in power has proved to be an institution that Washington feared and despised—political party. To compound the irony, Thomas Jefferson, who shared Washington's antipathy, created the first great democratic political party. Jefferson was a better builder than he was an architect. His vision was to create the party that would end party, that would erase the Federalist-inspired perversion of the Constitution and restore and strengthen it to such an extent that constitutional liberties would no longer require partisan defense" (Marc Landy and Sidney M. Milkis, *Presidential Greatness* [Lawrence: University Press of Kansas, 2000], 8).

35. E.g., J. David Gillespie, *Challengers to Duopoly: Why Third Parties Matter in American Two-Party Politics* (Columbia: University of South Carolina Press, 2012); Richard L. Hasen, "Entrenching the Duopoly: Why the Supreme Court Should Not Allow the States to Protect the Democrats and Republicans from Political Competition," *Supreme Court Review* (1997): 331–71; Richard L. Hasen, "Do the Parties or the People Own the Electoral Process?," *University of Pennsylvania Law Review* (2001): 815–41; Brian P. Marron, "Doubting America's Sacred Duopoly: Disestablishment Theory and the Two-Party System," *Texas Forum on Civil Liberties & Civil Rights* 6 (Winter 2001): 303.

36. Nathaniel Persily, "Toward a Functional Defense of Political Party Autonomy," *New York University Law Review* 76 (2001): 750–824, 823.

INDEX

ROBERT E. ROSS

is assistant professor of political science at Utah State University.

CPSIA information can be obtained
at www.ICGtesting.com
Printed in the USA
LVHW111824171219
640809LV00008B/254/P

9 780268 105495